THROUGH THE EYES OF THE ANCIENTS

THE BOOKS OF MOSES

THROUGH THE EYES OF THE ANCIENTS

THE BOOKS OF MOSES

R. DEAN DAVIS

Pacific Press®
Publishing Association
Nampa, Idaho | www.pacificpress.com

3ABN
books

Cover design by Gerald Lee Monks
Cover design resources from SermonView.com
Inside design by Aaron Troia

The author assumes full responsibility for the accuracy of all facts and quotations as cited in this book.

Unless otherwise noted, Scripture quotations are taken from the New King James Version®. Copyright © 1982 by Thomas Nelson, Inc. Used by permission. All rights reserved.

Scripture quotations marked ESV are from The Holy Bible, English Standard Version® (ESV®), copyright © 2001 by Crossway, a publishing ministry of Good News Publishers. Used by permission. All rights reserved.

Scripture quotations marked KJV are from the King James Version.

Purchase additional copies of this book by calling toll-free 1-800-765-6955 or by visiting http://www.adventistbookcenter.com.

Library of Congress Cataloging-in-Publication Data

Names: Davis, R. Dean, 1934- author.
Title: Through the eyes of the ancients : the Books of Moses / R. Dean Davis.
Description: Nampa, Idaho : Pacific Press Publishing Association, [2021] |
    Summary: "A comprehensive study on the books of Moses in the Bible"—
    Provided by publisher.
Identifiers: LCCN 2021000518 | ISBN 9780816367566 (paperback) |
    ISBN 9780816367573 (ebook)
Subjects: LCSH: Bible. Pentateuch—Criticism, interpretation, etc.
Classification: LCC BS1225.52 .D385 2021 | DDC 221.6—dc23
LC record available at https://lccn.loc.gov/2021000518

January 2021

Dedication

To God who sustained me.
To my wife, Vera, whose love carried me through this long process.
To my son, Bobby, who edited the manuscript.
To my daughters, Dolly and Linda, for encouragement.

Contents

Foreword

It's a rare author who makes humility his premise, and then consistently carries that value forward, even while offering insight, correcting misunderstanding, and providing guidance.

More typically, a writer tries to establish credentials, demonstrate scholarship, and give unique perspectives—all of which only widen and deepen the gulf between the reader and the author. In fact, novelty—or at least a new frame for familiar content—is the pitch that sells us books. The author knows what we don't, and the manner in which he or she delivers content is frequently intended to evoke experiences of admiration or even awe among readers like us. The author lives in the Himalayas, it seems, while we inhabit the flatlands.

Dean Davis's *Through the Eyes of the Ancients,* however, is a remarkable instance of both fine biblical scholarship and reader-friendly presentation—all because Davis includes himself among those who are still learning the backgrounds and context of the biblical story. In his compelling *Epilogue* at the conclusion of this volume, we find clearly stated what we've previously only sensed—that this journey through the Books Moses is only his latest one, and there will likely be more insights to come. The ten "lessons learned" with which he concludes are founded on the author's keen awareness that scholarship is often as much about unlearning as about acquiring new knowledge: "*Much of what I had previously been doing to understand the Pentateuch (the books of Moses) and its context was either incorrect or inadequate. I was reading much of my own thinking, context, and many of my concerns into the text.*"

After nearly forty years of interacting with brash theology students and over-confident lay expositors of the Pentateuch, I found myself wishing that Davis's ten lessons could somehow be posted at the door of each Old Testament classroom and inserted in the flyleaf of each Bible. The natural—but actually arrogant—assumption that we can easily understand the culture, language, symbolism, and thought structure of a people group who inhabited our planet thirty-five hundred years ago is but another illustration of the hubris of our age. We assume that ancient cultures were also somehow primitive, less developed, and incapable of our intellectual breadth and depth. The reality, as Davis amply demonstrates, is far different.

Understanding the biblical world, and specifically the early history of this planet recorded in the Books of Moses, requires a set of robust investigative tools, as well as a corresponding willingness to unlearn the often-simplistic versions of these stories we learned as children or teens. Davis brings the robust scholarly tools to the task, and asks only that we bring the teachable attitudes he also acquired on the way. This combination—some would say, this covenant—between author and readers provides us with a most companionable book, the kind one imagines enjoying again and again as we retrace the stories of God's interactions with those He loved and sought.

For that's the essence of *Through the Eyes of the Ancients*: it's a companion volume to read alongside each journey through the Pentateuch. Something less than a verse-by-verse commentary, but something more than a collection of well-structured lecture notes, the book reminds you of a good afternoon walk with a well-informed friend. You find yourself lingering a bit, unwilling for the stroll to end, because the friendliness and skill of the storyteller have made you see new meanings in old, familiar tales. It's one of the sweet ironies of this book that the motif of the journey—seen in the wanderings of the patriarchs, of Joseph, of Moses, and finally the entire Hebrew nation—becomes the way we reexamine stories we thought we knew. We walk, not run, through the text. The author stops to camp on major developments—covenant, law, sanctuary, and salvation—that require a thoughtful lingering. Those not used to deeper Bible study won't feel left behind in a wilderness of symbols and stories. In a word, this study of the Books of Moses is "accessible."

Dean Davis's fifty-plus years of mission service, pastoral care, and classroom teaching have coalesced in this volume to make available to thousands of readers what only a few Old Testament scholars know. The writing is clean and clear, never obtuse. The insights offered are fresh and vividly drawn, never pretentious.

I can hope that *Through the Eyes of the Ancients* will soon grace the study tables and libraries of many Christians. They'll find it, as I have, a highly useful tool for in-depth Bible study, and a volume that reminds us of the long arc of God's grace toward difficult, obstinate people like us.

—Bill Knott, executive editor, *Adventist Review*

Introduction

Have you ever puzzled over a biblical expression? Somehow, it sounds a little strange to "taste and see" that God is good, doesn't it? And why did Abel's blood "cry out" to God from the ground? Most of us are used to these phrases and don't notice them; however, a secular, Western thinker will almost certainly find them very odd.

I remember wondering why my thinking and language seemed so different from the ancients, but thought it was because I was reading the King James Version of the Bible, in its "ancient" language. As a young seminary student, I studied advanced Hebrew, but was never taught anything about their way of thinking.

I believe my eyes began to open when, as a young missionary in Brazil, I was asked to teach Old Testament courses in Portuguese, a language I could hardly get around in. What a tremendous challenge that was for both the students and me. As I became more proficient in that language, I realized that their way of thinking and their expressions were often different than my own. They *thought* differently. Certain things carried more importance for them than they did for me.

Soon, I learned that every culture and every language has its own emphasis, its own way of expression. I could not translate texts literally and have them make good sense.

Over the years I developed a great personal interest in the lives, customs, and expressions of the ancient Hebrews; and as a result, my eyes have been opened to some of the rich, layered treasures in the Holy Scriptures.

Somewhere around 1998, I was introduced to the book, *Our Father Abraham: Jewish Roots of the Christian Faith,* by Marvin R. Wilson. A large part of this book helped me understand that Western thought is very different from Hebrew thought.

First, I was led to understand that our rational or logical thinking came much later, with the Greeks. We reason things out, and don't always use our senses to interpret and describe our relationships. On the other hand, the ancient Hebrew way of understanding was based on their senses—what they saw, heard, touched, smelled, and tasted. They *experienced* what they knew.

Consider the emphasized words in the following texts: "Then on the third day Abraham *lifted his eyes* and saw the place afar off" (Genesis 22:4).

"Now when Moses went into the tabernacle of meeting to speak with Him, *he heard* the voice of One speaking to him from above the mercy seat that was on the ark of the Testimony, from between the two cherubim" (Numbers 7:89).

"Oh, *taste and see* that the LORD is good" (Psalm 34:8).

The Bible abounds in other colorful (and concrete) descriptions like "stiff necked" (stubborn, like a mule—see 2 Chronicles 30:8); "hard hearted" (lacking passion—see 1 Samuel 6:6); "setting one's face" (determined to go—see Numbers 24:1); and "girding one's loins" (getting ready—see 1 Kings 18:46).

Even noses are used in the Hebrew language to describe God in an unusual way! In Exodus 34:6 the Lord describes Himself as, "The LORD, the LORD God, merciful and gracious, longsuffering, and abounding in goodness and truth." The word "longsuffering" means patient, or slow to anger. But the Hebrew words for this are literally "long" and "nose."

God has a long nose?

This one puzzled me! As I studied the Hebrew word, *af,* or "anger," I discovered that it literally means "nose"! When a bull is angry, it's nostrils flare, it breathes hard, and snorts. With this in mind, to the ancients' way of thinking, the longer the nose, the longer it would take to expel the breath—and the slower one would be to anger.

But what about the New Testament books? Weren't they written in Greek? Yes—but although the writers used that global language, they were most definitely Jews (except Luke), and therefore, Hebrew thinkers. Consider how John speaks of Jesus: "That which was from the beginning, which we have *heard,* which we have *seen with our eyes,* which we have *looked upon,* and our *hands have handled,* concerning the Word of life" (1 John 1:1, emphasis added). It is obvious that he thought in terms of his senses.

The ancients were also fond of using symbols, and while we may puzzle over them, every Jewish child was taught their meaning from a very early age. Just as the children of old, we must understand them, too, or be hopelessly lost in books like Daniel and Revelation. Worse yet, if we try using our logical (or Greek) thinking on them, we are sure to distort the Scriptures, twisting the verses around to explain what *we* believe, instead of what the *authors* intended.

In this book, we'll look at many aspects of Hebrew thinking. One prominent aspect is the importance of action. To the ancients, God is primarily known for His actions. The record of the seven-day Creation story contains 114 verbs, and the overwhelming majority of them have God as their subject. This is in stark contrast to our way of describing Him, since we routinely use *adjectives* that reveal His attributes, like "God is loving; God is merciful; God is patient."

Normally, in the Hebrew language, the verb precedes the subject. The *action* is more important than who or what causes it—thus the *verb* is more important than the *subject*. The different parts of Hebrew speech are derived from the verbal root.

Much of the Christian world tends to look at the Bible in doctrinal terms, often using the "proof text" method, in which verses are chosen to prove the doctrine. This twists Scripture, and diverts our minds from getting the whole message it intends to give. Rather, we must comprehend the Bible as being written in a story form for people that generally needed a public reader. The Hebrews remembered stories and would retell the stories to the next generation, and since Hebrew is a verbal language, it expresses truth best through story form.

As you read this book, you will soon notice that we have deliberately placed all the stories in the present tense, hoping to capture some of the immediacy and emotion the ancients felt. My hope is that this book will shed new and wonderful light on your study of the Bible, as we look through the eyes of the ancients.

CHAPTER ONE

Tender Bonding

Based on Genesis 1 and 2

As we look at Scriptures through the eyes of the ancients, we discover they think from the general to the specific. Their narrative builds, detail upon detail. We see that the Creation story begins with the broad picture, or first level of detail: "In the beginning God created the heavens and the earth" (Genesis 1:1). This verse tells us all that really matters: God is the Creator. He created everything. A second level of detail begins with Genesis 1:2. God creates the world in six days, using the first three to create environments and the next three to populate each of them. However, beginning with the last part of Genesis 2:4, we see the third, and most important, level of detail given is man, who is the most important part of Creation.

The first thing we notice is how *personal* God becomes for man. Instead of referring to the Creator as God, or *Elohim* in Hebrew, the Bible suddenly starts calling Him the Lord God, *Yahweh Elohim*. Why this change? Because the author of Genesis is stressing the personal interest God takes in mankind. *Elohim* is the God of power, but *Yahweh* is the God of relationship.*

Watch as He takes the dust of the earth in His hands and tenderly shapes it into a man's form: "And the LORD God formed man of the dust of the ground" (Genesis 2:7). The word "formed" in Hebrew is *yatsar*, "to form, to fashion, as a potter." This is definitely a hands-on Creator! But it gets better.

---

* It should be noted that God is never referred to by using personal names. Instead, the Bible uses titles that identify Him. This comes from the Hebrew thinking that whoever knew your name had control over you. A father would give his son a name, therefore having control over him. In the case of Jesus Christ, Jesus is his human name, and Christ is His title. However, notice that He identifies Himself as "I am," the same title by which God identified Himself to Moses at the burning bush in Exodus 3. Jesus said of Himself, "I am the bread of life" (John 6:35); "I am the vine" (John 15:5); "I am the light of the world" (John 8:12), and "I say to you, before Abraham was, I AM" (John 8:58).

Now we see God tenderly breathing life into Adam's nostrils, then hovering closely to see his expression as he opens his eyes! Studies have shown the significant bonding that takes place between a newborn and its mother. In fact, babies under one month of age have a fixed focal length in their eyes of around eight inches—the approximate distance of a baby's face from its mother's while breastfeeding. When Adam opens his eyes for the first time and looks into the face of his Creator, an incredible bond is formed between the two!

The timing of this event is also significant. Adam is created on the sixth day, but he spends his first full day of life with his Creator on the first Sabbath. Imagine the intimate relationship the Lord God enjoys as He spends the Sabbath hours with His newborn—without a single distraction.

When Adam is created, he receives the distinction of being the Lord God's son—the firstborn son! He begins the line of sons on this earth. He is made in the image and likeness of God with the responsibility to spiritually reveal the knowledge and character of God to his offspring.

Poetry and song

The Genesis account contains another example of the Creator's personal concern for Adam. As God brings him each living creature to be named, it becomes distressingly clear that each one has a companion—but Adam does not. God's solution is to put him into a deep sleep (the first anesthesia), remove one of his ribs, and tenderly fashion a woman.

The Hebrew word for rib is *tesla,* and literally means "side." This suggests the connotation of equality and companionship. This word is frequently used in the construction of the sanctuary and Solomon's temple. The Hebrew verb in Genesis 2:22, "He made into a woman" is *banah,* a verb that is also often used with the sanctuary, and Solomon's temple. It is derived from the same verbal root as "house" and "family." Imagine the joy and bonding Adam feels when he awakens, and the first person he sees is his beautiful wife Eve! In ecstasy, he breaks into poetry, exclaiming,

> "This is now bone of my bones
> And flesh of my flesh;
> She shall be called Woman,
> Because she was taken out of Man" (Genesis 2:23).

Poetry and song are used in the Bible to signify something of great importance. In Exodus 15, after God delivers the Hebrews from certain annihilation at the Red Sea (all written in narrative form), Moses breaks into song—which is really poetry set to music.

Songs and poetry are special ways of remembering important events for generations to come, so therefore, anything in poetic form is *very important* in the Hebrew mind, since it contains the high points of the story.

Through the details of Creation, God provides a self-revelation to the Hebrews by showing He is a God of love in the way He creates their forefathers, provides for their needs, and fashions a lovely home for them.

CHAPTER TWO

A God of Detail

Based on Genesis 1 and 2

The only way we can know God for sure is to look at how He reveals Himself in story form throughout the Bible. While God reveals Himself in person to Adam and Eve, all those details have been largely lost by the time of Moses. Now God longs to reveal Himself to mankind, again.

The intended audience for the Creation story in Genesis is the Hebrews, who have just come out of hundreds of years of Egyptian captivity. They have largely lost sight of their history and the God of their ancestors, and now worship the false gods of their masters, instead. There are over two thousand Egyptian gods—the sun is a god, a tree is a god, a bull is a god—even a scarab or dung beetle is a god! The pagan thought is that the gods created man as an afterthought, to be slaves that carry out their wishes. They must even feed them!

Men spend their time trying to appease their gods, and are in constant fear of them. They give supreme worship to whichever god seems to be the most powerful—the god that might do something for them in exchange for their devotion. Their gods are all vulnerable to a stronger god that might come along, so the people follow the most powerful one they can find. Sadly, this is a diabolical distortion of the character of God.

Although the Lord tries to reveal Himself through His loving actions, He must first show them His power, because of their pagan beliefs. The Hebrew word for God in the Creation story is *Elohim*—emphasizing His power. He is not creation itself. He works *outside* of creation; He *controls* creation; He has the *power* to create.

Through His Creation, He reveals Himself as a God whose greatest interest is to provide for all man's needs. His character and actions are completely different from the Egyptian gods.

Environments

So let's start with God's manifestation of His power. The writer, who most conservative scholars believe is Moses, gives us the chaotic state of affairs in the beginning. Genesis 1 says there is deep water and darkness, and the earth is formless and empty; but now God begins to create order out of chaos. As His Spirit hovers over the waters and this empty mass, suddenly He speaks—and there is light! God calls the light "day," and the darkness "night;" and since light is necessary for nearly all living things, we understand why He creates it first.

On the second day, God creates the firmament, which in Hebrew means "expanse;" for us the word is derived from the Latin *firmamentum,* meaning "to support, prop, or stay." This giant air pocket suspends the waters above from the waters below.

On the third day, God gathers the waters below into the seas, and calls the dry land "earth." In this act, He creates an environment for all the creatures of the air and seas. He also provides the environment and food that His land creatures will need by creating grass and seed-bearing fruit.

Filling the environments

On the next three days, the Creator fills these environments. The first day's environment is filled on the fourth day by the sun, moon, and stars. Right here many scientists have problems with the Bible, because they try to apply logic, or Greek thinking, to this event. "How can there be light without the sun, moon, and stars?" they ask. The explanation is simple: The light in the first day is the light of God's presence. This is the same light that clothes Adam and Eve before they sin.

The sun and the moon of the fourth day are not given their usual names to prevent people from making them into individual gods. Instead, they are called "luminaries," created for the purpose of dividing day from night and marking off signs, seasons, days, and years. The word, "luminaries," is the same word that is used in the sanctuary for lamps. The sun and moon are lamps to illuminate the world, just as the lamps illuminate the sanctuary. Likewise, the Hebrew words for "signs" and "seasons" are the same words used in the sanctuary to mark off rituals and time for assemblies and yearly feasts. This indicates a close connection between Creation and the sanctuary.

On the fifth day, He fills the second environment by creating birds for the firmament, and sea creatures for the seas. Then, on the sixth day, He creates the animals that inhabit the dry land, culminating with His crowning act—the creation of man. This act is so important that a divine council is called, and a decision is made to create man in "Our" image and likeness. This supports a plurality of the Godhead and may indicate a plurality of man in that they are created male and female. The "image of God" should be understood broadly to include spiritual, functional, and physical aspects. It comes from the root *tselem,* "to carve," or "to cut off." Biblically, that word is used for physical things, such as tumors, idols, statutes of men, and so on. The word, *demuwth,* or "likeness," means "similar to," as when comparing one person or thing to another. This word refers to abstract qualities, rather than physical ones.

From this description, it is clear that God and man are closely related. Man is God's representative on earth. He is coruler, together with God, on earth. He is to participate in and help carry out God's plan for the earth.

Man is clearly the pinnacle of God's Creation, and the focus of the Creation story is on him—especially since he is created in the "image" and "likeness" of God. In the ancient pagan world, animals often represent the gods; and the gods are formed in the images of animals.

Do you see the parallels between the first three days and the next three days of Creation week? Clearly, the Creator is a God of order, but it also demonstrates His great care and love for each of His creatures.

A sanctuary in time

Now we come to a day that has no parallel with any other day of the week. After declaring that everything He created is very good, on the seventh day God finishes His work. This expression of "finishing work" is found again when Moses ends the seven stages of the building of the sanctuary (Exodus 40:33), and again, when Huram finishes building the temple for Solomon after seven years (1 Kings 7:40). This clearly indicates that the seventh day is linked with the sanctuary/temple, making it a sanctuary in time. On the seventh day, God rests from His finished work, making the "resting" part of His "finishing."

After designating the seventh day as the Sabbath, God blesses and sanctifies it. "To sanctify," means to set apart for holy purpose. The word "sanctuary" is derived from the same verbal root, and is used throughout the Scriptures to signify God's dwelling place with His people. In Exodus 25:8, the Lord says, "Let them make Me a sanctuary, that I may dwell among them."

Biblical numbers

Notice that God uses the number seven to designate the most important of the days of Creation—His special day, as well as the culmination of the

Creation process. Along with the seven days, there are other instances of sevens in the Creation story.

Biblical scholars clearly understand the importance of numerology in ancient Hebrew thinking. The Bible is full of repeated numbers—twos (as in the two witnesses), threes (used to indicate something of importance), fours (indicating something universal, or the whole earth), sixes (indicating man), sevens (God's favorite number), tens (indicating completeness), twelves (indicating Israel), forties (indicating a generation, and negative periods—such as the Flood, Jesus' temptations, etc.), and multiples of seven (in prophecy, etc.). In Genesis 1:1, the verse is composed of seven Hebrew words, and in verse 2, there are fourteen. In the seven days of Creation, the word "God" appears thirty-five times and "earth" is mentioned twenty-one times—all multiples of seven.

Between Genesis 1:1 and Genesis 2:3, the words "God created" and "and it was so" each occur seven times. This evidence indicates that the Creation story establishes the number seven as an archetype for the rest of Scripture. It is a number repeatedly associated with God; the agricultural year is based on it; the feasts follow it; the sanctuary and its services echo it; the blessings and curses linked with judgment and salvation are modeled on it.

To the Hebrews, the account of Creation clearly reveals that the Lord is a God of detail and order. Through this account, they also realize His love for them as they hear how He tenderly forms Adam with His own hands, creating him in His image and likeness, breathing the breath of life into him, and spending that first full day with him in intimate communion.

CHAPTER THREE

A Garden of Choices

Based on Genesis 2 and 3

The Hebrew word for garden is *gan*, meaning "an enclosed garden," and the word *eden* (Eden) literally means "pleasure" or "delight." God longs to live right in the center of things, surrounded by His children, so He creates the earth's first sanctuary—a sacred place where He can dwell with them in a special relationship.

God's careful attention to detail provides Adam and Eve all that they need to be happy and productive. He creates a river that flows from Eden and divides into four riverheads to water the whole earth. Biblically, the number four represents the whole earth (think of the "four corners of the earth" in Isaiah 11:12). Ezekiel 47:1 describes this same river of living water as coming from the temple, and in Revelation 22:1 it comes out from the throne of God.

The four riverheads that are formed from this river all have names. They are Pishon, Gihon, Hiddekel, and Euphrates. Since we are acquainted with the Euphrates, and the Hiddekel is known to be the Tigris, it is generally concluded that the Garden of Eden was located in what was later called Mesopotamia. But there may be more to the story than we generally think.

It has already been noted that there are close parallels between the account of Creation in Genesis 1 and the building of the sanctuary in Exodus 25–27; however, in the description of the garden in Genesis 2, there are other similarities to the sanctuary.

In the description of the river Pishon, mention is made of gold, bdellium, and the onyx stone. Precious stones are also mentioned in connection with Eden in Ezekiel 28:13, and again in the description of the New Jerusalem in Revelation 21:16–21.

Some scholars believe that Pishon and Gihon are closely related, since they surround the countries of Havilah and Cush. They also believe they may be related to the Nile, since Cush has been identified with Ethiopia, located just south of Egypt.

In the Table of Nations (Genesis 10), Cush and Havilah are closely associated, suggesting that they refer to the same general region. If this is correct, the Tigris and Euphrates rivers define the northern boundary of Canaan, while the Pishon and Gihon rivers define the southern boundary. Thousands of years after Creation, Canaan becomes the new sanctuary for the Hebrews, with God dwelling among them. This conforms to what God promises to Abraham in Genesis 15:18, and is echoed by later prophets in Isaiah 19:25; 35:8; and Zechariah 9:10.

Trees—and choices

The Lord God plants two trees in the midst of the Garden. In Hebrew thinking, anything that is singled out, or placed in the center of something, has great importance. Why have two trees, side by side, as if they're equal? The simple answer is that Adam and Eve are given a choice. Both trees bear fruit, which signify food and life; however, one choice brings life, and the other brings certain death. The tree of life represents God, who is the Source of life, and the tree of knowledge of good and evil represents man trying to exalt himself to the place of God. Because these two trees are in the midst of the Garden, they again parallel the sanctuary concept, where God is the central figure among His people.

In Hebrew, the word "life" is plural—so they understand the first tree to be the tree of *lives.* This indicates that life is to continue on without end, and that it is to follow on through successive generations. It provides life-sustaining food, and represents God as the Source of life.

The second tree is the tree of the knowledge of good and evil—which Adam and Eve are carefully instructed never to eat from, or they will most certainly die. Adam and Eve must regularly eat the fruit of the tree of life in order to live.

In Genesis 2:16, God uses the verb "command" for the first time in the Bible. This word signifies more than prohibitions and orders of what should or should not be done. God's commands are a *gift of grace* to mankind to avoid doing things that will harm their happiness and well-being. But God's instructions are unmistakable. If they chose to eat of the tree of the knowledge of good and evil, they reject God's wisdom, and follow the suggestion of the serpent that, "your eyes will be opened, and you will be like God, knowing good and evil" (Genesis 3:5). Through their act of disobedience, they might think to exalt themselves to divine status.

God provides Adam and Eve with everything they need: a beautiful home, food, water, work, companionship for their social needs, communion with Him for their spiritual needs, and a Sabbath rest in His sanctuary. His commands are designed to constantly fulfill the couple's needs and prevent anything that will disrupt their happiness.

In His wisdom, He knows they must form their own characters by continually making choices, so He gives them free will. Even Jesus Christ was not born with a developed character (see Hebrews 5:8, 9; 7:28). He had to choose His Father's will continually. In fact, everything written in Scripture about salvation indicates we have to choose God continually as well.

Man is clearly the centerpiece of God's Creation. He is His magnificent accomplishment—created in His own image and likeness. Adam has a special relationship with God, because he is the crowning act of Creation. He has rulership, under God, here on earth. Because of this, he can make choices: He can create words to name the animals, he can create offspring, and most importantly, he can choose to continually obey the Lord God, assuring his continued life.

God has given man free will to make important choices in life. The choices Adam and Eve have in the Garden of Eden are the same we have today. We can choose to have an intimate relationship with God and accept His gift of grace by following what He says to do or not to do, or we can choose to attempt to usurp His position by following our own will and relying upon ourselves.

CHAPTER FOUR

Wisdom at What Price?

Based on Genesis 3

The story of the fall of man in Genesis 3 offers an amazing display of God's grace.

Eve's first sin, motivated by her desire for self-exaltation, is the same sin that cost Lucifer his home in heaven (Isaiah 14:12–14; Ezekiel 28:13–15). Now known as Satan (see Revelation 12:9 and 20:2), he tempts Eve, disguised as a serpent.

Tricked

Eve isn't frightened. After all, this serpent is an innocent, nonthreatening, beautiful animal. But there's something different—this one speaks! "Has God indeed said, 'You shall not eat of every tree of the garden'?" the serpent asks (Genesis 3:1).

In response, Eve quickly recites her version of God's instructions, adding to what is recorded in Scripture by saying she is not even to *touch* the fruit, lest she die.

"You will not surely die," the serpent responds. "For God knows that in the day you eat of it your eyes will be opened, and you will be like God, knowing good and evil" (Genesis 3:4, 5). The serpent is explaining God's words with *his own* interpretation.

God has subjected every animal to Adam and Eve, but now the serpent implies that he's *wiser than Eve*. Even worse, he implies *he's as wise as God* by accusing Him of selfish motives in denying her this fruit!

Eve apparently follows the serpent's line of thinking by believing that the fruit is good for food, that it is delightful to look at, and that it will make her wise. Perhaps she feels she can attain even more wisdom than she has, because, after all, the serpent curled in the forbidden tree can speak! She decides she wants to be like God, as the serpent suggests—a position she can never attain—and eats the fruit. Feeling no ill effects, she becomes Satan's unwitting instrument in tempting her husband.

Naked

While Eve is tricked into eating the fruit, Adam eats it deliberately. Suddenly, their eyes are opened and they see that they are naked (Genesis 3:7). God's presence has been their clothing, but now they make their own clothes, consisting of leafy loincloths or aprons. They've acquired wisdom all right—the strange wisdom of having the knowledge of both good and evil—resulting in nakedness, shame, and alienation from God. Up to this point, God has clothed them; but now they usurp the role of God by independently providing their own clothing. In Genesis 3:21, God again clothes them fully, in contrast to the skimpy garments they make for themselves.

The word for "garment" or "tunic" is the same word often used for the priestly garments. In order for God to clothe them, innocent animals must die—suggesting the concept of substitution. This parallels the preparation of priests, who are to be fully clothed by others in preparation for ministry in the sanctuary (see Exodus 28:40, 41; 29:8; 40:12–14; Leviticus 8:13). In contrast, the ancient pagan Babylonian priests could minister in their temples without even covering their private parts. For us today, it explains why the sinner has to be completely clothed by God with Christ's righteousness in order to be saved.

The first investigative judgment

That evening, Adam and Eve hear "the sound of the LORD God walking in the garden in the cool of the day" (Genesis 3:8). The word "walking" is the same form of the Hebrew verb used of the God's presence in the sanctuary (Leviticus 26:12). Apparently, Adam and Eve are startled when they hear the sound of the Lord God, so they hide among the trees. The trees that have formerly been for food and beauty now serve as a place for hiding. Clearly, they are now separated from God and afraid of Him.

God immediately begins to ask Adam questions in what is known biblically as a covenant lawsuit, or investigative judgment (see Genesis 4:9, 10; 6:5–8; 11:5; 18:21). These questions are designed to bring out the evidence that will determine whether the judgment sentence is positive or negative. Any true justice must be based on evidence. God is playing the role of prosecutor in a court of law.

God asks Adam, "Where are you?" He answers, "I heard Your voice in the garden, and I was afraid because I was naked; and I hid myself" (Genesis

3:9, 10). His answer indicates he is conscious of his sin because he is naked.

God's second question is: "Who told you that you were naked?" (verse 11). The "who" implies that somebody besides Adam and God is involved in this whole affair. God's question, therefore, appears to be: "Who acted in My place in telling you that you were naked?"

Before Adam answers, God follows up with another question: "Have you eaten from the tree of which I commanded you that you should not eat?" (verse 11).

Adam answers, "The woman whom You gave to be with me, she gave me of the tree, and I ate" (verse 12). Notice that he answers the first question of "who" by blaming *God* for giving him the woman, who gives him the fruit. To the second question, Adam answers, "I ate."

Next God asks the woman, "What is this you have done?" She answers in a similar fashion, "The serpent deceived me, and I ate" (verse 13).

The phase of the investigative judgment is now over, and the sentencing phase of the judgment begins with a curse on the serpent (Genesis 3:14). The Bible indicates that the following verses are very important, since they are formatted in poetic form. No questions are asked of the serpent because *he has no excuse.* Since he was more cunning (shrewd, sly, and crafty and deceiving) than any beast of the field (Genesis 3:1), he is now cursed more than any other beast of the field. Apparently, his cunningness results in his curse.

His curse affects him physically. "On your belly you shall go" (verse 14), indicates that formerly, he moved about differently (see Isaiah 30:6). In Leviticus 11:42 he is classified with the "creeping things." Notice that the animals in this category are all considered unclean because their domain is closely linked with the earth that, at times, is associated with death (Exodus 15:12). The curse of the serpent changes its status from a high position in the animal kingdom, to the most base. As a result, it changes its classification from a clean to an unclean animal.

The first curse is on the serpent, and later in the passage, the second curse is on the earth. Since the curse includes, "eat dust all the days of your life," it indicates that the serpent's life will end (Genesis 3:14). Eating dust signifies *abject subjugation.*

This introduces the idea of "enmity" between the serpent and the woman of the Genesis 3:15 prophecy. Notice that this enmity will result in the serpent's head being fatally bruised. The Hebrew word for enmity is *eyba,* and is found in two other passages of Scripture (Ezekiel 25:15; 35:5) that have the same concept of continual and long-term enmity as does Genesis 3:15. God is the subject that puts this enmity between the serpent and the woman and between his seed and the woman's seed. Enmity is never applied to animals in Scripture, so the entity behind the symbolism of the serpent must be Satan.

Because God is the one who puts the enmity between the two, it indicates that there is enmity between good and evil and, as the verse states, between the seed of the serpent and the seed of the woman.

The result of the enmity is that the seed of the woman, who is indicated as "He," will bruise the head of the serpent. The word Hebrew word *shuwph,* or "bruise," carries the concept of crushing his head, indicating that the bruising will be fatal. However, when the serpent bruises the heel of the woman's seed, the concept is more of grabbing one's heel, or playing dirty because one is grabbed from behind. The serpent is playing dirty by being subtle, cunning, and deceptive. This concept is best illustrated through the biblical account of the birth of Esau, when his twin brother grabs his heel and is given the name of Jacob—meaning "supplanter" or "deceiver."

Both attacks in this conflict between good and evil are fatal; however, one is permanent, while the other is temporary. The scenario of bruising the woman's seed brings salvation for the righteous and is paralleled in the sanctuary ritual, where the life of the animal results in the forgiveness of the sinner. This same process is revealed in the substitute death of the suffering Servant in Isaiah 52 and 53.

In the Hebrew language, Genesis 3:15 is formatted as poetry—indicating that it is extremely important. It reveals the solution to the problem of Adam and Eve's sin. This poetic form continues as God informs Adam and Eve of the consequences of their sin. Notice that the word "curse" is not applied to them and that He gives them the blessed promise of hope and salvation through the seed of the woman, in contrast to the predicted demise of the serpent. However, all sin has consequences, so Eve must suffer "sorrow" in bearing a child, while Adam must "toil" to provide food. The Hebrew word, *itsabon* is the same for both "sorrow/pain" and "toil"—indicating that the consequence is similar for both man and woman. For Eve it means pain in childbirth and that her desire will be for her husband, who will "rule" over her. This sounds harsh and has caused terrible exploitive subjugation in many societies because the Hebrew word for "rule" is not understood—*even in Christianity.* The word *mashal,* or "rule" as used here—and in Genesis 4:7 relating to the relationship of Cain and his brother Abel—has a different connotation than what we usually understand. It carries the concept of "being responsible for," "protecting," and "loving" the person one "rules" over.

Let's look specifically at Genesis 4:7 for a moment. The meaning of *mashal* (to rule) is clear in the King James Version when the Lord addresses Cain, saying, "If thou doest well, shalt thou not be accepted? and if thou doest not well, sin lieth at the door. And unto thee shall be *his* desire, and thou shalt rule over *him*" (Genesis 4:7, emphasis added). It's very important to note that some of the modern translations of the Bible unfortunately use the word "it" instead of the correct pronouns, "his" and "him" in the latter part of this verse. The New King James (and many other versions) read,

> "If you do well, will you not be accepted? And if you do not do well, sin lies at the door.

> And *its* desire is for you, but you should rule over *it*" (verse 7, emphasis added).

This distorts the meaning of the text, making it sound as if the Lord is telling Cain that *sin* is desiring him, yet he must *rule over it*, giving the idea that we can somehow overcome sin by our own power—utter heresy to a Christian!

As we look at this verse carefully, using a more accurate translation like the one in the King James Version, it's clear that the Lord is saying that *Abel's desire (teshuqah* in Hebrew) is for Cain, the firstborn—he naturally trusts, respects, loves, and looks up to his big brother. Age is undoubtedly more significant and respected at that time than in our Western society, today. He looks up to him and generally follows Cain's directions—except in this case, where his brother defiantly brings an unacceptable offering to the Lord. By not offering the correct sacrifice, Cain, in essence, refuses to accept his firstborn status with the Lord. He further proves that he's unwilling to love and protect his younger brother when the Lord asks Cain,

> " 'Where is Abel your brother?'
> He said, 'I do not know. Am I my brother's keeper?' " (Genesis 4:9).

Back to the story of Eve, we note that she is created *equal* to her husband, but because of her sin, she must now look to him ("desire") as the one responsible for her, the one who will protect and love her. *The emphasis here is on the responsibility that the husband has in his relationship with his wife, not a right to demand his way in a selfish sense.* In other words, God is trying to arrange a positive relationship, even in a sinful, imperfect state. Later on, in the New Testaments, Paul makes this clear in Ephesians 5:25, when he writes, "Husbands, love your wives, just as Christ also loved the church and gave Himself for her."

The consequences for Adam's sin are now revealed to him. Because Adam has listened to the voice of his wife, rather than God's voice, the ground is cursed for his sake. In toil he shall eat of it all the days of his life. Notice, the ground is cursed for his benefit, hoping it will serve to keep him loyal to God. He will not continue in sin forever because his life will end. As he toils the ground, thorns and thistles will make difficult his work and diminish the harvest. His diet is changed from fruit and nuts to herbs of the field, making his diet similar to that of the cattle. His attention is turned from fruit that he was eating of the tree of life supplied by God to the ground where he must toil to obtain his own food.

Changing roles

Notice the inversion of roles that each one assumes in the temptations. Animals are subject to Adam and Eve, but the serpent takes a superior position to her. God made Eve from one of Adam's ribs (taken from his side, not from his foot nor from his head). She is his equal, but by tempting him, she assumes a superior position, implying she knows better than he does. Adam is over all of nature, including the trees—but not the two trees in the midst of the garden. Now he exercises authority over the tree of knowledge of good and evil by eating its forbidden fruit.

Each has stepped out of their place in God's creation, and each one has their former role reversed to an inferior one. As God calls them, they crouch among the trees, trembling and ashamed. How quickly sin has taken hold. They each blame someone else for their disobedience: the woman blames the serpent, and man blames his wife—and God for giving her to him!

But notice the reversal of roles, again, as God pronounces fair punishment for their self-exaltation in each transgression. The serpent, that exalted itself above the woman, now becomes a despised creature that must crawl on his belly. The woman, who exalted herself above her husband, becomes subject to him. Man, who had been over all of nature, will now toil and labor for his food—just as the woman will labor in childbirth. Both are now subject to nature by returning to dust after they die. All of these consequences for sin are designed to be *redemptive*. They help humans to realize the need of a Redeemer who will reverse the consequences of sin.

But don't miss this: After the curse on the serpent in Genesis 3:14—and before the punishment for Adam and Eve in Genesis 3:16, 17—God gives them the promise of a Redeemer in Genesis 3:15 who will pay the price for sin and restore humans back to God! The serpent will bruise the heel of the woman's Seed, but God promises that her Seed, Jesus, will bruise the serpent's head.

CHAPTER FIVE

My Brother's Keeper

Based on Genesis 4

When Eve has Cain, she undoubtedly believes she's given birth to the Messiah, because the Hebrew states literally, "I have gotten a man—the Lord." (In this phrase, "the Lord" is the direct object.) So, obviously, she saw no need for her second son, Abel. His name (*hebel* in Hebrew), is translated as "breath," as in, "Man is like a breath; his days are like a passing shadow" (Psalm 144:4); and also, "vanity," or nothingness—as in "Vanity of vanities, all is vanity" (Ecclesiastes 1:2).

In the process of time, Cain and Abel grow up and now must bring a sacrifice to atone for their sins. The instructions (later recorded in Exodus 29:39–41) have obviously been given to their parents, else Genesis 3:15 would not be understood by Adam and Eve.

The sacrificial offering requires a vegetable offering be brought to the Lord, along with the firstborn of the flock. Abel, the shepherd, follows the instructions God gave his parents to the letter—"Abel *also* brought of the firstborn of his flock" (Genesis 4:4, emphasis added). However, Cain, the farmer, only offers the Lord the fruit of his fields, *without* the firstborn of the flock. This difference may seem trivial, but Cain's omission is an act of defiance and a rejection of Jesus, whom the lamb represents. He feels no need for a Redeemer.

There is also a difference in the motives of each brother. Cain brings an "offering to the LORD," as if it is a gift, while Abel just offers. These represent two different views of worship. Cain considers his offering to be presented upward *to the Lord* as a gift, while Abel understands the meaning of the sacrifice as a gift *from* the Lord.

Abel's sacrifice is accepted; but the Lord has "no regard" for Cain's offering. This makes him angry, and his countenance falls—indicating that he becomes depressed.

Observe how the Lord tries to reason with him. "Why are you angry?" He asks, "And why has your countenance fallen? If you do well, will you not be accepted?" (verses 6, 7).

Sadly, Cain refuses to accept forgiveness and change. His anger boils over, and he murders his brother! Ironically, the first murder recorded in the Bible occurs at the same time of the first mentioned act of worship.

Investigative judgment

God comes looking for Cain and asks him, "Where is Abel your brother?"

"I do not know," Cain lies. "Am I my brother's keeper?" (Genesis 4:9). This is the first recorded human lie, and Cain's disdain for flock keepers is obvious, as he essentially says, "Am I my brother's shepherd?"

"What have you done?" God continues. "The voice of your brother's blood cries out to Me from the ground" (Genesis 4:10). Here, the word "blood" in Hebrew is the plural form; by ending Abel's life, Cain kills off all future generations of his bloodline.

Notice how the Lord conducts an "investigative judgment"—bringing to light all the facts, so everyone can see that He is just in His judgment. The questions He asks of Cain are the same type as those He asked Cain's parents. This is a technique ancient Hebrew narrators used; first they tell a story, then another, using details and language that recall and comment on the first.

The mark of cain

Finding Cain guilty of murder, God now pronounces judgment: "You are cursed from the earth, which has opened its mouth to receive your brother's blood from your hand. When you till the ground, it shall no longer yield its strength to you. A fugitive and a vagabond you shall be on the earth" (Genesis 4:11, 12). Since the earth has been forced to swallow his brother's blood, it will no longer produce crops for this farmer because sin has also affected the ground. Ironically, Cain is forced to be a wanderer—like a shepherd—and he complains bitterly! He also greatly fears for his life.

Notice the interesting way God's compassion is illustrated: In Genesis 1, the Creator is called "God," *Elohim* in Hebrew—the God of power. Later, when creating man in Genesis 2, He is called "the LORD God," *Yahweh Elohim*—the God of covenant (personal relationship) and power. But as He deals with Cain in Genesis 4, He's simply called *Yahweh* "the LORD" (the loving, personal God). Trying His best to reach His guilty child, the Lord senses his great fear and promises to protect Cain with a mark or warning to others. God vows to bring a heavy, seven fold judgment upon anyone who dares kill him!

While the Bible is silent about this mark, the Hebrew gives us a clue. Most modern translations call it a *token,* not some strange physical mark or skin pigmentation as some suggest. *This is not a mark of condemnation; it's a mark of protection!* What tenderness God shows him—even though he's unrepentant. Amazing grace indeed!

After Cain rejects God's grace and forgiveness, the Bible says he walks away going from the east (where God lives) to the west, away from the Lord. How sad that Cain begins this story drawing near to God and ends it by permanently leaving His presence. He settles in the land of Nod that has the meaning of "wandering," "flight," or "exile."

Two genealogical lines

The evil legacy of Cain continues in his genealogical line. Cain builds the first city, contrary to God's desire for man to commune with nature. He names the city after his firstborn son Enoch, whose name means "dedication." Apparently, this city is dedicated to his son and probably carries the idea of a religious act. Since God is not mentioned in this whole narrative, this city must be pagan, built by Cain's own labors. Ancient pagan cities were built as dwelling places for the gods rather than humans.

Cain's evil descendants try to lessen their guilt through personal achievements. Jabel gains fame for his herds, Jubal for musical instruments, and Tubal-Cain for his mastery of metals. But the most notorious descendant is Lamech, a bigamist so wicked, he kills a man for merely wounding him—and brags about it! He follows in the footsteps of Cain. It seems that God promised Cain to bring a sevenfold vengeance on anyone who dared murder him, but to Lamech He says, "If Cain shall be avenged sevenfold, then Lamech seventy-sevenfold" (verse 24).

The genealogy now turns from the wicked line of Cain to the righteous line. Again, a son is born to Adam with the name of Seth that means, "to put in the place of." Obviously, he is a replacement for Abel who was killed. At that time, "men began to call on the name of the LORD" (verse 26). This does not refer to worship but to the propagation of the name of the Lord in the earth, since it has been interrupted with the murder of Abel.

The seventh from Adam is Enoch, who walks with God three hundred years. The Bible says, "And Enoch walked with God; and he was not, for God took him" (Genesis 5:24). Enoch's "walking with God" is what Adam and Eve did before they sinned, because *after* they sin, God comes walking and looking for them. Walking with God indicates a close relationship with Him that is linked with life and becomes a key concept connected with salvation through the divine covenant in Genesis 17:1, 2. Enoch is the righteous counterpart to the evil Lamech, who is the seventh in line in Cain's genealogy.

Enoch is the first man to be translated without seeing death and becomes the archetype for all those who follow.

The ninth from Adam is the righteous Lamech, who says of his son Noah, "This one will comfort us concerning our work and the toil of our hands, because of the ground which the LORD has cursed" (Genesis 5:29). Noah's name is derived from the word "rest" that is linked with the toil caused by sin. The word "comfort" can also carry the connotation of revenge that is linked with judgment (see Ezekiel 5:13). Here we see Lamech's hope that Noah will be the Redeemer who brings relief from the toil of sin and the rest of salvation. Noah is the tenth in the righteous line of Adam. The genealogy list pauses with Noah and only resumes again after the Flood story.

CHAPTER SIX

Giants and the Unpardonable Sin

Based on Genesis 6

Family is extremely important to the Hebrews; married sons build onto their fathers' houses, and patriarchs extend their tents to cover three and four generations. Family descent is closely traced in their way of thinking. In Genesis 4 and 5, two lines of genealogy show—one godly and one wicked—intermingling in Genesis 6, as "the sons of God" marry "the daughters of men" and have offspring (verse 2). The "of God" and "of men" seem to clearly distinguish these two different lines. These unholy marriages greatly displease the Lord.

The *nephilim*

The Bible says that giants, or *nephilim* in Hebrew, lived on the earth in those days (verse 4). This word has caused great confusion. Some speculate that the *nephilim* are giants in stature, while others believe they are notorious rulers. Still others believe they are fallen angels.

However, *nephilim* literally means "fallen ones." They cannot be fallen angels, since neither heaven nor angels are mentioned; they cannot be rulers, since no kings or kingdoms are mentioned; and as far as giants, there's no immediate contextual evidence indicating physical height. Instead, the detailed lineages mentioned in the previous chapters indicate "the fallen ones" to be those who have fallen into sin. They are giants, all right—giants in wickedness, not in stature! They're notorious evildoers, and the next verse confirms this, when "the LORD saw that the wickedness of man was great in the earth, and that every intent of the thoughts of his heart was only evil continually" (verse 5). The wicked ones continually reject the Holy Spirit's pleadings, and now they endanger the righteous!

Seeing all this evil, the Bible says, "the LORD was sorry that He had made man on the earth, and He was grieved in His heart" (verse 6). Therefore, the Lord decides, "My Spirit shall not strive with man forever, for he *is* indeed flesh; yet his days shall be one hundred and twenty years" (verse 3).

This isn't a reference to man's lifespan, since Noah's descendants certainly lived longer than that. Instead, it indicates how long the Holy Spirit will continue pleading with men. Indeed, Noah preaches for 120 years before the Flood comes, but men harden their hearts to the point where the Holy Spirit cannot reach them—the truly unpardonable sin (see Matthew 12:31).

The Lord regretted

Before the Lord sends the Flood, He conducts an investigative judgment and sees that the wickedness of man has reached an intolerable level. The Bible now makes a sad conclusion: "And the LORD was sorry that He had made man" (Genesis 6:6).

The danger here is to make the Lord human, since the writer, by necessity, must use human words to describe the Lord's feelings. But did He change His mind? Can the Lord make mistakes?

What we do know is that He "grieved in His heart" because of how far humans had advanced in sin (verse 6). The word "grieve" in Hebrew is associated with sadness that is the opposite of joy and contains nuances of grace and love. This brings a strong element of the hope of salvation through the Flood. We stretch to understand Hebrew thinking; we must stretch much more to understand the Lord!

CHAPTER SEVEN

Righteousness Rewarded

Based on Genesis 6–8

The Lord's amazing grace is displayed as He vows to strive with the wicked antediluvians for 120 years. Throughout this probation period, His faithful servant, Noah, pleads passionately with them, but the Lord's great heart grieves as He watches Noah's family walk into the ark, alone.

Noah finds grace in the Lord's eyes as the result of an extremely close relationship.

Genesis 6:9 says, "Noah walked with God," a phrase used only one other time previously, to describe Enoch (Genesis 5:24). The emphasis of this story is not on the wicked—it's upon righteous Noah, "For the eyes of the LORD are on the righteous, and His ears are open to their prayers" (1 Peter 3:12). He is also considered "perfect," not that he is sinless, as we tend to think, but complete in his actions because he is wholly dedicated to his Lord.

Detailed instructions

The ark is to be made of gopher wood (probably cypress) that will resist decay for centuries. It will have many rooms for animals and people, be covered with pitch or resin, and be approximately 450 feet long, 75 feet wide, and 45 feet high.

Then the Lord instructs Noah to preserve His creatures by bringing a male and female of each of the animals on board. Of the clean animals, and all the birds, he's to bring in seven pairs, as well as one pair of every creeping thing. (Clearly, mankind knew about clean and unclean animals long before the time of Moses.)

The wicked are stunned into silence as the long procession of animals walk past them into the ark, guided by an unseen hand! However, after the Lord closes the door, implying that they are completely in His hands, nothing happens for seven days. Now the people are *convinced* of Noah's lunacy and they mock him. However, God will not be mocked, and after seven days, the skies turn black with rain and the vast "fountains of the deep" break open, shooting up into the sky! Above the noise of thunder and rushing waters, the terrified cries of man and beast can be heard as they trample each other, seeking higher ground. What a sad end to the Lord's beautiful world.

Interesting numbers

Notice the very specific numbers mentioned in Genesis 7. The Lord is undoing His Creation, returning the earth to its original state of watery chaos. He does so by destroying all the nonaquatic, air-breathing creatures with rain for forty days and nights.

A careful study of the number forty in the Bible reveals that it's often associated with bad times: The Israelites wander in the wilderness for forty years as punishment for refusing to obey the Lord; Moses lives in exile for forty years for killing an Egyptian; then, while he was on Mount Sinai for forty days, the Israelites thought they had lost him. Elijah fasts for forty days as he flees Jezebel's wrath; and Ezekiel suffers forty days of punishment for the sins of Judah, while the people suffered for forty years. Even in the New Testament, Jesus endures forty days of fasting and temptation.

Genesis 7:24 brings us another significant number, as the Bible tells us that the flood waters remain on the earth 150 days until the ark comes to rest on Mount Ararat. This lunar five-month period is a familiar number for the ancients—it is the timespan between the planting of grain and the end of the harvest. During the Flood, the Lord completes the "harvest" of the wicked—a point that Noah and his family undoubtedly understand.

However, the Bible says, "God remembered Noah, and every living thing, and all the animals that were with him in the ark" (Genesis 8:1). The God of the universe is totally focused on the preservation of a tiny ark floating on the violent waves. What tender mercy and personal attention He shows His creatures! In fact, the word *Elohim*, or God, is used throughout Genesis 7 after verse 1—a name used to indicate the great power of God that is here being displayed in the Flood and in the protection and salvation of His righteous ones.

As a reward for his righteousness, Noah and his family are now the remnant who preserve the righteous line and human life on this planet—even as God prepares to start over. The word "remnant" carries the idea that what is left at the end serves to continue life into the next generation. Applying this concept to grain, the remnant seed that is left over is used for the next planting and harvesting.

CHAPTER EIGHT

A New Beginning

Based on Genesis 8 and 9

Hebrew storytelling often uses elements from a previous, similar story, largely repeating them to make a point. Although we miss many of them, consider how the author of Genesis uses this technique with the Flood story.

The Flood has submerged everything; the highest mountains are topped by fifteen cubits—over twenty-two feet—of water (Genesis 7:19, 20). In doing so, God has essentially put the earth back into its pre-Creation state, where it was covered with water and was without form and void (Genesis 1:2).

Noah is the new Adam. He has three sons, just as Adam had, and because his family is the only one that survived, he is the second father of all humans.

Notice some of the parallels between Creation and re-creation:

Creation	Re-Creation
God's Spirit hovers over waters (Genesis 1:2)	God sends wind over waters (Genesis 8:1)
Dry land created (Genesis 1:9)	Waters recede, dry land appears (Genesis 8:3–5)
Vegetation created (Genesis 1:11, 12)	Plants reappear (Genesis 8:10, 11)
Birds created (Genesis 1:20, 21)	Birds released (Genesis 8:19)
Animals created (Genesis 1:26, 27)	Animals released (Genesis 8:19)
Man created (Genesis 1:26, 27)	Noah and his family released (Genesis 8:18)

Adam commanded to be fruitful and multiply (Genesis 1:28)	Noah commanded to be fruitful and multiply (Genesis 9:7)
Sabbath and worship established (Genesis 2:1–3)	Worship reestablished (Genesis 8:20)

Before exiting the ark, Noah sends out birds to gain information about conditions outside. He opens a window in the roof of the ark and releases a raven, an unclean bird that can fly for long periods of time. Noah knows that ravens live mainly on carrion, which will be available in abundance, but when the bird returns, he realizes the surface of the earth is still covered in water.

Next, he sends out a dove—a clean bird that will only eat seed. With a limited ability for sustained flight, the dove returns, indicating to Noah that there is not yet much dry ground. Seven days later, he releases it again, and once more, it returns—this time with a fresh olive leaf in its beak, and after another seven days, the dove is sent out and doesn't return at all—indicating that the waters have dried up. However, God does not release Noah from the ark immediately after it rests on Mount Ararat. He must wait more than seven lunar months until sufficient food is available for him and all the animals.

It's interesting that the total time that Noah was in the ark with all the animals is specifically recorded—a period of exactly one year and one week. The Bible says that "In the six hundredth year of Noah's life, in the second month, the seventeenth day of the month," (Genesis 7:11) the Flood began. "And in the second month, on the twenty-seventh day of the month, the earth was dried," (Genesis 8:14) allowing Noah and his family to exit from the ark. The time period between Genesis 7:11 and Genesis 8:14 is exactly twelve lunar months (354 days) and eleven days (for a total of 365 days) afterward. There is historical evidence that the Babylonians and Egyptians were acquainted with both the lunar and solar calendars before Moses' time, but obviously, God laid the foundation for these calendars in Genesis 1:14, where He set the sun, moon, and stars up "for signs and seasons, and for days and years."

God's bow in the clouds

We can only imagine the mixture of joy and sadness Noah and his family must feel when they finally exit the ark. An entire year has passed, and while Noah and the animals are happy to be released, the surface of the earth has been totally changed; in fact, it is impossible to describe.

God's perfect world has been torn apart. Where there was once perfect symmetry, there are jagged rocks. Hills and mountains have been moved, and the beauty of the earth has been permanently scarred.

However, Noah's focus is on gratitude to the Lord. He builds an altar, and offers burnt offerings of every clean animal and bird. Clearly, God instructed Noah's forefathers to sacrifice in this manner, and his sacrifices are both a petition to be forgiven and an offering of thanksgiving for being saved from the Flood.

This is pleasing in God's sight, and He says in His heart, "I will never again curse the ground for man's sake, although the imagination of man's heart is evil from his youth; nor will I again destroy every living thing as I have done. While the earth remains, seedtime and harvest, cold and heat, winter and summer, and day and night shall not cease" (Genesis 8:21, 22).

Now God makes a covenant with man and every living creature, promising to never again destroy the earth with water. Moreover, He gives them a sign of His covenant by saying, "I do set my bow in the cloud, and it shall be for a token of a covenant between me and the earth" (Genesis 9:13, KJV). Many versions of the Bible have translated the word *qesheth* as "rainbow;" but although this term is correct, the original Hebrew word is "bow."

Notice how we think in Greek terms: When we see a rainbow, we see a pretty arc of color in the sky. Most of us know that it's the result of sunlight shining on the droplets of moisture in the earth's atmosphere; some even know that there are seven colors displayed in a rainbow (not surprising, since that seems to be God's favorite number). But while we're interested in the scientific explanation (Greek thinking, again), the ancient Hebrews see something quite different. To them, it's God's bow. It's bright, colorful, and huge, and it only appears after a rainstorm—which still terrorizes those who remember the Flood. While we're interested in its colors, the ancients are interested in its shape. This bow represents God's WMD, His "weapon of mass destruction"! This is His bow (think bow and arrow as they thought), but it's hanging in the clouds *without arrows* for all to see. He has laid down His weapon of war! He promised, and He is faithful.

Of course, the irony of it all is that God's bow is made of water—the very substance He used to destroy the earth with a flood!

The rainbow symbol is echoed in the biblical descriptions of God's glory in Ezekiel 1:26–28, and His throne in Revelation 4:3. His beautiful bow represents His mercy and fidelity to the ancients—and to us.

CHAPTER NINE

An Important Message

Based on Genesis 9

Jews and Christians alike have long considered Moses to be the author of the book of Genesis, which covers everything from Creation through the life of Joseph. It's important to know that the book's first intended audience is the Hebrew people in the time of Moses.

As we have seen before, Hebrew storytelling often uses elements from a previous, similar story, largely repeating them to make a point. This is the means used by the author to tie together self-contained narratives into a larger line of stories. By placing the story of Noah's sin at this point in Scripture, the author is deliberately drawing the parallels between his fall, and the fall of Adam.

Canaan's curse

In Genesis 9:18–29 Noah emerges from the ark and begins farming, just as Adam did when he cultivated and kept the Garden of Eden. Noah plants a vineyard, crushes the grapes, drinks the wine, and becomes drunk. He lays in his tent, naked—just as Adam found himself after he sinned.

Noah's son Ham sees "the nakedness of his father" (verse 22) and greatly dishonors him by not covering him. Then he tells his brothers about it! However, unlike their brother, Shem and Japheth honor Noah by entering the tent walking backward with a garment laid upon their shoulders to cover him—just as God did for Adam by clothing him with animal skins.

When Noah awakes from his drunkenness, he knows what his son has done to him (Genesis 9:24) and then pronounces a curse on Canaan, Ham's son—just as God did with Adam and his posterity. Once again, notice the similarities: Adam had three sons, two were righteous, one was wicked; Noah has three sons, two are righteous, and one is wicked. However, the curse is not mentioned as being on Ham but his son Canaan.

Noah prophesies that Canaan will be a servant to Shem and Japheth, while Shem and Japheth will receive God's blessing.

But why is Canaan cursed, rather than Ham?

The clue lies in the fact that the Hebrews in the time of Moses were the first intended audience for the book of Genesis. Canaan is mentioned by name because the people are to settle in *his* land. *This is a very important message for them!* It warns them that the descendants of Canaan are a wicked and immoral line and that they should neither marry nor associate with them—as the descendants of Seth and Cain did before the Flood. They must destroy them because their cup of iniquity is full and the land must be cleansed before the Hebrews occupy it. This story anticipates and foreshadows the wickedness and sexual immorality of the Canaanites, especially at their high places, where they performed many of their religious immoral practices.

Additional facts

This story brings up several other important facts. First, in modern American history, the curse on Canaan has often been used to justify slavery. This interpretation is still heard at times today and has resulted in the unfair demeaning of a large part of earth's population. However, if we interpret this passage in its proper context, this interpretation is not only incorrect but also is actually insulting and should never be used!

Also, the notion of covering one's "nakedness" was apparently so important that Moses includes it in the regulations for the priests that serve in the tabernacle (see Exodus 28:42, 43). He also deals with it in the correction of the immoral relationships in Leviticus 18. When they approach the presence of the Lord at the altar, they must cover their nakedness by wearing linen undergarments. In contrast the pagan priests have no need to cover their private parts.

The message from this story is clear. There are two groups: one that follows in wickedness and one that follows in righteousness and is blessed by God. While God never takes away anyone's free will, He does prophesy what the majority of this world's people will do.

CHAPTER TEN

What Is in a Number?

God used the ancient Hebrew writers to communicate profound truths in skilled and intricate ways. These include the use of numbers, which are used to reveal deeper meanings throughout Scripture that are commonly missed by casual readers. We will focus on this subject, not as a spiritual lesson, but in preparation for important applications later.

As Pastor Doug Batchelor has pointed out, "Throughout history, men with great minds, like Augustine, Isaac Newton, and Leonardo da Vinci, showed more than just a passing curiosity regarding the importance of biblical numbers." He goes on to say, "Jesus said, 'The very hairs of your head are numbered' (Matthew 10:30), so obviously, Bible numbers should be carefully considered."*

However, I will insert a strong caution here: While understanding the significance of these recurring biblical numbers is useful as an aid in studying Scripture, *I certainly do not condone numerology*—a practice associated with the paranormal, alongside astrology and similar divination arts used to predict the future. These are *counterfeits,* and therefore, a perversion of what God intended us to see in His use of numbers.

Seven

So what do biblical numbers show us? We will start with the number seven. It is the most common and important one, by far, since it appears many hundreds of times in both the Old and New Testaments.

Just glancing over the Old Testament, we find that Noah brought seven pairs of every clean animal and bird aboard the ark, and seven days later it

---

* Doug Batchelor, "The Key to Bible Numbers," BibleUniverse.com, Amazing Facts, accessed November 28, 2020, http://www.bibleuniverse.com/articles/the-keys-to-bible-numbers.

began to rain. The Egyptian Pharaoh dreamed of seven fat and seven lean cattle, which represented seven years of plenty and seven years of famine. Led by seven priests with seven trumpets, the Israelites marched around the city of Jericho seven days—and seven times on the seventh day—before its walls crumbled. The annual covenant agricultural feasts use sevens and multiples of seven.

The New Testament is also full of sevens: Jesus used seven loaves to feed four thousand, people and had seven large baskets of leftovers, He commanded us to forgive seventy times seven, and cast out seven demons from Mary Magdalene. But nothing represents this number's importance more clearly than the fact that it is found in the prophetic books of Daniel and Revelation dozens of times. As others have pointed out, Revelation alone mentions seven churches, seven spirits, seven candlesticks, seven stars, seven lamps, seven seals, seven horns, seven eyes, seven angels, seven trumpets, seven thunders, seven heads, seven crowns, seven plagues, seven vials, seven mountains, and seven kings!

There are even seven amens—and John adds his own to them!

Let's go back now and look at the amazing intricacy of the first story in the Bible—the first account of Creation found in Genesis 1:1 through 2:3. The Bible says our world was created in a literal seven-day week of evenings and mornings; and God's Sabbath, the day He rested from His labor and blessed, is clearly listed as the seventh day.

There are interesting multiples of seven that occur here as well. *In the Hebrew text,* Genesis 1:1 has seven words, and Genesis 1:2 has fourteen words. In addition, if we count the words "It was so," "It was good," and "God saw," in the story of Creation, we find that they all appear seven times, while the word "earth" appears twenty-one times.

There are many more examples, but the repeated use of the number seven and its multiples clearly indicates the extreme importance of both God's seven-day Creation week and His seventh-day Sabbath.

Numbers in genealogy

Notice the multiples of seven in the lineage of Jesus. Matthew 1:17 says, "So all the generations from Abraham to David are fourteen generations, from David until the captivity in Babylon are fourteen generations, and from the captivity in Babylon until the Christ are fourteen generations." But let's look at two genealogical lines from the Old Testament; the non-covenant-keeping line of Cain (Genesis 4:17–24) and the godly line of Seth, which the Bible begins with Adam (Genesis 5:1–32). Cain's lineage lists seven names, and the seventh one is Lamech—the most violent man of Cain's wicked line, who killed a man for merely striking and wounding him. Notice his peculiar use of numbers when he boasts, "If Cain shall be avenged sevenfold, then Lamech seventy-sevenfold" (Genesis 4:24).

It's interesting to note that another Lamech, from Seth's righteous line, is mentioned as living 777 years (Genesis 5:31). There are also ten generations listed in the covenant-keeping line of Seth. The seventh name on this list is Enoch, who walked with God and was taken to heaven without seeing death. Obviously the seventh person in each line balances out the other.

The number ten also has significance in biblical genealogy. The righteous line of Seth lists the tenth man as Noah. He is extremely important because he builds the ark and is saved from the Flood. He is, in essence, the second Adam, since our world's population descends from him. Now let's look at one of Noah's sons. Shem's righteous line (Genesis 11:10–26) lists the tenth name as Abram, with whom God makes a covenant, and through whom He establishes a holy nation.

The number four also emerges as a new and significant number in Shem's line. His fourth descendant is Eber, after whom the Hebrews were named. According to the Old Testament prophets, if they were to remain faithful to God, they would ultimately fill and rule the earth. So the number four comes to represent the whole earth.

Seventy

Genesis 10 lists the genealogy of the sons of Noah—seventy in all— from whom the whole earth is repopulated. Thus, this number becomes symbolic of all the nations of the earth.

God uses this same number later, when He instructs Moses to take seventy of the elders of Israel up Mount Sinai (Exodus 24:1, 9). If they remain faithful, His plan is to set them up as administrators over all the nations of the earth.

Then, when Jesus instructs His followers to spread the gospel, He sends out "the 70" to all the nations of the earth (Luke 10:1–20). These, and many other numbers used by the ancient Hebrew writers heighten the richness and unity of Scripture. The ancients understand their significance, and Satan also seems to use members to produce his counterfeits. Six, "the "number of a man" (Revelation 13:18), refers to his creation on the sixth day. In Revelation 13:18, the six is tripled to 666. Numerology was used as early as Babylonian times. Nebuchadnezzar uses the number six and its multiples to build a self-exalting statue. It is six cubits wide and sixty cubits high—a tall, thin statue way out of human proportions. It towers into the sky, trying to elevate him to the status of a god. Study of the Bible will constantly yield new insights into the depth and richness of God's Holy Word. The fact that so many writers at different times and places in history could have written such a cohesive Book under God's inspiration is simply amazing!

CHAPTER ELEVEN

Trying to Become Gods

Based on Genesis 11

The context for the Tower of Babel story begins in Genesis 10 with Noah's seventy descendants who make up what's known as the Table of Nations. Notice that both an evil and a righteous line emerge from Shem's descendants—just as they did with Cain and Seth's children, recorded in Genesis 4 and 5.

Although Joktan belongs to Shem's righteous line, he and his descendants become decidedly evil. Instead of heeding God's command to multiply and fill the earth, they travel southeast to the Plain of Shinar to build a city.

The Bible says, "And it came to pass, as they journeyed from the east, that they found a plain in the land of Shinar, and they dwelt there" (Genesis 11:2). Here some difficulty arises among Bible translators, since the Plain of Shinar (located where the ruins of Babylon are in Iraq) is definitely *southeast* from where the ark settled in the Ararat Mountains in Turkey. The Hebrew word *miqqedem* can literally mean "from the east" *or* "eastward" depending on how it's translated, so let's look at how it is translated elsewhere.

Both the King James and New King James versions translate *miqqedem* in Genesis 11:2 as "from the east." However, these same versions translate it in Genesis 2:8 as "eastward," and in Genesis 3:24; 12:8; and 13:11 as "east." Many newer translations have picked this up and translate *miqqedem* as "toward the east," or "eastward."

East—where God lives

Is this direction important? Certainly, since the Bible often associates God with the east. Consider this: After sinning, Adam and Eve worship God at the *east* gate of the Garden of Eden, the tabernacle and temple both face *east,* and the wise men follow a star in the *east.* In addition, God often sends an *east* wind to fulfill His intentions. An *east* wind blows the locusts into Egypt, an *east* wind blows open the Red Sea, and God sends a hot *east* wind to overheat Jonah. Jesus is called the Morning Star (in astronomical terms, the morning star refers to Venus, which appears in the east each morning). Even the Second Coming is described as being like lightning streaking from *east* to west.

Pagan cities

Ancient pagans don't build cities to live in—they build them for their gods.

However, Joktan's descendants say, "Come, let us build *ourselves* a city, and a tower whose top is in the heavens; let us make a name for *ourselves,* lest we be scattered abroad over the face of the whole earth" (Genesis 11:4, emphasis added). "Let us" is using the same expression as Genesis 1:26 when the members of the Godhead decide to make man in His image.

These rebellious men disobey God's command to populate the earth, congregating, instead, and building a city *for themselves.* By traveling eastward, they seek to build their city where God lives—elevating themselves to the status of God. In fact, the Tower of Babel in ancient Babylonian texts is interpreted as "the gateway of the gods." They call this type of tower a ziggurat, allowing the gods who live on top to travel back and forth between heaven and earth.

Undoubtedly, these men fear another universal flood, in spite of God's promise.

They intend to build a tower that will reach the heavens (where God lives) and stay above any flood He might send. But most of all, they want to make a name for themselves.

Mercy

It's interesting to note that *Yahweh* is used in this story—the name for a tender, personal God. This is very appropriate, considering how He deals with them: "The LORD came down to see the city and the tower which the sons of men had built" (Genesis 11:5).

Instead of destroying them, He shows the builders of Babel mercy. He does away with their universal language, and by confusing their communication, He effectively stops the construction of the tower that becomes known as Babel or confusion. By sparing their lives, He ends their rebellion and scatters them over the face of the earth, ultimately accomplishing His purpose.

Following this story, the Bible lists the descendants of Joktan's brother, Peleg. His righteous line did not participate in the building of the tower—but brings forth righteous Abram and the patriarchs, instead.

The ancients understand God through their senses and by His actions. Once more, it becomes clear that the age-old sin of self-exaltation can only end in failure.

CHAPTER TWELVE

A Call to Calamity?

Based on Genesis 12

Confusing the languages does not stop the wickedness of the tower builders of Babel. They build many cities in Mesopotamia, including the city of Ur.

When Abram is born, Ur is already famous for its advanced knowledge of mathematics and astronomy and its wealthy kings. Along with the northern city of Haran, it is also known for its worship of the moon god. But among these wealthy, idolatrous people, Abram stands out. He becomes the center of the book of Genesis. He is known by his faith and the fact that God reveals His covenant to him.

A huge test

Genesis 11:31 makes clear that God first appears to Abram while he's still living in Ur of the Chaldeans. That is located in the region of Babylonia that is associated with the tower of Babel. "Get out of your country and from your family and from your father's house, to a land that I will show you" (Genesis 12:1). This leaving Ur becomes the archetype for future scriptural use of the concept of coming out of wicked Babylon (contextually Babel) and the return to God's covenant.

The enormity of this command is lost on us today. We can write, call, text, or even videoconference those we love, and a few hundred dollars plus a day of air travel can usually take us to our family. However, this is not so for the ancients. They place the utmost importance on family and land, and now God asks Abram to leave both behind. He is to establish a new identity in a new land with an unknown future. Clearly, God is starting something radical and new with Abram.

Family is important to the ancients. Parents need children to sustain them in their old age and keep the family name alive, since the greatest of calamities is to have their genealogical line die out. Land ownership is also extremely important because it meant inheritance—land should forever remain in the family.

The second reason God's command seems overwhelming is because He doesn't tell Abram where he's going. Instead, He commands him to move away from everything he knows, loves, and values—away from everything that offers him security, "to a land that I will show you."

God might take him through lands where he, his flocks, and family might be attacked; He might take him to a land that is rocky and poor. However, Abram's faith overrides his fear and he strikes out with his father's family on a journey that surely seems like a call to calamity!

Honor

Although God's command is directed to Abram, the Bible says that his father, Terah, leads the move. In ancient times it would certainly be disrespectful of Abram to *not* allow his father to take charge.

As they set out, they travel northwest to Haran, a city some say is over seven hundred miles away. While the Bible doesn't tell us why, the reason they pause in this city most likely has to do with Abram's respect for his father's age, and his attempt to make Terah's last days more comfortable.

Terah dies in Haran some time later, and after he is buried, the Lord calls Abram again. "Get out of your country, from your family and from your father's house, to a land that I will show you. I will make you a great nation; I will bless you and make your name great; and you shall be a blessing. I will bless those who bless you, and I will curse him who curses you; and in you all the families of the earth shall be blessed" (Genesis 12:1–3). In Genesis 10 the whole earth is represented by the Table of Nations, now the same concept occurs with the blessing to "all families of the earth."

The land where God guides him is Canaan—a place inhabited by many different peoples who are all trying to claim it for themselves. Historical sources reveal that travel through this unfamiliar frontier land must be terrifying, since encounters with wild animals and the locals may happen at any time.

When Abram departs from Haran, he takes his wife Sarai, his nephew Lot, and all the people whom he has acquired in Haran with him. These people are not slaves, so they must be people that he has influenced religiously though his relationship with his God.

Abram has now literally given up his earthly security, his identity, his inheritance, and his future—placing them all in God's hands. Now God places him as an alien in a land belonging to the wicked descendants of Canaan, on whom He placed a curse several generations before! And even as Abram passes this test of his faith, he must wonder how God will fulfill His promise, since he is over seventy-five years old and still childless.

CHAPTER THIRTEEN

From Jeopardy to Redemption

Based on Genesis 12

Ancient Hebrews follow the concept that similar things can be equated with each other, whether they are stories, persons, situations, events, or colors. Good examples are found in the stories about Abram and his descendants. They contain great similarities, both in the jeopardy humans keep imposing on God's covenant plan and in His amazing remedies.

An example

Genesis 12 finds Abram in Canaan, but a severe famine makes him leave the Promised Land for Egypt—a place abundant in food, so long as the Nile has its spring overflow. He's keenly aware that his life will be in jeopardy if an Egyptian desires beautiful Sarai and discovers that she's his wife, so he asks her to say that she's his sister. After all, she *is* the daughter of his father—but *not* his mother (Genesis 20:12).

Most will understand this to mean that she's his half-sister, the daughter of Terah.

This means Abram is telling the truth on one hand, but on the other, he's clearly telling a lie to Pharaoh.

But there may be another interpretation, since we have no clear biblical reference stating that her father is Terah. Because they are childless, their wealth will be in jeopardy if Abram dies, since there is no male heir to take care of Sarai. However, according to an ancient law, this can be remedied if Abram's father adopts Sarai as his daughter.

Pharaoh's princes see Sarai and commend her to him, so the king takes her into his house and showers Abram with great gifts of many animals and servants. But God is not pleased with this, and brings great plagues on the Egyptian king. Pharaoh then calls Abram, reprimands him for not disclosing that Sarai is his wife and expels him from his country—although he's careful to protect him with a guarded escort to the border.

Abram errs, but God remedies the situation and fulfills His covenant promises by taking him out of Egypt and restoring him back in Canaan— along with the blessing of the great riches Pharaoh gives him.

Another example

Two generations later, this story is essentially repeated. Abram's grand-son, Jacob, asks for Rachel's hand but is tricked into marrying both Rachel and her older sister Leah. But in spite of clearly favoring Rachel, only Leah gives him children.

When Rachel finally has a child, baby Joseph quickly becomes his father's favorite, creating a rift between him and his older half-brothers. Eventually, their resentments cause them to sell Joseph into slavery, but God miraculously establishes him as the Egyptian prime minister (vizier). Then He reveals that a famine is coming, so Joseph heads up a program to stockpile grain. In reality, he becomes a savior to Jacob and his family as well as that entire area of the world by providing food.

Finally, Joseph calls his father to Egypt, and God assures Jacob that He'll go with him and surely bring him back to the Promised Land. But after several generations, the Hebrews essentially adopt the pagan gods and are enslaved by the Egyptians. Once again, God's covenant promises appear to be placed in jeopardy by man. However, He begins to remedy the situation and fulfill His covenant promises by bringing ten plagues upon Egypt. The Hebrews are virtually expelled from the land, but as they leave, the Egyptians shower them with articles of gold and silver, as well as rich clothing.

And another

Many generations later, a similar situation arises with the most impor-tant of Abram's descendants, Jesus Christ. After hearing of His birth, King Herod believes Him to be a threat and orders all of Bethlehem's male children two years and younger to be put to death. However, God appears to Joseph in a dream and instructs him to flee to Egypt.

After Herod's death, Joseph, Mary, and Jesus return, fulfilling the Messi-anic prophecy, "Out of Egypt I called My Son" (Matthew 2:15; see also Hosea 11:1 and Numbers 24:8). Once again, man places God's covenant plan in jeopardy, and once again, He remedies the situation. And in this case, the riches given Christ are the ones He saves.

CHAPTER FOURTEEN

Separation

Based on Genesis 13 and 14

After Abram returns from Egypt with Sarai and his nephew Lot, he settles near Bethel, and calls on the name of the Lord. Both he and Lot have such an abundance of livestock that the land cannot support them, and the herdsmen of each begin to quarrel. However, there may be more to the story than just a shortage of pasture space. Abram appears to be deeply religious, while Lot seems to be more interested in material wealth than in the Lord. When the two men part ways, Lot chooses the more fertile land of the well-watered plain of Jordan and soon moves into the wicked city of Sodom, outside of the territory of the Promised Land. Meanwhile, Abram stays in the less fertile hill country, but soon the Lord says, "Lift your eyes now and look from the place where you are—northward, southward, eastward, and westward; for all the land which you see I will give to you and your descendants forever" (Genesis 13:14, 15).

In order for the ancients to grasp the extent of the land, they must experience it. Therefore, God says, "Arise, walk in the land through its length and its width" (verse 17). Then Abram moves his tent and dwells by the terebinth trees of Mamre at Hebron, where he builds an altar to the Lord.

War breaks out in the region because five kings of city-states of the Jordan plain have formed a coalition and revolt against a coalition of four kings from the east that have been their oppressors. The cities of the Jordan plain are defeated and Lot is captured.

An escapee comes and informs Abram that Lot has been taken prisoner, and Abram immediately arms 318 of his trained servants for battle. If his military organization is like that of a later time, a captain is placed over every twenty men, and a higher officer is placed over every five captains. This may explain why the odd number of 318 is given, since there would be three hundred soldiers and eighteen officers. Abram divides his men into two groups and makes a surprise attack at night, routing the enemy and rescuing Lot.

As Abram returns home, he meets Melchizedek, king of Salem—the ancient name for Jerusalem. He brings out bread and wine to Abram and blesses him. In turn, Abram tithes of all the spoil of war. Melchizedek is a compound word that means king of righteousness. Although he is not a Hebrew, he is called "the priest of God Most High" (Genesis 14:18).

Apparently, God is using him as His representative among the people of his time. He is linked with the future Davidic Messiah in Psalms 110:4, and his unique pattern of priesthood is used by Christ in Hebrews 6:20–7:28.

Abram also encounters the king of Sodom, who tells Abram to keep all the spoils of war in return for all the persons of his city who have been rescued. Abram refuses, however, saying that he's sworn to the Lord that he will keep no spoils, except for what his men have eaten.

After seeing all the details of this chapter, we can see a great contrast between Abram's and Lot's spirituality. It demonstrates that the reason why they could not dwell together is much greater than just the lack of pasture for their livestock:

At the time of separation, Lot sees the material advantages of the Jordan plain and chooses to go there, while Abram remains where his altar is, and where he called on the name of the Lord.

Lot journeys to the east (which is associated with God), thereby trying to usurp the place of God, as Noah's descendants did in building the Tower of Babel. Meanwhile, Abram remains humble in his relationship to God.

Lot moves into the wealthy and wicked city of Sodom, while Abram moves to Hebron, where God makes His covenant with him (Genesis 15), and remains there for most of his life, and Isaac's life as well.

Lot lives in Sodom in the midst of political and military tensions. Meanwhile, Abram lives in peace with his neighbors.

Lot is taken captive, while Abram rescues him.

Lot loses everything, while Abram recovers everything.

Lot ignores God in all of his difficulties, while Abram is blessed and communicates with the Lord. Clearly their spiritual perspective is so different that they cannot dwell together.

CHAPTER FIFTEEN

A Divine Covenant

Based on Genesis 12; 15; and 17

When God calls Abram to Canaan, He makes a covenant with him, and our need to understand this covenant cannot be overstated; so let's look at it through the eyes of the ancients.

The divine covenant is very different from covenants made between two parties today. First, it is *designed by God* with no human input; second, it is *God who takes the initiative.*

Suzerains and vassals

God uses a Canaanite model for His covenant with Abram, since he's familiar with it. The Hittite kings (called suzerains) make covenants with other kings, allowing them to live and reign under them as vassals.

If a vassal rebels, the suzerain doesn't kill him, but extends a covenant of grace in return for his loyalty. The vassal's only choice is to accept or reject the covenant—he cannot bargain with the suzerain about his terms.

The divine covenant is so similar to the Hittite model that it's called a suzerainty-type covenant. As sinners, we deserve to die for our disloyalty and rebellion against God, but He offers us eternal life through divine grace, instead—as long as we remain loyal to Him. We cannot modify His covenant of grace—we can only choose to accept or reject it. Note that God's plan of salvation is referred to as *His covenant* in the Old Testament, and in the New Testament, it is usually called *the gospel.*

Covenant promises

God promises Abram: "I will make you a great nation; I will bless you and make your name great; and you shall be a blessing. I will bless those who bless you, and I will curse him who curses you; and in you all the families of the earth shall be blessed" (Genesis 12:2, 3). The fulfillment of God's promises are simply a commitment on *His* part. They are wholly dependent on *His* action.

God constantly repeats His blessing to Abram and his descendants throughout Genesis. However, the plural *descendants* narrows to singular in Galatians 3:16, where the Bible says, "Now to Abraham and his Seed were the promises made. He does not say, 'And to seeds,' as of many, but as of one, 'And to your Seed,' who is Christ." Here the Bible makes it clear that it is Christ who brings the blessing of salvation.

God also promises Abram that He'll make his name great. The tower-builders of Babel determined to make their own names great, but only God can do that. David is the only other person in the Bible to receive this promise in 2 Samuel 7:9. As a descendant of Abram and an ancestor of Christ, God promises David that his line of kings and his kingdom will last forever. This will be fulfilled when Christ becomes King of this earth. His kingdom will last forever.

Blessings and curses

God's judgment always brings blessings for the righteous, and curses for the wicked.

His promises to Abram include blessings for his faithfulness and curses on those who curse him. In the same way, Christ's final judgment brings blessings for the righteous and curses for the wicked.

It is important to note that in the Bible, curses are designed for those who have not accepted the divine gift of grace, or who have strayed away from God's will. *They are redemptive in nature.* Each curse is designed to be a difficult experience for the wicked that will cause them to realize their need. Hopefully they will change and turn to God to receive the benefits of salvation. However, those who do not accept His divine covenant are ultimately destroyed.

This is important!

We think of covenants in strictly legal terms today. But while both the Suzerainty and divine covenants are legally binding, they are very different from our covenants, because at their core, their emphasis is primarily *relational.*

God's divine covenant creates a relationship that lasts as long as each party lives—and for man, that's forever, if he receives eternal life. Through this close, mutual relationship, the divine blessings of God's covenant become reality for us. But while God longs to fulfill His covenant promises to us, He's bound by His terms. He can only do this through our faithful relationship to Him.

Significance of the covenant

Most of us do not understand the significance of the covenant promises made to Abram. In simple language, the covenant is *the plan of salvation,* the restoration of sinful humans back to God with a pre-Fall status. God promises Abram three things: seed (offspring), land, and blessing.

First, he will have seed (offspring), in the collective sense, that will expand into many nations (see Genesis 12:2, 3; 15:4, 5; 17:2–7). Based on the promise to Eve (Genesis 3:15) and the covenant promise to David (2 Samuel 7:12, 13), he will also have seed, in the special singular sense, in the coming Messiah, who will redeem sinful man.

Initially, the promise of inherited land is to be the Promised Land of Canaan.

However, when the remainder of Scripture is considered, the land will ultimately be the whole earth (see Revelation 21:1–5).

Then, God promises that Abram's descendants will be a blessing to the earth, serving, in a missionary sense, to bring the plan of salvation to the world. Exodus 19:5, 6 says they are to be a kingdom of priests to God, and to the world.

Many years later, King David wants to build a temple for the Lord, but the Lord tells him that *He* will build the temple through one of the king's offspring—the Messiah.

However, because the people have a difficult time understanding the true *spiritual* temple that will be built by the Messiah, God allows Solomon to build a *physical* building, which is called Solomon's Temple.

The concept of a temple stems from the covenant sanctuary of Exodus 25:8 where God wants to *dwell with His people.* The earthly tabernacle is built for the ancients to visually illustrate God dwelling with His people. However, in 2 Samuel 7:11–13, the real spiritual temple is prophesied to be built by the Messiah that will once again unite sinners to God, like it was before the fall of man.

In Revelation 21:3 and 21:22, the real spiritual temple becomes reality, since God is dwelling with His redeemed *without* a building. When this occurs, the covenant has been fulfilled, and the plan of redemption is complete!

CHAPTER SIXTEEN

God's Guarantee

Based on Genesis 15

Perhaps the most fascinating story about Abram centers on God's covenant with him, just after his battle with the invading kings, and freeing his nephew Lot. Abram is a man of peace, so the carnage of battle must be revolting. His foes are sure to return for revenge, but even more troubling is the fact that he's grown old without receiving the Promised Land—or an heir.

Then God comes to him in a vision in Genesis 15, saying, "Do not be afraid, Abram. I am your shield, your exceedingly great reward"(verse 1). However, Abram can't help wondering aloud if his servant, Eliezer, might have to become his adopted heir.

"This one shall not be your heir, but one who will come from your own body shall be your heir," God replies. Taking him outside, He shows him the stars, and adds, "So shall your descendants be" (verse 4, 5).

Remember, the ancients thought literally, so when Abram sees the stars with his own eyes, his faith has something literal to be based on. He believes and God "accounted it to him for righteousness" (verse 6).

Solemn covenant

Next God reminds Abram that He brought him out of Ur and promised him Canaan as an inheritance, but Abram begs, "Lord GOD, how shall I know that I will inherit it?" (verse 8).

The Lord, who knows our hearts and answers accordingly, now takes the extraordinary step of reassuring His faithful servant by condescending to enter into a solemn covenant using the customary form of the ancients. He instructs Abram to sacrifice a three-year-old heifer, female goat, and ram—the best of young mature animals—along with a turtledove and a young pigeon. All these continued to be used as sacrificial animals by the

Hebrews for centuries. Abram reverently cuts them in half and places the pieces next to each other, leaving a path in between. The small birds are left whole. Notice that while today we "make" covenants, the ancients would "cut" a covenant—for obvious reasons.

Both parties would pass between the carcasses in ancient covenants of this type, indicating that if they didn't fulfill their obligations the result would be death; subsequent sacrifices were a reminder of that death penalty. As Abram solemnly walks between them, he faithfully guards the sacrifices from vultures—creatures the ancients believed were an evil omen. He is worried since there is no visible evidence that the Lord God is doing anything.

As the sun sets, Abram falls into a deep sleep, and "horror and great darkness fell upon him" (verse 12). Then God reveals the omen: Abram's descendants will serve in a foreign land and be afflicted for four hundred years—a period beginning when Abram enters Canaan, rather than four hundred years of actual slavery. Three other things are revealed to Abram: after the four hundred years, they will come out of Egypt with great possessions; Abram will die at a good old age; and the deliverance will be delayed until the fourth generation because the iniquity of the Amorites is not complete until that time. However, God reassures Abram by giving him the boundaries of the Promised Land: "To your descendants I have given this land," He says, "from the river of Egypt to the great river, the River Euphrates" (verse 18).

Darkness and light

After dark, "a smoking oven and burning torch" appear and pass between the carcasses (verse 17). Both darkness and light are symbols associated with God: "I form the light and create darkness, I make peace and create calamity; I, the LORD, do all these things" (Isaiah 45:7). God is a light to His people and darkness to the wicked.

The ancients had no trouble with opposites when it pertained to God. Remember the story in Exodus 14, when the Hebrews were trapped between the Red Sea, the mountains, and the Egyptian army? The Bible says the "Angel of God," in the form of a "pillar of cloud" went behind the people, bringing darkness to the Egyptians but light to His chosen.

The Lord God alone provides Abram with literal guarantees of the fulfillment of His covenant promises: First, in the stars; and second, in ratifying His covenant by personally passing between the sacrificed animals. In ancient Near Eastern treaties, the inferior party of the covenant must walk between the cut pieces of animals; but here it is the Lord God who passes between the cut pieces. He unilaterally ratifies this covenant to prove that He is faithful in fulfilling His promise to give Abram a son. And Genesis 15:6 says that Abram "believed"—*he'emin* in Hebrew—from the same root as the word *amen.* This verb not only expresses trust but also *continual* trust in God.

Reference to the borders of the Promised Land with the mention of the river of Egypt and the Euphrates suggests that this is a deliberate intention to connect with Genesis 2 in describing Canaan as the new Garden of Eden.

The Lord God's promise to Abram appears to be more than a nationalistic statement about the historic settlement of Canaan. It is a vision of the Messianic return to the global Garden of Eden of Revelation 22. This Messianic interpretation of the passage is supported by the apocalyptic features of the story: the scene of Abram's struggle against the vultures, the atmosphere of darkness and horror that fell on Abram, and the appearance of fire (smoking oven and a burning torch) that is used in Scripture as a cleansing agent to eradicate sin. This is further strengthened by the list of ten nations or peoples that occupy Canaan. In Psalm 83, ten nations are also mentioned that will be totally destroyed (Psalm 83:13) as the Lord establishes His universal kingdom (Psalm 83:18).

CHAPTER SEVENTEEN

A Very Bad Idea

Based on Genesis 16 and 17

When Abram leaves Ur he is childless, and by the time he leaves Haran for Canaan, he's seventy-five years old. Ten years later, Abram and Sarai still have no children—and she blames God. Childlessness is considered a divine curse in ancient times, often bringing social difficulties, disdain, and even divorce. Inversely, having children is a sign of God's favor and a fulfillment of His promise to Adam and Eve to be fruitful and multiply.

From bad to worse

In Sarai's eyes, God's covenant promise of a son is in jeopardy, so she uses her style of thinking and suggests Abram take her slave as a second wife to provide him an heir—a common practice in her country.

Hagar, Sarai's slave, is Egyptian, although her name is not. She may have been a gift to Abram when Pharaoh unknowingly took Sarai to be his wife in Genesis 12. Slave women were considered both property and extensions of their mistresses, so Hagar might fulfill household tasks and bear children for Sarai. She would be Abram's concubine—a lesser but legal wife, different from her mistress in that she wouldn't receive a dowry.

Polygamy often came about from a first wife's barrenness, but contemporary Canaanite moral standards would hardly have called concubinage polygamy.

Abram goes along with Sarai's suggestion. Believing this will fulfill God's promise of an heir, he takes Hagar as his second wife and she conceives. But by consummating the marriage, both Abram and Hagar suddenly become Sarai's instruments. *She's* now giving the orders!

However, Hagar knows that she'll now produce an heir, so she becomes insufferable. So much so that Sarai accuses Abram of being the cause of her plight—similar to what Eve did to Adam. Realizing her husband's dependence on Hagar for an heir, her wrath ends in a virtual curse. "My wrong be upon you!" she says to her husband. "The Lord judge between you and me" (Genesis 16:5).

Abram struggles with this huge dilemma, since Hagar is his wife, and the mother of the unborn child he thinks God's promised him! Finally, he answers, "Your maid is in your hand; do to her as you please" (verse 6). With his permission, Sarai now deals "harshly" with her maid—probably implying corporal punishment—and Hagar flees. Their attempt to help God fulfill His promise has created serious new jeopardies: If God fulfills His promise, there's the jeopardy of competing heirs; and with Hagar gone, Abram is in jeopardy of losing his son *before he's even born!*

Amazing compassion

Notice how God steps in and deals with this major problem. The angel of the Lord finds the suffering and abandoned Hagar by a spring in the wilderness. Pregnant and terrified, she is on her way to Shur, fleeing south, toward her native Egypt.

Then God speaks to her through His messenger. Referring to her position, he calls out, "Hagar, Sarai's maid" (verse 8), then asks where she's coming from, and where she's going. When she answers him, he instructs her to return to her mistress—even though she must suffer at Sarai's hand. This return implies more than a physical return, it also involves repentance for her pride and haughtiness toward Sarai. However, God assures her that He sees her affliction. He names her unborn child Ishmael, meaning "God hears," but tells her that he will be a wild man—literally an onager, or wild ass—living a roving, untamed life in which "his hand shall be against every man, and every man's hand against him" (verse 12).

But notice how God then gives Hagar the same amazing promise He gave Abram: "I will multiply your descendants exceedingly" (verse 10). What grace, compassion, and love God extends to this woman! And although Hagar doesn't recognize His voice at first, as He speaks through the angel, she eventually comes to her senses. Calling Him "The God Who Sees," she's astonished she's still alive, and exclaims, "Have I also here seen Him who sees me?" (verse 13).

Again, Hebrew thinking has no trouble with opposites, as we sometimes do. The angel of the Lord first points out her sin of arrogance and pride. It's obvious that she has mistreated her mistress, and this needs to repent—regardless of what Sarai does or does not do. On the other hand, God shows her great personal attention, first by seeing her plight and naming her unborn child, and then by promising to multiply her descendants—using words similar to those He spoke to Abram.

CHAPTER EIGHTEEN

When God Appears

Based on Genesis 17 and 18

When the Lord appears to humans, we call it a *theophany*—a special and thrilling event that's often very dramatic. Scripture mentions two types of theophanies: majestic appearances, like the one on Mount Sinai where He appears amidst smoke, fire, and an earthquake; and nonmajestic, where He appears in visions or in a form not instantly recognized.

Abram's encounters

The Bible says He appears to Abram three times, revealing new covenant details on each occasion.

Genesis 12:7 records the first theophany. While Abram has heard God's voice calling him to Canaan, he's startled by His appearance and His promise to give the land of Canaan to his descendants.

The Lord appears to Abram again in Genesis 17:1, calling Himself *El-Shaddai*, or God Almighty, for the first time. This indicates He has the power to do the humanly impossible in fulfilling His promise to make of Abram a great nation. God then gives Abram and Sarai new names—another unusual event, considering the importance placed on one's name in those days. To have God change your name when you are old is very rare, indeed!

Their new names have great significance, since they reflect His covenant promise, and that they are His chosen servants. Abram means "exalted father," but his new name, Abraham, means "father of a multitude." Sarai means "my princess," but Sarah means "*a* princess,"—not just Abraham's princess, but a princess in a royal line. Together, they will give rise to a line of kings that will last forever, since God's covenant is eternal.

All these shocking and mind-boggling promises demand a response from Abraham: He must circumcise all the males in his household. Circumcision now becomes a sign of the divine covenant promise of many descendants because, in their literal thinking, it's linked with reproduction, which in turn shows they all belong to God's covenant family. For the ratification of the covenant in Genesis 15, Abraham was instructed to "cut" the sacrificial animals into two parts. In Hebrew one "cuts a covenant," so for humans to enter into a covenant relationship with the Lord, the foreskin of males must be "cut off." However, beyond the cutting, there is another important component of a covenant—blood. Both the cutting and the blood are combined in circumcision, demonstrating a clear link to the covenant.

Abraham laughs at God

Thirteen years have passed since Abraham's hopes first focused on Ishmael as his promised heir, and now he's ninety-nine years old. In blessing Sarah, God specifically states she'll have a son the next year, in spite of her age.

Abraham's immediate reaction is to laugh and say in his heart, "Shall a child be born to a man who is one hundred years old?" (Genesis 17:17). Then he says to God, "Oh, that Ishmael might live before You" (verse 18), but God does not accept this at all, and states that his promised son will be called Isaac, meaning "he laughs," reflecting the joy the baby will bring for one who is childless—and perhaps reminding Abram that he laughed at being a one-hundred-year-old father. Hebrew and biblical studies suggest that Isaac implies the name of God, and if this is the case, it implicitly suggests that it is God who laughs last.

Sarah laughs too!

The third theophany comes in Genesis 18:1. Abraham sees three men approaching his tent one summer, and following the ancient custom, he runs to offer them water to wash their dusty feet, shade to rest in, and a morsel of bread—suggesting pita bread. This show of hospitality can transform potential enemies to at least temporary friends!

Ancient custom then requires a meal be served that exceeds what is first offered, so Abraham asks Sarah to make a huge banquet, including cakes fried in fat and milk, using three measures (or twenty quarts!) of fine flour. Then he runs to get a fatted calf that is reserved to feed visitors and a young servant to prepare it, before personally placing both curdled and sweet milk before his guests and standing by, as a servant, while they eat.

"Where is Sarah?" one of the strangers asks (Genesis 18:9). In ancient custom, strangers would never refer to a wife by name, so undoubtedly Abraham begins to suspect these guests are not mere men.

"Here in the tent," he answers (verse 9), and the conversation that follows confirms his suspicions. One of the strangers states that He'll return "according to the time of life" (literally spring of the next year) when Sarah has a son (verse 10).

Listening at the door of the tent, Sarah laughs to herself at the notion of having a child at her age (just as her husband did)—then denies she laughed when the stranger calls her on it (verses 10–15).

"Is anything too hard for the LORD?" He asks, clearly revealing that He is God (verse 14).

The Lord is true to His promise and revisits Sarah again the next year, when Isaac is born (Genesis 21:1).

CHAPTER NINETEEN

The High Cost of Bad Choices

Based on Genesis 19

The three strangers Abraham welcomes to his tent in Genesis 18 turn out to be two angels and the Lord, Himself. After the angels leave, they have to hurry to cover the approximate forty miles to Sodom. The Lord remains with Abraham for a while, telling him that they've come to investigate the outcry against Sodom and Gomorrah before passing judgment on those wicked cities.

Abraham is gravely concerned, since his nephew, Lot, lives in Sodom.

"Would You also destroy the righteous with the wicked?" he asks (Genesis 18:23), as he begins a series of seven questions that intercede in the customary style of the ancients. Beginning with fifty righteous men, he descends in numbers to see if the Lord will still destroy the city if there be only ten, and each time the Lord answers that He will not (verses 24–32). The number ten is represented by *yod*, the smallest letter of the Hebrew alphabet. In later Judaism it is the minimum number required to have a worshiping community.

Lot's concern

Meanwhile, Lot sits at the city gate where the elders sit. This is where business transactions are made and legal disputes are judged. As the strangers approach, he bows and greets them, inviting them home for the night. They refuse at first. It's common for travelers to spend the night on the street in this mild climate, wrapped in their warm outer robe. This will also provide them ample opportunity to gather evidence about the city, but Lot is so concerned for their safety that they finally accept his invitation.

He's not the only one who's noticed the strangers, though. Soon a mob gathers at Lot's door, demanding he send out the strangers so they might violate them. Exiting his home, he closes the door behind him and pleads with them not to act so wickedly. He even offers his two daughters to them instead of the two guests they are demanding.

When Lot calls the men "my brethren," he puts himself on the same level as the Sodomites. But instead of accepting Lot's request, the men lunge at the door while calling him judgmental and threatening to do even worse to him!

Suddenly, the angels reach outside and pull Lot in—as they strike the mob with blindness! Their investigative judgment is complete, and as the realization of who these strangers really are begins to dawn on Lot, they urge him to flee the city with his relatives before it's destroyed, because grace must precede justice. He fails to convince his married daughters and sons-in-law to go because they think he is joking, and the angels finally have to take Lot, his wife, and his two unmarried daughters by the hand and rush them outside the city. The strangers then order them to flee to the mountains and not look back for any reason, but Lot lingers and begs to go to the nearby city of Zoar, instead of leaving the area.

Destruction

As the Lord swiftly destroys Sodom and Gomorrah with fire and brimstone (sulphur) from heaven, Lot's wife disobeys the dire warning, and looks back. She instantly becomes a pillar of salt—a visible and lasting omen for those who place their home and possessions above their own salvation!

Fearing that the Lord might destroy Zoar next, Lot runs for a cave in the mountains with his two daughters. In their isolation, these women fear they will die without offspring, so they scheme to get their father drunk, producing children to preserve his lineage through incest. Their children, Moab and Ben-Ammi, become the fathers of the Moabite and Ammonite nations, who one day will be hostile toward the Israelites heading for Canaan.

By rescuing Lot and his daughters, the Lord fulfills His promise during Abraham's intercession. However, this story vividly demonstrates the consequences Lot suffers for pitching his tent toward Sodom, and later moving into that wicked city. Despite this, we can marvel at God's grace in forcefully taking him and his family by the hand and leading them to safety.

Lot's decision to move to Sodom costs him dearly. He loses his wife and his possessions and ends up in a cave with two unmarried daughters who treat him shamefully, assuring he will spend his old age in infamy.

CHAPTER TWENTY

Repeated Error

Based on Genesis 20

For unknown reasons, Abraham moves from near Hebron far to the south for a period. Then he moves back northwest near to the Mediterranean coast to a place called Gerar. This land is more fertile and well-watered, but it is also Philistine country, where Abimelech is the regional ruler. The name Abimelech is probably a title-name, since it means "Melech is my father," or "the king is my father."

Once again, Abraham is presented with a dilemma. Abimelech is stunned by Sarah's beauty, and when he asks Abraham about her, he repeats the error he made in Egypt by calling Sarah his sister.

As a result, Abimelech takes her into his harem, and the Lord is not pleased! Back in Egypt, Pharaoh's scouts found Sarah very beautiful at sixty-five years of age, and apparently, Abimelech still finds her beautiful at the age of ninety! She is certainly not near the end of her life yet, since she will live another forty years.

Although Abimelech has no idea that Sarah is Abraham's wife, God communicates with him through a dramatic dream and calls him a "dead man!" (Genesis 20:3). This phrase in Hebrew literally means, "You are about to die."

As we look at this story, it's important to see it through the eyes of the ancients. When He calls Abimelech a "dead man," God does not mean that he will be instantly killed, but that his family will die out. Genesis 20:4 states, "But Abimelech had not come near her; and he said, 'Lord, will You slay a righteous nation also?' " This indicates that it was clear to the ruler that God would prevent him from having heirs, effectively ending his genealogy and his kingdom.

The fact that Abimelech has "not come near her" clears him of adultery, and even though he is a Philistine, he pleads to the Lord to save his nation—just as Abraham did when he pleaded for the righteous in Sodom.

Abimelech continues to defend himself, asking God, "Did he not say to me, 'She is my sister'? And she, even she herself said, 'He is my brother.' In the integrity of my heart and innocence of my hands I have done this" (verse 5).

As far as Abimelech knows, he has done nothing wrong, and God even confirms this by saying, "Yes, I know that you did this in the integrity of your heart." Then God declares that He had prevented a tragedy, by saying, "For I also withheld you from sinning against Me; therefore I did not let you touch her" (verse 6).

Ironically, Abimelech is righteous, while Abraham and Sarah are not, since they have both told a half-truth. God orders Abimelech to restore Abraham's wife, and if he doesn't, he will surely die, along with all who belong to him. God also says, Abraham "is a prophet, and he will pray for you and you shall live" (verse 7).

Abimelech takes this all very seriously and arises early in the morning to call all his servants and announce to them what has happened. Next, he calls Abraham and says,

> "What have you done to us? How have I offended you, that you have brought on me and on my kingdom a great sin? You have done deeds to me that ought not to be done. . . .
> What did you have in view, that you did this thing?" (verses 9, 10).

Abraham's answer is classic, "Because I thought, surely the fear of God is not in this place, and they will kill me on account of my wife" (verse 11). He truly believes only he and his wife can be righteous in Philistine territory, and in his mind, this rationalization gives license to deceive.

Abimelech gives Abraham sheep, oxen, and male and female servants, saying, "See my land is before you; dwell where it pleases you" (verse 15). With the gifts and the land, Abimelech literally reassures Abraham of his good intentions in this whole affair. It also gives Abraham legal license to settle in Canaan. Then, the ruler rebukes Sarah by saying in irony, "Behold, I have given your *brother* a thousand pieces of silver [about twenty-five pounds—more than a worker can earn in a lifetime]; indeed this vindicates you before all who are with you and before everybody" (verse 16).

Now we see why Abraham is called a prophet, since he serves as the intermediary between God and Abimelech. He prays to God who heals Abimelech, his wife and female servants so they can now have children. In their case, being childless is a terrible calamity, resulting in the family name dying out and the demise of Abimelech's kingdom—making him a "dead man," indeed.

All of this happens because of Sarah, Abraham's wife—and the irony is that Abimelech is denied children as long as Abraham is denied his wife.

This whole story has some very significant points. Abraham has not learned his lesson stemming from his former error of lying about his wife. This brings far-reaching consequences, since it affects Abraham, Sarah, Abimelech, his servants, and his wife. It also affects the Philistine view of God, because Abraham and Sarah are known as His followers. It also demonstrates that in Abraham's thinking, there could be no God-fearing people there, except him and his wife.

Most important, he places God's promise in jeopardy that he would have a son born of Sarah. Had Abimelech taken Sarah and produced a son, Isaac would never have been born, and God's promise would never have been fulfilled. But even when man fails, God always brings something good from the chaos. God promised Abraham a son through whom the Redeemer would come, and now this is placed back on track. God also promised Abraham the land of Canaan, and now Abimelech, the Canaanite, graciously offers a gift of land, rather than to have it taken violently from him.

CHAPTER TWENTY-ONE

Beginning of Covenant Fulfillment

Based on Genesis 21

The beginning fulfillment of the covenant promise of descendants to Abraham and Sarah now occurs with the birth of Isaac. The emphasis of the passage is that the Lord is faithful in fulfilling His word since within the first two verses of the passage reference is made three times of the Lord having spoken to them. In Genesis 21:1, the Lord "visited" Sarah. This verb has the connotation in Hebrew of "remembering." The child is born to Abraham "at the set time of which God had spoken to him" (verse 2). Abraham is now one hundred years old and it has been twenty-five years since he first received the promise of a son. The child is given the name Isaac, as the Lord has said. Since the name has the connotation of laughter, Sarah is no longer laughing with cynicism and unbelief as she has done previously, but with great joy because a miracle has taken place.

Abraham is obedient to the Lord's former instruction and circumcises Isaac on the eighth day, indicating that he is a son of the covenant. In the ancient world, a child is weaned somewhere between three to five years, although the Hebrews usually wean them between two or three. At this point, the ancients believe the child becomes physiologically independent of their mother, and celebrate the weaning with a ritual feast where the child eats solid food for the first time. In Abraham's case, he provides a "great feast," since his child is a special gift from the Lord (verse 8).

Consequences of jealousy

The feast, however, incites the jealously of Isaac's half-brother Ishmael, who did not receive a feast at his weaning. The birth of Isaac and the feast make it apparent to him that he is being replaced by Isaac. Sarah observes Ishmael "scoffing" (the Hebrew verb for scoffing is also translated as laughing or mocking in many translations). In Galatians 4:29, Paul interprets this as persecuting Isaac. Ishmael is probably about seventeen years old, and very sensitive when all this occurs. Sarah speaks to Abraham to "cast out this bondwoman and her son; for the son of this bondwoman shall not be heir with my son" (verse 10). Her attitude causes Abraham great consternation because of his love and hopes for Ishmael.

God instructs Abraham to do as Sarah has said, because his promised seed would be through Isaac. Early in the morning, Abraham provides Hagar and Ishmael with food and a goatskin of water (about three gallons) and sends them away. Being an Egyptian, Hagar apparently heads for Egypt, but becomes hopelessly lost, and wanders in the wilderness of Beersheba. Their drinking water runs out and the boy is literally dying of thirst. In desperation, Hagar places her son in the shade of a shrub and sits down weeping some distance away to avoid seeing him die.

But an angel of God calls to her, "Arise, lift up the lad and hold him with your hand, for I will make him a great nation" (verse 18). Suddenly, she sees a well and fills her goatskin, giving Ishmael a lifesaving drink of water. The lad grows up in the wilderness of Paran, and becomes a mighty hunter, providing food for himself and his Egyptian wife.

It is interesting to note that the Hebrew verb for "wandered" implies to "err" or "go astray." Apparently, God allows Hagar and her son to be lost in the wilderness, rather than settling in Egypt, since the prophecy about him in Genesis 16:10–12 predicts that he will become a "wild man," or literally, "a wild ass of a man"—a figure of speech describing the wild onager that roams the desert wilderness.

Difficult story

This story tends to make modern-day people think of God negatively. We are troubled with His apparent harshness and disregard for Hagar and Ishmael. Why does He seem cruel? Why would He treat them this way?

It is necessary to approach this dilemma by remembering that Abraham, at Sarah's demand, made a very serious mistake that must be dealt with to avoid derailing God's covenant plan. He must show that Isaac is the legitimate offspring, rather than Ishmael and makes it clear that His plan must still be carried out.

However, despite Abraham's error, God displays mercy and protection on both Hagar and Ishmael. By sending her an angel, and providing water, He spared their lives. Moreover, He honored His word to Abraham, and multiplied Ishmael's offspring into a great nation through his twelve sons.

A covenant with Abimelech

Now the center of attention shifts to the story of the covenant between Abraham and Abimelech—the king who had previously taken Sarah, and had been warned by God that he had taken Abraham's wife. King Abimelech perceives that Abraham has been blessed by his God and that a closer association with him would be advantageous. Along with his army commander, Phichol, Abimelech approaches Abraham to enter into a covenant treaty.

Clearly Abraham has the superior position, since Abimelech asks him to swear by his God and not deal falsely with him or his offspring, on account of the kindness he has previously shown him. Abraham does this, and then Abimelech swears by his god. But before concluding their treaty, Abraham rebukes Abimelech because his servants have seized one of his wells. A good well is extremely important, since flocks and herds cannot survive long without water.

Abimelech responds by saying that he knew nothing of the situation until that day. So Abraham takes the initiative in making the covenant by giving Abimelech sheep and oxen to be used in the sacrifice connected with the ceremony. The covenant is legally ratified by cutting the animals in two parts with one part representing each of the two entities. They walk between the two parts and promise they will faithfully fulfill the terms of the covenant. If either breaks the covenant, he is to die, just as the animals did.

After the ratification, Abraham separates seven ewe lambs from his flock. When Abimelech asks why he's done this, Abraham answers, "You will take these seven lambs from my hand, that they may be my witness that I have dug this well" (verse 30). These lambs are not a part of the covenant treaty. They are either a gift or payment for the well, and serve as a witness that Abraham dug the well, even though it is apparently on Abimelech's property.

Abraham calls the name of the place Beersheba, meaning either "well of swearing" or "well of seven." At that time the Hebrew words did not have vowels, so "swearing" and "seven" were identical, in written form. Abraham plants a slow-growing tamarisk tree as a memorial, and calls on the name of the Lord, the Everlasting God. This gives the covenant permanence.

This chapter reveals the beginning of the fulfillment of the covenant made previously with Abraham. He is promised descendants and that will come through his and Sarah's son, Isaac, who has now been born and weaned. The threat from Ishmael as the promised son has been eliminated. Abraham has acquired possession of a well at Beersheba through a covenant treaty with Abimelech, and the seven lambs are a legal witness that the well is his property. He concludes this covenant by planting the tamarisk tree and calling on the name of the Lord.

Abraham recognizes that it is the Lord who has accomplished all of this, and gives Him thanks. He now has the hope of settling permanently in the Promised Land.

CHAPTER TWENTY-TWO

A Terrible Test of Faith

Based on Genesis 22

Because Abraham had doubted the promise of a son through Sarah, God finds it necessary to develop his faith more fully, with a test. One purpose of testing is for God "to know what is in your heart" (Deuteronomy 8:2). Another aspect of testing is seen in Exodus 20:20, when Moses says, "Do not fear; for God has come to test you, and that His fear may be before you, so that you may not sin." Here we see that testing and fear of God are closely linked, resulting in both divine judgment and atonement, in connection with God's covenant of grace.

The Lord asks Abraham to offer Isaac as a burnt offering on a mountain in the land of Moriah (later the site of Solomon's temple). Notice how the ancients think: all must be revealed through action to indicate who you really are, whether you are Abraham or God. This chapter is so important for the ancients that it serves as the center of Genesis, and the central message of the book.

Abraham is clearly stunned by this. The Canaanites commonly sacrifice their firstborn, but this doesn't seem to fit with God's promise of a son, nor with what he's learned about the true God. There is a great difference between the two sacrifices, however, the pagan offering suggests man goes up to God with his gift, while the Israelite offering implies the descent of God with a gift for man.

What is spoken to Abraham about his son makes it even more confusing—"Take now your son, your only son Isaac, whom you love . . ." (Genesis 22:2). Isaac is to be offered as a burnt offering—requiring the total annihilation of the animal, which in this case is Abraham's son. Satan undoubtedly uses this chance to tempt him by questioning, *What kind of God would ask such a thing?*

Genesis 22:1 makes it clear that God is testing his *faith,* rather than actually expecting him to carry out this heinous act; however, in Abraham's mind, this is all about sacrificing his promised heir!

Agony

Imagine Abraham's agony as he prepares to carry out the Lord's request. *How can I tell Sarah?* he wonders. *Will I actually have the courage to do this? Will Isaac allow me, old and weak as I am, to kill him? Oh God, why do You ask me to do this?*

Slowly and methodically, the story unfolds, leaving us caught in the suspense.

Rising early in the morning, Abraham saddles his donkey. Then he takes Isaac and two young men, splits the wood for the burnt offering, and begins the three-day journey of about fifty miles to the place God has indicated. As the mountain comes into view on the third day, he tells the young men to stay there with the donkey while he and Isaac complete the journey and worship. For the ancients, anything linked with the number three is always very important.

Slowly and painfully they climb the mountain—a 120-year-old man with coals of fire and a knife, followed by a lad of about twenty, with a bundle of wood on his back.

"Where is the lamb for a burnt offering?" Isaac wonders out loud (verse 7).

"God will provide," his father answers slowly, as he struggles on with a breaking heart (verse 8). As the two proceed up the mountain together, it gradually dawns on Isaac that *he* must be the lamb.

Finally, they reach their destination, build an altar, and place the wood in order.

Then with a trembling voice, the old man finally reveals to his son what God has asked him to do.

Imagine the terror Isaac feels—but he is also a believer in his father's God, so he willingly submits himself to be bound. As Abraham stretches out his hand with the knife to slay his son, the story reaches its climax. The Bible says the angel of the Lord calls to him from heaven, saying, "Do not lay your hand on the lad, or do anything to him; for now I know that you fear God, since you have not withheld your son, your only son from Me" (verses 11, 12).

Suddenly, a ram caught in a thicket by its horns catches Abraham's attention, and he leaps with joy. God has provided a substitute! The angel of the Lord then reiterates God's covenant with Abraham and his descendants, swearing by His own name to affirm it. Notice that Isaac refers to a lamb for the burnt offering, but the Scripture states that God provides a *ram*. In Leviticus 16:3, 5 a ram is offered for a burnt offering on the Day of Atonement—and not a lamb. The burnt offering is completely burned on the altar day and night and represents the substitute for man's sinful nature and not specific sins. The ram on the Day of Atonement does not represent Abraham's son, but *God's Son*. Further evidence that this story prefigures the Day of Atonement and Christ's death can be seen in the name that Abraham gives to the place, "The-LORD-Will-Provide; as it is said to this day, 'in the Mount of the LORD it shall be provided' " (Genesis 22:14). Abraham has ended his journey. He has arrived at the place that is the common designation for the temple where God's Son is the burnt offering for the covenant of grace.

Abraham has passed the test. He is now judged as a man of faith. His faith that has been seen as incomplete in the past, has now matured. Never again will it be in doubt, because he has truly understood the gospel of the covenant of grace. Abraham also perceives God's abhorrence of his forefathers' pagan beliefs (Joshua 24:14), which include human sacrifices so prevalent in Canaan. The idea that man, through works, can provide nothing for salvation is indelibly etched in his mind. Only God can provide the sacrifice for sin.

Through this experience, he now graphically understands the pain the Father will feel as He gives His only Son! He has finally reached an understanding of the covenant—God's amazing plan of salvation.

CHAPTER TWENTY-THREE

God Chooses a Bride

Based on Genesis 23 and 24

After the great test of faith that Abraham went through, the Genesis story shifts to the death of Sarah at 127 years of age. She is the only Old Testament woman whose age is recorded at death—an indication of how significant she is in covenant history. She dies in the land of Canaan, a foreign land, far from her native Mesopotamia.

Abraham now "stands up," indicating that he has been sitting in mourning. It is now time for action, but he owns no land for burial. He approaches the sons of Heth, for a place to bury Sarah. They are apparently elders of the city who can use their influence in helping secure property and expedite its sale.

They refer him to Ephron who owns the cave of Machpelah that means double. The "double" may mean that it is a double cave. Business transactions are made at the city gate and Ephron speaks to Abraham, "I give [the field with the cave of Machpelah] to you" (Genesis 23:11). To us this means an outright gift, but to the ancients everyone knows that he is unwilling to sell the cave without the field.

Hittite law explains why Ephron did not sell the cave without the field. If Abraham bought only the cave, Ephron would still have to pay tax on all the property, according to his feudal obligations. If the field is sold with the cave, the tax obligations are transferred to the new owner.

Abraham speaks to Ephron, "If you will give it, please hear me. I will give you money for the field." Ephron responds, "The land is worth four hundred shekels of silver. What is that between you and me? So bury your dead" (verses 13, 15).

The whole transaction is done in typical Middle Eastern bargaining style. Each party is stating that he is "giving" to the other. Ephron states it three times and Abraham uses it four times. Abraham weighs out the silver—about ten pounds. This is an exorbitant price, several times more than the land is worth, but now the cave and the land are "deeded" to him to bury Sarah. God's covenant promises are beginning to be fulfilled. Isaac has been born, and Abraham now possesses land in Canaan.

The setting has now been established for a new generation, since Sarah has died, and Abraham is old. Sarah will be replaced by Rebekah, and Isaac will replace Abraham as the patriarch. Sixty-seven verses are used to describe how Rebekah becomes Isaac's wife—indicating the writer believes this story is extremely important.

Abraham is very old, and concerned for the next generation of the divine covenant.

Calling his chief servant, he instructs him to find a wife for Isaac in his homeland of Mesopotamia. The ancients think quite literally, so when he seeks assurance that his servant won't bring back a Canaanite to corrupt the covenant lineage, Abraham asks him to place his hand under his thigh—the seat of procreative powers—and swear by the Lord that he will select a woman from Abraham's relatives. Then he adds that the Lord will send His angel to indicate who that might be.

The sign

The servant begins the five hundred-mile journey to Nahor (a city named after Abraham's brother) on ten camels—a rare and luxurious mode of transportation at that time. After several weeks he arrives at the city's well, and asks the Lord to indicate the right woman by having her give him a drink of water, *and* offer to water his camels.

Before he's finished praying, Rebekah appears with a pitcher on her shoulder.

Running up to her, he asks for a drink of water. "Drink, my lord," she answers, adding, "I will draw water for your camels also, until they have finished drinking" (Genesis 24:18, 19).

Rebekah descends the steps to the well, draws about three gallons, and climbs back up to the watering trough. She repeats this until each animal has had its fill—and considering a thirsty camel can drink up to twenty-five gallons, she may have made more than eighty trips!

The servant watches silently, making sure this is the Lord's chosen one. Then he gives her jewelry as a token of his appreciation.

"Whose daughter are you?" he asks (verse 23), and she answers that her father is Bethuel. Then he asks if her father's house might have room to lodge him, and when she answers yes, he bows his head and thanks the Lord for bringing him to his master's relatives.

Rebekah runs home, and soon her brother Laban (who's probably blond or an albino, since his name means "white") runs back to meet the servant. Undoubtedly impressed by his gifts and camels, Laban invites him home and offers him food. However, Abraham's servant will not eat until he recounts his mission and journey, and that Isaac will inherit great wealth and support Rebekah well. He also recounts how God has answered his prayer with the appearance of Rebekah and her offer to water his camels.

"The thing comes from the LORD," Laban and Bethuel say (verse 50). God has pointed out Rebekah—and they dare not oppose Him. Detailed negotiations follow about the bride money to be paid her family, and Rebekah is given more silver and gold jewelry, as well as fine clothing. Her brother and mother also receive valuable gifts. The gifts are considered the formal dowry.

Although her family begs her to stay at least ten days, the servant is anxious to leave in the morning, so Laban asks Rebekah to make the decision, and after a family blessing, she chooses to leave immediately. Her decision echoes that of Abram, when he chose to leave Mesopotamia and enter into Canaan. Their journey to Canaan probably took about a month. On the evening of their arrival, Isaac is located near the same well where Hagar was saved by the angel of the Lord. He has gone into a field to meditate when he sees camels coming. Rebekah sees him, dismounts from her camel, and asks the servant who the man is. The servant identifies him as his master, and Rebekah immediately covers herself with a veil. The servant tells Isaac all the things he has done.

A different concept of love

The Bible is short on Isaac's wedding details, focusing instead on the fact that when they married, Rebekah comforted him on the loss of his mother—indicating that she is replacing Sarah. The Hebrew concept of love and marriage is quite different from our western view. In the case of Isaac and Rebekah, "[Isaac] took Rebekah and she became his wife, and he loved her" (verse 67). Although love may not be lacking in some cases before marriage, it refers to a more mature love than a purely emotional love like it tends to be in western thinking. It refers to a love that develops and blossoms after marriage.

They love each other because they live together; they do not live together because they are in love. Love implies faithfulness, commitment, and enjoyment. It is closely linked with the biblical concept of religion, as expressed in the divine covenant. Marriage is constantly used in Scripture to express man's relationship to God. When God asks sinners to love Him, He is not asking for sentimental love but a commitment to live with Him.

This same type of love is to be portrayed in human conjugal relationship. Much can be said about arranged marriages, but in this case Isaac's *heavenly* Father was the one who chose his wife—and God never makes mistakes!

CHAPTER TWENTY-FOUR

Abraham's Descendants

Based on Genesis 25 and 26

After the death of Sarah, Abraham lives another thirty-eight years and marries his concubine, Keturah. Her name means "incense," and likely she is a comfort to Abraham as Rebekah is to Isaac after the loss of his mother. She bears Abraham another six sons, who in turn produce several grandchildren. These offspring, no doubt, gladden the heart of the old patriarch during his final years.

Abraham ultimately gives "all that he had to Isaac" because he is the promised son, but he gives gifts to Keturah's offspring and sends them east to Arabia (Genesis 25:5, 6). This is an implication that they are being separated from God's people in the Promised Land. Then Abraham dies at the "good old age" of 175 (verse 8), fulfilling the promise given him long before. Both Isaac and Ishmael lovingly bury him "with his people" in the cave of Machpelah, next to Sarah, indicating how important the family or clan is, even in death.

Ishmael

After his death, the biblical writer first focuses on Ishmael, the son of Abraham and Hagar, his Egyptian concubine. Although Abraham has many other sons, Ishmael is considered to be the most important one after Isaac because, initially, his father believed him to be his promised son.

God promised to Abraham that Ishmael would have twelve sons (like Jacob will have in the future) and become a great nation. Ishmael's descendants dwell in the east, indicating they are separated from Isaac's offspring, who dwell in Canaan, the Promised Land.

Isaac

Now, the biblical writer turns to Abraham's most important son—the

87

son of the covenant promise—Isaac, who marries Rebekah at the age of forty. However, as the years pass, it becomes clear that his wife is barren, as Sarah was, until God intervened. Isaac pleads with the Lord on her behalf, resulting in Rebekah conceiving twins. She feels her sons struggling within her womb, and becomes very apprehensive. She inquires of the Lord as to why all this is happening, and the Lord responds, stating that two nations are within her womb, *but the older son will serve the younger.* This idea is contrary to the normal custom, where the firstborn inherits a double portion of his father's wealth as a "birthright."

Twins

It is common for the ancients to note any peculiar appearance or actions of their children as they are born, and to name them accordingly. As Rebekah's twins are delivered, Esau, her first son, is reddish in color and very hairy, so she names him Esau, meaning "red." It's interesting to note that his name is probably from the same root as Edom—a place of red earth—where he eventually settles. His abundant hair becomes the most significant feature of his physical appearance.

The first thing noted about the birth of Jacob is that his hand takes hold of Esau's heel in the birth process. This causes his parents to give him the appropriate name of Jacob, meaning "supplanter" or "deceiver." The Hebrew word *'ageb,* or "heel," is related to the verb *'agab,* "to take by the heel," and both have the connotation of "deceiver." One who grabs another's heel from behind is considered one who plays dirty. Much of Jacob's life reveals the appropriateness of his name.

As the two boys grow and develop, they soon prove to have very different interests.

Esau is a man of the field who likes open spaces and becomes a skillful hunter, while Jacob is more domesticated, and a mild man that dwells in tents. Esau bonds closely with his father, while Jacob bonds more fully with his mother. This favoritism of each parent for a particular son creates a rift between them, as well as between the twins.

A stolen birthright

According to the custom of the ancients, all inheritance is split equally between all their sons; however, the firstborn receives a *double* portion, effectively decreasing the portions the others receive. In Isaac's case, he will give his entire wealth to his two sons, but since Esau is his firstborn, he will receive two-thirds of his wealth, while Jacob will receive one-third. The firstborn also has the distinction of being the family religious leader and priest.

One day, as Jacob is cooking a stew of red lentils, his brother Esau arrives from a hunt, seemingly famished. He begs for some of his brother's stew, and Jacob cunningly proposes to sell him the stew in exchange for Esau's birthright.

Esau answers, "Look, I am about to die; so what is this birthright to me?" and Jacob quickly replies, "Swear to me as of this day" (Genesis 25:32, 33).

The transaction is legally confirmed through an oath, and Esau's hunger is satisfied with bread and red lentil stew. This incident starkly reveals each brother's character and values, and serves as an omen for their future life!

A story repeated

Circumstances now change for Isaac as a famine sweeps through the southern part of the Promised Land. This famine echoes the story of Abraham, where he leaves Canaan and goes to Egypt, and declares that Sarah is his sister. Isaac apparently plans to leave the Promised Land to go to Egypt, where famines do not occur along the Nile because of yearly inundations. However, the Lord appears to him and instructs him not to go down to Egypt as Abraham had foolishly done, but to stay in the Promised Land. Canaan is much higher in elevation than the land along the Nile, so one literally goes down to Egypt.

The Lord then repeats to Isaac the covenant promises that He made to Abraham. As a result, Isaac remains in Canaan and settles in the land of Gerar, in Philistine country.

This fertile area is far better watered than the remainder of the southern portion of the Promised Land, and is ruled by Abimelech and his army commander, Phichol. Much time has passed since Abimelech and Phichol met with Abraham, so it appears that these are not the same persons. Apparently, Abimelech is a royal title while Phichol is the title for the army commander.

When Isaac settles in Gerar, the men of the place soon notice his beautiful wife Rebekah, and ask about her. Isaac immediately puts her in danger by stating that she is his sister—just as Abraham lied to the Pharaoh in Egypt, and later to Abimelech, the Philistine king. This incident occurs when her twins are about seventeen years of age, demonstrating that she is still stunningly beautiful.

After a time, Abimelech observes Isaac showing Rebekah affection, and states, "Quite obviously she is your wife, so how can you say, 'She is my sister'?" (Genesis 26:9).

Isaac responds, "Because I said, 'Lest I die on account of her' " (verse 9).

Abimelech rebukes him by stating that an immoral act could have occurred that would have brought guilt upon his people. Then, with magnanimous ethical consideration, he decrees, "He who touches this man or his wife shall surely be put to death" (verse 11).

Fighting over wells

Isaac begins farming and is blessed by the Lord with a hundredfold harvest. But unfortunately, his great prosperity causes tremendous envy among the Philistines. They react by stopping up all of Abraham's wells, which Isaac's men are using. These wells were guaranteed to Abraham in perpetuity by the king of Gerar. However, Abimelech tells Isaac to go away because he has become much mightier than his people.

Isaac leaves and pitches his tent in the valley of Gerar, opening the stopped-up wells and reaffirming their original names. Restoring their original names is Isaac's way of reestablishing his ownership. In addition, his servants dig a new well, but again, the herdsmen of Gerar quarrel over it. Isaac then gives the well the name Esek, meaning "quarrel."

A new well is dug, and again they quarrel over it, so Isaac names it Sitnah, meaning "accusation." Moving to a new location, his men dig a third well that the men of Gerar do no quarrel over, so he gives it the name of Rehoboth, meaning "spacious." Isaac apparently now feels that he has enough room to settle in peace.

Isaac eventually moves north to Beersheba, his father's old homestead, and that same night, the Lord appears to him and repeats the covenant promises made to Abraham. Immediately, Isaac builds an altar there and calls on the name of the Lord.

Cutting another covenant

Abimelech comes to visit Isaac with Ahuzzath (which the Bible calls "one of his friends" [verse 26] but is probably a civil officer serving as his counselor) and Phichol, his military commander.

Isaac asks, "Why have you come to me, since you hate me and have sent me away from you?" (verse 27).

They answer saying, "We have certainly seen that the LORD is with you," then lie, "We have done nothing to you but good and have sent you away in peace" (verses 28, 29). Next, they propose to establish a covenant of peace with him.

The fact that Abimelech asks for a covenant is an indication that he considers Isaac to be more powerful than he is and, potentially, a threat. Isaac kindly does not call Abimelech on his lie, but responds positively by providing the covenant meal—a confirmation of his superior position.

On the day of the covenant, Isaac's servants inform him that the well they had previously dug has now filled with water, so Isaac gives it the name Sheba, meaning "oath," commemorating the treaty made with Abimelech.

Abraham has followed God's plan with his descendants, especially with Isaac.

Keturah's offspring have received gifts, but not inheritance—and they settle outside the Promised Land. Ishmael has twelve sons and also settles outside Canaan. All Abraham's wealth has been protected for Isaac, who settles in the Promised Land.

The Lord has repeated the promises to Isaac that He's given to Abraham—the land of Canaan, and that the Redeemer will be born of his descendants.

CHAPTER TWENTY-FIVE

A Tragic Tale of Deceit

Based on Genesis 27 and 28

Isaac is about 137 years old, and because of his age and blindness, he thinks he is about to die (although he lives for another forty-three years). It is time, he thinks, to put his house in order by bestowing the birthright blessing on his eldest son. Although he knows that the angel has revealed to Rebekah that their eldest son Esau will serve the younger Jacob (indicating that Jacob will receive the birthright blessing), he is determined to give it to Esau, who is apparently his favorite.

A celebration ceremony involving a feast normally accompanies such an event. The food for this feast is determined by Isaac's appetite, he loves the wild game that Esau brings home. He sends Esau out to the field with his weapons to obtain venison that would be cooked until it is tender and seasoned with herbs.

In the unfolding of this story, the family rivalry becomes evident. Esau is clearly favored by Isaac and called "his son," while Rebekah favors Jacob, who is designated as "her son." Rebekah overhears Isaac's instructions to Esau, and confides in Jacob that his father intends to bless Esau "in the presence of the Lord" (Genesis 27:7). She has added this phrase herself, implying that it would be with the Lord's approval and would negate what the angel said to her that the older would serve the younger. In her mind this justifies her plan to have Jacob deceive his father to bestow upon him the birthright blessing.

Rebekah now speaks as if she has the authority of a prophet when she tells Jacob to obey her command and bring in two choice young goats so she can prepare savory food for Isaac. Jacob is to take this food to his father and receive the birthright blessing. He immediately reacts, "Look, Esau my brother is a hairy man, and I am a smooth-skinned man. Perhaps my father will feel me, and I shall seem to be a deceiver to him; and I shall bring a curse on myself and not a blessing" (verses 11, 12). He appears to be more worried about suffering a curse than sinning by deceiving his father.

Rebekah responds, "Let your curse be on me" (verse 13). In reality, neither a blessing nor a curse is transferable, only the consequences of a wrong decision can come to her. The Lord is the enforcer of the curse, but Rebekah will suffer the consequences of the curse, rather than the curse itself. As a result of her plan she suffers the consequences for the rest of her life—including never seeing Jacob again.

The deception

Rebekah prepares the goat's meat to taste like the savory venison by using the same herbs Esau uses. Next, she clothes Jacob with Esau's choice garments, using the young goats' skins on his hands and neck in an effort to imitate Esau. That goat's hair could fool Isaac may seem a bit of a stretch, however, some Oriental goats have silky black hair that resembles human hair. Rebekah has planned well, and now sends Jacob to his father with bread and savory food in an effort to deceive him.

As Jacob arrives before his father he says, "My father" (verse 18).

Isaac responds with his first doubt, "Here I am. Who are you, my son?" (verse 18).

Jacob with lying lips says, "I am Esau your firstborn; I have done just as you told me; please arise, sit and eat of my game, that your soul might bless me" (verse 19).

But Isaac responds with his second doubt, "How is it that you have found it so quickly, my son?" (verse 20).

One lie leads to another as Jacob replies, "Because the LORD your God brought it to me" (verse 20).

Isaac now expresses his third doubt, "Please come near, that I may feel you, my son, whether you are really my son Esau or not" (verse 21).

As Jacob comes close to be felt, his father expresses his fourth doubt by saying, "The voice is Jacob's voice, but the hands are the hands of Esau" (verse 22). Evidently his blindness has made his hearing more acute.

Then he expresses his fifth doubt by appealing to Jacob's honesty when he asks, "Are you really my son Esau?" (verse 24).

Jacob again lies and responds, "I am" (verse 24).

Isaac now wants to eat the savory food to take away his sixth doubt. After eating the food, he asks Jacob, "Come near now and kiss me, my son" (verse 26). As he comes near and kisses his father, the seventh doubt of his father is expressed when he smells his clothing to see if it smells like Esau. All of the doubts have been removed except that of the voice that sounds like Jacob—and not of Esau. But in Isaac's mind the preponderance of evidence seems to indicate that the son before him must really be Esau. Notice how Isaac acquires his knowledge in the typical way of the ancients by using his senses in touching him, hearing him, smelling him, and by tasting his food.

The blessing

Isaac now blesses Jacob, and as he does, the narrative of the story changes to poetry, indicating this is the most important part of the whole story. The blessing reflects the principal elements of the Abrahamic covenant. The first part of the blessing is the fertility of the land. The second part is domination over other nations, and the third part applies the terms of the Abrahamic blessing as he says, "Cursed be everyone who curses you, and blessed be those who bless you" (verse 29).

As soon as Jacob has left the presence of his father, Esau arrives with his savory food. He says, "Let my father arise and eat of his son's game, that your soul may bless me" (verse 31).

Isaac says, "Who are you?" (verse 32).

Esau responds, "I am your son, your firstborn, Esau" (verse 32).

Isaac immediately panics, trembles violently, and says, "Who? Where is the one who hunted game and brought it to me? I ate all of it before you came, and I have blessed him—and indeed he shall be blessed" (verse 33).

When Esau hears these words, he bursts out with an exceedingly bitter cry and begs, "Bless me—me also, O my father!"

Isaac recognizes the fact that he has been deceived and can do nothing about it. The birthright blessing is final and cannot be reversed. With deep sadness he responds, "Your brother came with deceit and has taken away your blessing" (verse 35).

Esau says, "Is he not rightly named Jacob? For he has supplanted me these two times. He took away my birthright, and now look, he has taken away my blessing!" (verse 36).

Esau refers to Jacob's name as a deceiver or supplanter, indicating that the name given to Jacob is appropriate. Still desperately hoping, he asks, "Have you not reserved a blessing for me?" (verse 36).

Isaac answers, "Indeed I have made him your master, and all of his brethren I have given to him as servants, with grain and wine I have sustained him. What shall I do now for you, my son?" (verse 37). Here Isaac recognizes that God's plan of the older serving the younger will indeed be fulfilled, and admits that his plan to reverse what God said has failed.

In utter despair, Esau again begs his father, "Have you only one blessing, my father? Bless me—me also, O my father!" (verse 38). Then, in bitter anguish, Esau begins to wail and weep, not in true repentance but sorrowful that he has lost his birthright blessing. In response, Isaac seems to *try* to bless him, but in reality, it is not a blessing at all, but an *antiblessing*.

The first part of this antiblessing is that Esau's "dwelling shall be of the fatness of the earth, and of the dew of heaven" (verse 39, emphasis added). The Hebrew preposition *min* (often meaning "from" or "of") is used here in the sense of *away from* the fatness of the land and the dew of heaven, as many other reputable translations state.

These seem more accurate than the King James and New King James translations, because Esau will live by hunting game, instead of living off the land.

The second part of the antiblessing states that Esau will live by his sword and that he will serve his brother. Both parts of this antiblessing are a reversal of what Jacob receives. They indicate a negative future for Esau. It is also significant that the sequence of Jacob's blessing emphasizes heaven, by mentioning it first: "May God give you of the dew of heaven and of the fatness of the earth" (verse 28, ESV), while Esau's curse emphasizes earth, by mentioning it first: "Behold, away from the fatness of the earth shall your dwelling be, and away from the dew of heaven on high" (verse 39, ESV). This places Esau outside the divine influence and on his own, forcing him to live by his sword.

Esau now has an intense hatred for Jacob and in his heart says, "The days of mourning for my father are at hand, then I will kill my brother Jacob" (verse 41). In deference to his father, he will kill Jacob only after his father dies.

When Rebekah hears of Esau's intentions, she informs Jacob and gives orders for him to flee to her brother Laban in Haran. She thinks Esau "comforts himself" (verse 42) with the plan to kill his brother because that would bring him revenge and also enable him to receive his inheritance rights. She thinks Jacob will only have to stay in Haran a short time until Esau's intense anger abates. "Why should I be bereaved also of you both in one day?" (verse 45). She not only fears for Jacob's life but also for Esau's, because she knows there is the possibility of retaliation by blood revenge.

Rebekah goes to Isaac and tells him her life isn't worth living because of the two Canaanite wives of Esau. She astutely uses this reason to save her son, by suggesting that Isaac should send Jacob to her brother Laban in Haran to get a non-Canaanite wife. This made sense to Isaac, since his father Abraham had done this for him. This is Rebekah's last recorded act in Scripture.

Isaac accepts Rebekah's plan and calls in Jacob to give him the customary farewell blessing. Before the blessing, he charges Jacob to marry a wife from the daughters of Laban. His blessing on Jacob is similar to the birthright blessing that includes elements from the covenant with Abraham.

After the farewell blessing, Isaac sends Jacob off, and he immediately becomes a fugitive. Meanwhile, when Esau sees that his brother has been sent away to find a non-Canaanite wife, he marries Mahalath, the daughter of Ishmael (and Abraham's granddaughter), thinking this might please his father.

Jacob's ladder

When Jacob leaves his father, he travels in utter terror without stopping, covering fifty to sixty miles. It surely must have taken more than a day and night to cover this distance!

He tries to avoid contact with anyone, because Esau might find out where he is.

Finally, completely exhausted, he lays down on the ground to sleep with a stone under his head.

He dreams about a ladder or staircase that reaches from earth to heaven, and he sees angels traveling up and down on it from the Lord, who stands at the top. Jacob understands the imagery. His Mesopotamian ancestry built ziggurats or towers next to their temples where their imaginary heavenly messengers traveled between the earth below and their gods in heaven.

Through the dream, Jacob realizes that the Lord is with him. He promises him the land of Canaan as an inheritance, and a great posterity (including the Messiah) through which all earthly families will be blessed. Then He promises to never leave him, and to bring him back home safely.

"How awesome is this place!" Jacob exclaims, adding that this is the "House of God" and "the gate of heaven!" (Genesis 28:17). He understands that he does not ascend to God as they tried to do at Babel, but that the ascending and descending belongs to the heavenly order, and not to humans. He names it Bethel, meaning "house of God"—indicating it is a temple, sets his headrest upright as a pillar, and anoints it with oil to consecrate it as a permanent marker. Then he utters the first recorded scriptural vow: "This stone, which I have set up as a pillar, will be God's house, and of all that You give me I will surely give a tenth to You" (verse 22). Then he continues his long journey to Mesopotamia by traveling northeast around the desert.

God gets His way

The story of the birthright blessing is a demonstration of how patient God is with sinful humans. Amazingly, each family member chooses not to follow God's express commands, and as the story unfolds, it reveals a saga of human errors.

This story begins with Isaac, who knows that God has communicated to Rebekah that the birthright is to go to Jacob in that the older brother will serve the younger. But Isaac favors Esau, and is determined to give the birthright blessing to him, rather than fulfilling God's plan.

Esau demonstrates no spiritual interest in the birthright, and sells it to Jacob when he comes in one day from hunting, and is hungry.

Rebekah overhears Isaac asking Esau to hunt game for savory food to be used in the ceremony where he will bestow the birthright blessing. Taking matters into her own hands, she quickly tells Jacob how to deceive his father into giving *him* the birthright blessing.

Jacob accepts the deceptive plan and executes it through a series of lies.

Isaac gives Jacob the birthright blessing, while believing he is giving it to Esau.

And when Esau discovers that Jacob received the birthright blessing, he is livid with anger and vows to kill his brother.

Looking through the eyes of the ancients, we realize there are no agnostics or unbelievers in Isaac's family. There is also no human choice or legal recourse when it comes to the birthright. What God determines, happens, *in spite of* human error and stubbornness.

CHAPTER TWENTY-SIX

A Deceiver Meets His Match

Based on Genesis 29

Jacob continues his approximate three-week journey of about 450 miles to Haran, in Mesopotamia. Although this location is stated to be in the East, geographically, Haran is northeast of Canaan. To avoid traveling through the great Syrian Desert, one must travel north through Canaan, then turn east in Mesopotamia to arrive at Haran in the region of Padan Aram.

As Jacob is arriving at his destination, he comes to a well that has three flocks of sheep lying beside it. He asks the shepherds where they are from, and they answer that they are from Haran. He asks if they know Laban, and they say yes. He asks if Laban is in good health, and again they say yes, adding that his daughter Rachel is arriving with her sheep.

Jacob mentions that it is the heat of the day, and suggests they water the sheep. But the shepherds tell him they must wait until all the flocks are gathered, and the large stone is rolled off the mouth of the well. This stone protects the well from contamination or poisoning. But it may also be a means of preventing other herdsmen in the area from drawing more water than is their right, since water is scarce. Although this text suggests it would take several men to roll the stone away, Jacob rolls it away single-handedly—perhaps to show off a bit!

Falling in love

The story of Rachel, in typical Hebrew style, echoes the story of Rebekah at the well, and the Lord's leading in the whole affair. Jacob is so taken by Rachel's appearance that he not only removes the large stone but also waters her sheep as well. Then he kisses her and begins to weep, because he, as a tired and lonely fugitive, has found a relative.

Although this may seem strange to us today, Jacob's greeting is typical of their custom of kissing each cheek and then embracing. When he tells her that he's Rebekah's son, she immediately runs to tell her father, who runs back to Jacob, embracing and kissing him too. Jacob is brought to Laban's house, where he informs them about his family, and the circumstances that bring him there.

Laban recognizes that Jacob is a true relative, so he keeps him in his house for a month. During that time, Jacob becomes useful to him because of his diligence, and his previous experience with animals.

Tricked!

Laban has two daughters, Leah and Rachel. Leah's eyes are "delicate," apparently expressing the idea that they are weak. The Greek translation of the Old Testament renders her eyes as "dull." To the ancients, beauty is especially concentrated in eyes that sparkle, and apparently, Leah's do not. On the other hand, Rachel is described as beautiful of form and appearance, and Jacob falls in love at first sight.

Laban is no fool and quickly figures out what Jacob feels toward Rachel. Now he cunningly takes advantage of this by insisting that Jacob name his price for his services. Enthralled by Rachel's beauty, Jacob—who is penniless and has no money for the bride price—offers to work for seven years in return for her hand in marriage. The price Jacob proposes for her at that time is considered very generous, however, after seven years, Jacob has to remind Laban that he has completed the service period for his wife.

Laban organizes a wedding that normally would include processions from and to the bride's house, the reading of the marriage contract, and a large meal offered to the family and guests. He also plans to switch Leah as the bride, instead of Rachel. At the wedding, the custom of veiling the bride, the darkness of the night, Leah's silence and Jacob's emotion all contribute to Laban's deception. Jacob, the great deceiver, has now met his match!

The next morning Jacob discovers that his wife is Leah, and not Rachel. The shock of it all is expressed by the words "behold it was Leah" (Genesis 29:25). He immediately confronts Laban with the words, "What is this you have done to me? Was it not for Rachel that I served you? Why then have you deceived me?"

Laban's lame excuse is that it is tradition to marry off the oldest daughter before the youngest. He tells Jacob that if he completes the seven days of the wedding feast, at the end, he will receive Rachel for his wife. However, he must work for Laban another seven years! Jacob, in his naivete, accepts this whole plan and works for another seven years.

Jacob, the deceiver, is living a hard life. He has fled from Esau to avoid being murdered; he has had to take a long flight as a fugitive; he lives with a deceptive father-in-law; he has gotten a wife that he neither wants, nor especially loves; he has had to work very hard for fourteen years, because he had no money to pay the bride price.

Jacob is learning firsthand about the negative effects of deception, but for him to change, he needs to suffer more at the hand of Laban, the arch deceiver.

Truly, Jacob has met his match!

CHAPTER TWENTY-SEVEN

Sister Struggles

Based on Genesis 29 and 30

Jacob has two wives, Leah and Rachel who are sisters. Soon it is clear that Jacob loves Rachel more than Leah, and this bigamous marriage sparks a lifelong conflict between the sisters. Even the names of their children reflect their hopes—and rivalry!

Looking for love

Our merciful Lord sees that Leah is not loved, so He intervenes and gives her a son whom she names Reuben (literally, "Behold a son!"). The fact that she produces a son for Jacob makes her exultantly exclaim, "Now therefore, my husband will love me" (Genesis 29:32). Clearly, she has an intense longing to be loved and accepted by Jacob. Then she bears a second son, whom she names Simeon (meaning "Heard"), saying, "Because the LORD has heard that I am unloved, He has therefore given me this son also" (verse 33).

When her third son is born, she names him Levi (meaning "Attached"), saying, "Now this time my husband will become attached to me, because I have born him three sons" (verse 34). After the birth of each son, she is confident that she will be loved and accepted by Jacob. However, she still does not win her husband's affection.

The fourth son she names, Judah (meaning "Praise"). Notice how her focus changes from her relationship with her husband, to her relationship with *Yahweh*—the God of relationship, by exclaiming, "Now I will praise the LORD" (verse 35).

Envy

Each time Leah conceives, Rachel's envy grows more intense, since she is barren. In desperation she cries, "Give me children or else I die!" and

Jacob angrily answers, "Am I in the place of God, who has withheld from you the fruit of the womb?" (Genesis 30:1, 2).

Following a bad example

Soon Rachel repeats Sarah's mistake from years ago by taking the place of God and giving her maid to Jacob, to bear a child for her. Bilhah bears a son, and Rachel calls him Dan (meaning "Judge"). "God has judged my case; and He has also heard my voice and given me a son" (verse 6). Notice she uses the Hebrew word *Elohim* for God—a name that emphasizes His power, rather than the name *Yahweh,* that emphasizes a personal God.

This indicates that only Leah has a personal and intimate relationship with her God.

Rachel repeats the same strategy as Bilhah bears a second son, which Rachel names Naphtali (meaning "My wrestling"). Boasting, she says, "With great wrestlings I have wrestled with my sister, and indeed I have prevailed" (verse 8).

When Leah sees Rachel's success in having two sons through her maid, she gives her own maid, Zilpah, to Jacob to produce more sons. Zilpah bears a son, whom Leah names Gad. This name is translated by some from a Jewish post-biblical tradition as "a troop"; however, the Septuagint, an ancient Greek translation, gives it as "Luck" or "Good Fortune." This name gives no reference to God, reflecting only her personal impression. Leah names Zilpah's second son Asher (meaning "Happy"), saying, "I am happy, for the daughters will call me blessed" (verse 13).

During the wheat harvest, Leah's son Reuben, finds some mandrakes in the field and brings them to his mother. Because of the mandrake roots appearance, the people of the Near East associate it with enhanced fertility. Immediately both Rachel and Leah take interest in the plants—Rachel because she is barren, and Leah because she has ceased to bear children. Rachel begs for the mandrakes, hoping to end her infertility, and Leah agrees to give them to her in exchange for a night with Jacob, because she feels that Rachel has taken away her husband.

As a result, Leah bears a fifth son, whom she names Issachar (meaning "Wages"). She says, "God has given me my wages, because I have given my maid to my husband" (verse 18). She seems to believe that giving Zilpah to her husband has resulted in God rewarding her with Issachar and that her action, stemming from jealously, is an evidence of her self-denial.

Then, Leah bears another son, Zebulun (meaning "Dwelling"). She states, "God has endowed me with a good endowment; now my husband will dwell with me, because I have borne him six sons" (verse 20). With this statement she recognizes that God, through His grace, has endowed her with another son. She hopes this will cause her husband to dwell with her as his first wife.

Finally, God remembers Rachel, and she bears Joseph (meaning "He will take away," or "He will add"). Triumphantly, she proclaims, "God has taken away my reproach"; and then predicts, "The LORD shall add to me another son" (verses 23, 24). Rachel has had to wait seven years after her marriage, and fourteen years after her betrothal, to bear her first child. This long period has changed how she references God. She now calls Him "LORD" (*Yahweh*—a personal God), indicating she's finally on intimate terms with Him.

Jacob now has eleven sons, and may also have several daughters, which are not usually mentioned in biblical genealogy. We do know that he has at least one daughter, Dinah, but only because she is involved in a tragic incident later on. Imagine how unhappy Jacob must be, living with two concubines and two jealous and unhappy wives—Leah, who feels unloved; and Rachel, who craves more children. He also has a ruthless father-in-law, who is constantly and deceitfully trying to take advantage of him. Surely, the thought of facing his brother's wrath terrifies him, but his current situation is becoming intolerable as well!

CHAPTER TWENTY-EIGHT

Blessed

Based on Genesis 30

Through a dream at Bethel, God promises Jacob an inheritance, prosperity, and to bless all nations through him. He also promises to bring him back to Canaan after his exile in Haran with his uncle, Laban.

Jacob has labored fourteen years to accumulate bride money for his wives, Leah and Rachel. These bride monies are normally given to the women at marriage in case their husband dies, divorces, or abandons them. However, Laban hasn't fulfilled his duty to his daughters—and he's not arranged to pay Jacob, either!

Slow to pay

Jacob has to remind his uncle that his fourteen-year contract for the bride money has been completed. Now it's time to be released from his work so that he can take his family and return home to his own country.

However, Laban responds, "Please stay, If I have found favor in your eyes, for I have learned by experience that the LORD has blessed me for your sake" (Genesis 30:27). Essentially, Laban recognizes that Jacob is right, and that he has worked for free, because he now tells him to name his wages; yet he wants to take advantage of his free service, if possible.

Jacob answers, "You know how I have served you." (verse 29; the Hebrew word for "served" that Jacob mentions three times has overtones of the condition of slavery in Exodus 1:13, 14!) Since Laban has used the argument of God's blessing, Jacob prepares Laban to accept his proposal by using the same argument. He states that Laban had little before he came, but through his service, the Lord has greatly increased Laban's wealth. Then he asks, "When shall I also provide for my own house?" (verse 30).

Again, Laban asks what wages he wants, but Jacob knows how hard it is for Laban "to give." So Jacob immediately responds, "You shall not give me anything, if you will do this thing for me, I will feed and keep your flocks" (verse 31). Then he proposes to keep all the speckled and spotted sheep and goats, and the brown lambs. Laban thinks this is a foolish deal for Jacob but a good deal for him.

In the Near East, goats are usually black or dark brown, and rarely white; but sheep are generally completely white, and seldom black or speckled. The deal is that all the white sheep and brown goats will be Laban's property and any multicolored animal will be Jacob's property. Jacob strengthens the deal by involving his "righteousness" to guarantee that if any nonmulticolored animal is found in his possession, it should be considered stolen. To Laban, this whole proposal appears as if Jacob is not asking for anything! In his selfishness, this appears to be a good deal, so he immediately agrees to support the contract on Jacob's terms.

Beating the odds

As part of the agreement, Jacob plans to separate all the multicolored animals from the flocks, himself, but the willy Laban thinks to cheat Jacob from having them at all. He takes the multicolored sheep and goats and gives them to his sons—who take them three days away so they cannot mate with the white animals. Without these, Laban's flock is now made up of solid colored animals; however, through his ruse, Laban is about to unwittingly highlight God's supernatural intervention on Jacob's behalf!

Since he's starting with only solid-colored animals, the odds of Jacob ever having a sizeable flock of multicolored sheep and goats seems remote, if not impossible.

However, he follows an ancient superstition that offspring markings can be affected by what their mothers see during the prenatal period. He takes branches from green poplar, almond, and chestnut trees and peels strips in the bark, giving the branches the appearance of being striped in brown and white. He sets them before the mating animals, and this seems to work. Soon Jacob has a sizeable flock (through divine providence, of course, rather than superstitious beliefs).

Scientifically, some of the animals of solid color apparently carry recessive genes that produce multicolored ones. When bred with each other, the recessive genes reappear in the next generation, producing the multicolored animals. Hybrid animals are noted to be sturdier and stronger than purebred animals, resulting in a stronger and healthier herd. Jacob also wisely keeps the first offspring the mothers produce every spring, because they tend to be stronger than later offspring of the same season. The feebler offspring, he does not keep, but delivers them to Laban.

God must have added his special blessing to Jacob, because recessive genes will not normally show up in such a marked manner as indicated by Genesis 30:43. This verse says that Jacob "became exceedingly prosperous, and had large flocks, female and male servants, and camels and donkeys."

The Hebrew word translated as "exceedingly" has been first used for Laban's wealth, but it is now used for Jacob's—indicating an explosion of wealth for both men at different times. This repetition also suggests that Jacob is now wealthier than his uncle—which makes Laban very unhappy.

Truly, God has fulfilled the promise of prosperity He gave to Jacob in his dream at Bethel, even as he was fleeing from his brother Esau's death threat.

CHAPTER TWENTY-NINE

A Strained Separation

Based on Genesis 31

Jacob works for Laban fourteen years for his two wives, and six more years to accumulate wealth for him and his family. Laban does everything to keep him poor and subservient, but the Lord blesses him with prosperity. As his wealth increases, Laban sons begin to complain, saying, "Jacob has taken away all that was our father's; and from what was our father's he has acquired all this wealth" (Genesis 31:1). Jacob also observes that Laban's countenance toward him is no longer favorable. Then the Lord communicates to Jacob, "Return to the land of your fathers and to your family, and I will be with you" (verse 3).

Jacob, who is away from home tending the flocks, calls his wives to the field and tells them privately what has happened with his work and relationship with their father and their brothers. He wants assurance from his wives that they are willing to leave their father's house and presents his reasons for leaving. He refers to Laban's hostility and deceitfulness in changing his wages ten times—in contrast to his faithfulness in serving their father. Then, he adds that the Angel of God has shown him in a dream that the Lord has prospered him, but that he must leave and return to his father's land.

Jacob's wives answer him with the same two arguments to buttress their leaving.

They refer to their father as disinheriting them and selling them by not returning the bride price to them, but retaining it for himself. They also add that God has taken away their father's riches, since it was really theirs and their children's. As a result, they support Jacob's decision to follow God's instructions and leave.

Stolen gods

As Jacob prepares to go, he sets his family on camels, loads his possessions, and prepares his cattle to travel while Laban is away shearing his sheep. This is usually in April or May, and is an occasion for family festivity; however, Jacob and his family have not been invited.

In Laban's absence, Rachel steals her father's household idols, which are likely small wooden or clay figurines, two to four inches long, that are often associated with ancestors or patron gods. Most of them are female in form, usually nude, and often with exaggerated features that are probably thought to enhance fertility. This may be one of the reasons why Rachel steals them, since she doesn't have nearly as many children as her sister Leah.

These gods are very important, since they are part of one's inheritance. If a man has sons, the household gods cannot be inherited by the daughters. This may be another reason why Rachel steals them, since her father never gave her the bride money that Jacob paid through his service. It also shows that her attachment to her husband's God is not strong, and that she still has an attachment to at least some aspects of her father's religion.

Jacob's departure without informing Laban is described as "he fled," seemingly an echo from his fleeing from Esau with the same emotions of fear and perhaps guilt. By the third day, Laban is informed of their departure. He immediately hotly pursues Jacob and by the seventh day of the journey, overtakes him in the mountains of Gilead. This is a distance of about 275 miles that could only be done in this short time by riding camels. A very fast camel could travel that distance in about seven days.

Obviously, it would be impossible to drive the flocks and herds much more than nine or ten miles in a day, so this seems to indicate that the family on camels is apparently well ahead of the animals because of their fear of Laban and his sons. This great distance includes the fording of the Euphrates River in the spring, when it is swollen from rains.

Accusations

During Laban's pursuit of Jacob, God warns him through a dream not to say or do anything that is harmful or unfavorable to Jacob. When the two meet, Laban begins with a series of accusations. "What have you done, that you have stolen away unknown to me, and carried away my daughters like captives taken with the sword?" (verse 26). Then he says, "Why did you flee away secretly, and steal away from me, and not tell me . . . ? And you did not allow me to kiss my sons and my daughters" (verses 27, 28).

Then Laban adds that he cannot do him harm, since "the God of your father" warned him not to in a dream (verse 29). This indicates that Laban does not fully accept Jacob's God but still believes in his own gods. Then comes what really bothers him: *"Why did you steal my gods?"* (verse 30, emphasis added).

Jacob answers that he left secretly because he was afraid Laban might take his wives away by force. As to the stolen gods, he says that whoever is found to be guilty should be put to death—in accordance with Mesopotamian law.

The custom of the time is to have the husband and each wife living in separate tents, and Laban searches Jacob's tent, Leah's tent, and in Rachel's tent, but can't find them.

Unbeknown to Jacob, Rachel has hidden the gods in her camel's saddle, which she now sitting on. She says to her father, "Let it not displease my lord that I cannot rise before you, for the manner of women is with me" (verse 35). Rachel's menstruation (whether true or not) now serves as the means to obstruct her father's search. Ironically, this leaves Laban powerless and fooled by a woman—the woman he had deceived twenty years before!

Rebuke

Jacob is angry and rebukes Laban, setting forth his innocence by referring to the quality of his service over twenty years of unselfish caring for Laban's flocks. In ancient law, the shepherd is not responsible for stolen animals or those that are killed by wild beasts, but Laban has forced him to replace them.

Next, he reminds Laban of the harsh working conditions he has endured—drought by day, frost by night, and constant sleep deprivation.

Finally, he shows how he has been abused and deceived by Laban—not being paid for fourteen years, and having his salary changed ten times over the past six years! Then he refers to how even God has taken his side—warning Laban not to harm him, or send him away empty-handed.

Laban's response is, "These daughters are my daughters, and these children are my children, and this flock is my flock, all that you see is mine" (verse 43). But since God has warned him, *he can do nothing* instead, he proposes they enter into a formal covenant, defining the issues between them.

Jacob remains silent, but takes a stone and sets it up as a pillar; then he insists that his brothers-in-law do the same. Laban names the place Jegar Sahadutha in Aramaic, meaning "a heap of witness," while Jacob names it Galeed, which has the same meaning in Hebrew.

Since Laban initiates the covenant, he gives the first speech, making reference to the two parties involved and the extra name for this place—Mizpah, meaning "watchtower." This name makes reference to God as a

Sentinel, when he says, "May the LORD watch between you and me when we are absent one from another" (verse 49). Instead of a blessing, this statement serves as a stern warning that God will watch this boundary when they are not present. He also says that the two pillars will serve as two witnesses that will not permit either party to pass beyond that point to harm each other. The fact that there are two pillars, makes the covenant legal beyond a doubt, since they serve as two legal witnesses.

It is worth noting that Jacob has not spoken a word to Laban after the covenant has been proposed, but only acts. However, now he offers a sacrifice and calls on them to seal the covenant with the customary ceremonial meal. Once they're through, the peace treaty is ratified.

The next day, Laban kisses his daughters and their sons, blesses them, and leaves to return home. Nothing is said about whether he kisses Jacob or speaks to him before he leaves; however, this final separation appears to be strained.

Jacob has seen what his own name, "deceiver" or "supplanter," really means through his dealings with Laban. However, the Lord has liberated Jacob from Laban's clutch, and he can now return home, as the Lord has promised.

CHAPTER THIRTY

A Night of Terror

Based on Genesis 32 and 33

After the separation from Laban, Jacob follows God's command to return to Canaan, but is in great fear of being killed by his twin brother Esau, whom he cheated out of his birthright twenty years before. At this point, God sends angels who appear and reassure him of divine protection, and Jacob names the place, Mahanaim, or "two camps." Many scholars believe that this indicates two camps of angels—one who camped before him, and one behind. These two bands serve as two divine witnesses, guaranteeing God's protection.

Trying to appease

As Jacob travels, he follows his normal scheming approach by devising a plan to appease the anger of his brother. He sends messengers to Esau, who is in Edom, saying, "I have dwelt with Laban and stayed there until now. I have oxen, donkeys, flocks, and male and female servants; and I have sent to tell my lord, that I may find favor in your sight" (Genesis 32:4, 5). The mention of his wealth is to impress Esau, and to gain his favor by showing he does not need his brother's inheritance, after all. However, Jacob's hopes are dashed when the messengers return saying, "Esau is coming with 400 men!" In his great fear, Jacob divides his family, servants, flocks, herds, and camels into two companies, reasoning, *If one group is attacked, the other might escape.* He understands that in order to restore his relationship with God, he must restore his relationship with Esau, but his fear is overwhelming. Jacob then turns to prayer, imploring God for help, based on His promise at Bethel to bring him back to Canaan. He knows that fulfillment of this promise is dependent on God's mercy, rather than on his own goodness.

Still trying to appease his brother, Jacob takes two hundred female goats, twenty male goats, two hundred ewes, twenty rams, thirty milk camels with their colts, forty cows, ten bulls, twenty female donkeys, and ten foals—about 550 in all—and sends them ahead as a present to Esau. In this way, he tries to show his brother that he is returning the birthright stolen from him years ago. These animals are entrusted to his servants, who are divided into multiple groups so Esau will get them one after another, and serve as a buffer. Each servant is to say, "Behold your servant Jacob is behind us" (verse 20). The Hebrew word translated as "appease" in Genesis 32:20 means to "atone," indicating that in attempting to reconcile with his brother, he is also reconciling himself with God.

"I will not let you go!"

That night Jacob sends his two wives, his two female servants, and his eleven sons to ford the Jabbok to its southern side, while he stays on the northern side, apparently wanting to be alone with God. All of sudden a "Man" wrestles with him. The struggle intensifies all night, and Jacob thinks it is a mortal enemy. Neither one gains a clear victory, until the break of dawn, when Jacob's antagonist, who so far has fought with only human strength, reaches out and atrophies the sinew on Jacob's hip with a single touch. As his hip comes out of joint, Jacob immediately becomes aware that his opponent is not human at all.

"Let Me go, for the day breaks," the Man cries, concerned the light of day will expose His face to Jacob and kill him, since none can see the face of God and live (verse 26). However, Jacob desperately clings to Him, saying, "I will not let you go unless you bless me!" (verse 26). He knows he is in the presence of God, and that only He can forgive his past cheating and deception.

"What is your name?" the Man asks.

"Jacob," he answers (verse 27).

"Your name shall no longer be called Jacob, but Israel," the Stranger says, "for you have struggled with God and with men and have prevailed" (verse 28).

A change of name is a change of identity. Jacob is no longer a "deceiver" of men, but a "victor of God," or an "overcomer." His new name literally means, "God fights," although the explanation that follows indicates that he is the subject, meaning, "He fights with God" or "He prevails over God."

The theological implications of his new name are many:

1. Jacob's relationship with God depends on his relationship with men.
2. The word Israel, meaning "God fights" is a reminder of his personal

struggle that taught him to let God fight for him.

3. Jacob prevailed because he allowed God to prevail over him. At this point, he is totally converted. His old self is dead because he has submitted to God as his Lord, rather than trying to function on his own.

Jacob now inquires the name of his opponent, and His response is, "Why is it that you ask about my name?" (verse 29). Throughout Scripture, asking the name of a supernatural being is essentially asking for control over them, so no name is given. However, when Jacob receives his new name of Israel, God has control over him. In the end, God fulfills Jacob's request by blessing him.

Biblical stories tend to correspond to previous stories, and Jacob's story of the divine blessing parallels his previous story of the blessing from his father Isaac. On each occasion, Jacob forces the blessing out of them and is occasioned with an identity crisis.

Isaac asks, "Who are you?" and the Man who wrestles with him asks, "What is your name?"

Both his father and the Man touch him—one questioning his identity, and the other giving him his identity.

Jacob previously lied about his name, but now he discloses who he is, and exposes himself.

Seeing the face of God

Jacob names the place of his encounter with the divine Being as Peniel, "The face of God." The Hebrew expression "face to face" does not mean that he *sees* God's face, but rather that he has had an encounter with God.

The experience at Peniel also echoes Jacob's previous experience at Bethel. There, his name was confirmed as Jacob ("the deceiver"), while the Peniel experience gives him a new name, Israel (one who "prevailed with God.")

At Bethel, the blessing comes at night when he is fleeing from Esau, while at Peniel, the blessing comes at daybreak, when Jacob is returning home from exile.

These parallels and contrasts clearly demonstrate that the old Jacob has been replaced by the new Israel.

Meeting Esau

Jacob now moves forward to encounter his brother, who has apparently set out to kill him with four hundred men. He puts the maidservants with their children in front, followed by Leah with her children, and Rachel and Joseph last. The order reflects who he esteems most. However, Jacob, now a transformed man, and no longer a coward, leads the way. Before he actually encounters his brother, he progressively bows down to the ground seven times as he gets closer and closer. Unexpectedly, Esau runs the final distance to him, embraces him, falls on his neck, kisses him, and weeps. Naturally, Jacob also weeps.

Esau asks about all the people with Jacob whom he has never seen, and Jacob says they are the children God has graciously given him. Then the maid servants and their children come near and bow down before Esau. They are followed by Leah and her children, and Joseph.

Esau asks the meaning of all the animals sent ahead of his brother's family, and Jacob responds, "These are to find favor in the sight of my lord" (verse 8).

"I have enough, my brother," Esau answers, "keep what you have for yourself" (verse 9).

Jacob insists, "No please, if I have found favor in your sight, then receive my present from my hand, inasmuch as I have seen your face as though I had seen the face of God, and you were pleased with me. Please take my blessing that is brought you, because God has dealt graciously with me, and because I have enough" (verses 10, 11). With that urging, Esau accepts the gifts. He kindly suggests they journey on together, but Jacob answers that the children and cattle will make their trip too slow.

The story of Jacob is very significant in that he begins as a deceiver from birth and lives his life as a hardened schemer. Then, in one night of terror, he struggles with a divine being until he accepts God as the Lord of his life. God in His wisdom and grace knows it will take a crisis to completely change him from Jacob to Israel.

CHAPTER THIRTY-ONE

Seven Great Sorrows

Based on Genesis 34–37

After Jacob returns to Canaan, he suffers terrible and sorrowful events. He settles in Shechem, where he buys a parcel of land. His daughter Dinah is identified as the daughter of Leah, and not as the daughter of Jacob, as would be the usual identification. This unusual introduction is apparently to link her with Simeon and Levi, who are her full brothers, and closely linked with her history.

Dinah goes out unaccompanied to see the daughters of the land. Since "daughters of the land" does not convey a positive image, doubt is cast on the intentions of the girl, since she is probably only about fifteen years of age. Shechem, the son of Hamor and prince of the country, sees her and humiliates her through rape. However, he is strongly attracted to her and requests his father to arrange their marriage.

When Jacob learns of this, he is apparently stunned into silence. This incident brings forth ceremonial uncleanness, and strongly affects his family's honor. It is clearly a very disgraceful thing, and when Dinah's brothers come in from the field, they are grieved and extremely angry. It is interesting to note that the father and the brothers are considered the legal guardians of Dinah, but Jacob has become passive, and defers all the decisions to others.

Caught in a tough spot

Hamor approaches Jacob proposing a marriage contract. This puts Jacob in a very difficult situation. To refuse the marriage proposal would result in the ill will of the Shechemites; but to accept it would be in clear violation of God's command not to associate with the evil inhabitants of the land. A further complication to the whole situation is that Dinah is still in the house of Shechem, and at this point, there is no plan on how to get her back home.

Hamor's marriage contract proposal is basically a business deal that will result in intermarriage between the two clans. It will bring business advantages for Jacob and his family, in that they can buy land and acquire possessions. Shechem, however, enters the negotiation by focusing on aspects that are of particular interest to Jacob and his sons, by referring to the bride price and even offering extra money as a gift.

The sons of Jacob immediately reject Hamor's proposal, and deceitfully say they cannot give their sister to one who is uncircumcised, because that would be a reproach to them. Instead, they follow what they observed of their father growing up and deceitfully propose that the marriage would be acceptable if all the Shechemite males are circumcised.

This proposal pleases Hamor and Shechem, but now they must plead their case before the men at the city gate to get their consent. Their only argument for the marriage and circumcision is economic, since they will be able to acquire Jacob's animals and property. They agree, and all those who live in the city, and all the farmers who do business in the city, are circumcised.

Massacre!

On the third day after being circumcised, when their pain is the greatest, two of Dinah's older brothers, Simeon and Levi, take their swords, enter the city, kill Hamor and Shechem, and all the men of the city. Then they rescue their sister from Shechem's house, plunder all the wealth of the city, and take all the animals within and without, along with their wives and children.

Ironically, Hamor arrives at an appropriate bride price for Dinah, who was taken forcibly, but now her brothers impose their own price by forcibly taking the life and goods of the whole city. Clearly, they are satisfied that the humiliation of their sister has been avenged.

Immediately, Jacob issues a stern rebuke to Simeon and Levi for this cruel deed, saying it will make him obnoxious among the inhabitants of the land. He believes this will cause a backlash that may kill him and his household. However, the two brothers, who have been bothered by their father's willingness to compromise, answer, "Should he treat our sister like a harlot?" (Genesis 34:31).

This story clearly demonstrates that what Jacob plans and schemes for his own comfort is, in the end, turned around by God to accomplish His own will. First, Jacob should not have settled down in Shechem among the Canaanites, but if they don't move now, they are in physical jeopardy. Second, if the marriage contract had become a reality, Jacob and his sons would have been heavily influenced over time by their new relatives.

Jacob's faith in God's promises about his seed and the Promised Land needs adjusting. God speaks to him and says, "Arise go up to Bethel and dwell there; and make an altar there to God, who appeared to you when you fled from the face of Esau your brother" (Genesis 35:1).

Jacob, in turn, tells his family and those with them, "Put away the foreign gods that are among you, purify yourselves, and change your garments" (verse 2). Many of these idols are no doubt part of the spoil from Shechem and the household gods that Rachel has stolen. They give Jacob all their foreign gods and jewelry (which are possibly amulets), and he buries under a terebinth tree at Shechem. With this act, he ends his ill-fated sojourn at Shechem.

On the way to Luz (called Bethel by the Hebrews), God protects them by instilling His fear on the inhabitants of the surrounding cities, since they can easily attack them in revenge for the slaughter of the Shechemites. There, Jacob builds an altar to the Lord, naming it El Bethel, "God of Bethel." He pours oil upon it, like he did on his previous visit, and they are purified from all their idolatry. This visit to Bethel renews Jacob's relationship with the Lord and His promises.

More sorrows

Jacob's next great sorrow comes from the death of Deborah, whose name means "bee." She has been Rebekah's nurse, and at this time, she may have been part of Jacob's household, after tenderly caring for him during his infancy and early life. She is buried south of Bethel, under an oak tree.

While there, God appears to Jacob, and His message echoes much of his previous experience at Peniel. He blesses him and repeats that his name will be Israel, instead of Jacob. He restates His covenant promises of fruitfulness, and inheritance of the Promised Land. Jacob sets up a pillar of stone as a monument, and pours a drink offering over it, as well as oil.

From Bethel, Jacob travels about fifteen miles toward Hebron, where another great sorrow comes to him—his beloved wife Rachel dies in childbirth. As she is dying, she gives her child the name, Ben Oni, or "son of my sorrow;" however, Jacob calls him Benjamin, or "son of the right."

The concept behind "right" has special significance in Scripture, since it refers to the south, which is on the right, when one is facing the east. The Hebrews fixed all the cardinal points by first facing east—apparently echoing back to the Garden of Eden, where they looked east toward God and His dwelling place. It also alludes to Jacob's future arrival in the south, if coming from Padan Aram in Mesopotamia and Benjamin's inherited land in the south of Canaan.

In Daniel 11, the Messiah is ultimately linked with the king of the south, and the southern quadrant of the tabernacle court is also linked with the cleansing of the animal burned on the altar of whole burnt offering.

Even more sorrows

Jacob travels south to the watchtower of Eder, from which shepherds can watch over their flocks. This tower seems to be synonymous with Mount Moriah, Mount Zion, and Jerusalem (Micah 4:7, 8). Here, he suffers another sorrowful event when his firstborn son Reuben sleeps with Bilhah, Jacob's concubine and Rachel's maid. Again, this act may resonate with what Simeon and Levi did, humiliating their father for his previous attitude toward their mother. It also may very well be a way for Reuben to claim his leadership and defile the memory of Rachel and the birth of Benjamin. The Bible records, however, that Reuben repents of his sin much later, as is evidenced by his concern for Joseph.

Jacob hears about what Reuben has done, but again, remains calm and does not retaliate. He apparently places this in God's hands and allows Him to deal with the situation, thereby demonstrating that his new name, Israel, is appropriate.

After thirty-six years of separation, Jacob now arrives in Hebron, where his aged father Isaac lives. They live together for another twenty years, then Jacob suffers the sorrowful experience of losing his father at age 180. Esau comes, and the brothers bury their father, probably in the cave of Machpelah, where Abraham and Sarah are buried. Afterward, Esau leaves Canaan permanently for Edom, while Jacob remains in the Promised Land.

Jacob settles down in Hebron on a permanent basis, in contrast to his father Isaac, who was a stranger or sojourner. Jacob is now heir to the beginning of the fulfillment of the promises and blessings of the divine covenant. His flocks increase, and his sons tend them, often far from home, particularly during the dry season. Joseph is tending the flocks with his brothers who are the sons of Bilhah and Zilpah, his father's concubines, and when he returns, he gives a bad report of his brothers to his father that sours relations between them.

The greatest sorrow

Joseph is the son of Jacob's beloved wife Rachel, and the son of his old age. He loves him more than all his children, and gives him a special coat of many colors (which can also be translated as a coat with long sleeves). This coat is worn by those of noble rank, suggesting that Jacob is perhaps making him his firstborn over Reuben, his chronological firstborn. Because of the father's special love and coat, Joseph's brothers hate him.

To make matters worse, Joseph has dreams that humiliate his brothers, since dreams are considered a divine sign of spiritual superiority. He tells them that in his dream they are binding sheaves in the field when his sheaf stands upright, and their sheaves all bow down to his. Since sheaves represent food, they understand that someday they will be economically dependent on him, and that he will rule over them. Naturally, this increases their hatred.

He has another dream that he relates to his father and brothers. In this dream the sun, moon, and eleven stars bow down to him. His father rebukes him asking, if he, his mother, and his brothers are going to bow to him. This results in his brothers hating him more, and his father pondering the dream.

Jacob's brothers go to pasture their flock at Shechem during the dry season of April to October. This region is about sixty miles north of Hebron, and Jacob has previously bought property there. Since considerable time has elapsed without word from them, Jacob sends seventeen-year-old Joseph to bring him word of their welfare. After all, they are in the territory of the Shechemites, who hate them. When Joseph arrives, they are not there, but he is told they have gone to Dothan, another sixteen miles to the northwest.

His brothers see him coming and say to themselves, "Look, this dreamer is coming!" (Genesis 37:19) and conspire to kill him and throw him into a deep pit, later telling their father that a wild beast has devoured him. When Reuben hears of it, he says, "Let us not kill him" (verse 21), secretly planning to take him back home.

When Joseph arrives, they strip him of his coat of many colors and throw him into a deep dry pit that serves as a cistern during rainy season. They sit down nearby and eat a meal, knowing that eventually Joseph will probably die of starvation. Dothan is situated on the great caravan highway from the north to Egypt, and a group of Midianite (also called Ishmaelite) merchants are passing by. Judah takes the initiative and proposes to his brothers to sell Joseph as a slave, to avoid having his blood on their hands. They sell him for only twenty shekels of silver—a very cheap price, since the average price is thirty shekels of silver for a slave. It should be noted that to become a slave during this era is a fate more feared than death.

Reuben, the firstborn, apparently is not there during this transaction, for when he returns and discovers what his brothers have done, he tears his clothes, identifying with his father, who will do the same.

The brothers decide to kill a young goat and dip Joseph's coat in its blood. Then they take it to their father, saying, "We have found this. Do you know whether it is your son's tunic or not?" (verse 32).

Feigning ignorance, they let their father assume that a wild animal has killed Joseph, and their plan succeeds. Jacob now suffers the greatest sorrow of his life. He tears his clothes, puts sackcloth around his waist; then he weeps and mourns. His children try to comfort him, but he says, "I shall go down into the grave to my son in mourning" (verse 35).

Jacob has suffered great sorrow seven different times after entering Canaan.

However, these experiences have allowed God to work out His plans, rather than Jacob working out his own. He has trusted God by essentially remaining willing to follow His leading, and allowing God to fight his battles for him. His change of name from Jacob to Israel has now become reality.

CHAPTER THIRTY-TWO

Tricked Into Justice

Based on Genesis 38

Judah's first act of intercession for others comes when he arranges to sell Joseph to the Midianite traders, rather than have him die of starvation in the pit his brothers have placed him in. However, Judah has a long way to go to become the man he needs to be for Lord.

He leaves his brothers and marries a Canaanite daughter of Shua, and they have three sons, Er, Onan, and Shelah. Er marries Tamar, but because of his wickedness, the Lord causes him to die. It is now the responsibility of Onan, his next oldest brother, to enter into a levirate marriage with Tamar. This type of marriage is to produce a male offspring for the older son, so that the family name does not die out, and his inheritance is passed on to his son. Onan refuses to fulfill his duty to his brother by wasting his seed on the ground. This action is considered evil in the sight of the Lord, who causes his death. Onan's refusal to perform his duty to his brother is probably because it would decrease the inheritance share that his own future son would receive.

It is the obligation of the father-in-law to arrange a husband for the widow as soon as possible after the mourning period so she can be cared for and produce offspring before she becomes too old to have children. Therefore, Judah has the obligation to arrange the marriage of his youngest son Shelah to Tamar.

Widows wear special garments that designate them as such. Like married women, they do not wear a veil; and in Israel, they have the right to glean at harvest time and receive a certain portion of the tithe, because they have no inheritance rights. At this point, Shelah is too young to marry Tamar, so Judah sends her away to her parents until Shelah grows up. However, only the daughter of a priest could return home after being widowed.

Judah's excuse for sending her home is, "Lest he also die like his brothers"

(Genesis 38:9). This suggests that Judah is blaming Tamar for the death of Er and Onan, and he does not intend to fulfill his obligation to give Shelah to her in marriage.

After some length of time, Judah's wife dies, and he is comforted—something that is not stated when his two wicked sons die. This is the third death in the family, and the number three is extremely significant in Scripture. Clearly it is to communicate to Judah that things are not going well for him and that God is telling him he needs to change. However, change is difficult, and takes time to happen.

It is spring, and Judah goes with his friend Hirah to Timnah to shear his sheep.

Tamar finds out, so she takes off her widow garments and puts on a veil—indicating that she is betrothed to be married. She goes to an open space on the road to Timnah, and sits down, waiting for Judah. The reason for these actions is that Shelah is grown up, but she hasn't been given to him in marriage.

After sheep shearing is done, it is a time for harvest festivity. For the Canaanites, it is associated with religious rituals of "sacred" prostitution, hoping for a bountiful harvest of wool. The pagans observed that in nature, reproduction came through sexual intercourse, and in the religious realm the gods controlled fertility. Since intercourse with the gods is not possible, religious prostitutes took their place to assure divine blessing on the harvest. By this means the pagans try to reenact the divine marriage.

Judah is traveling to Timnah, hoping for a bountiful harvest of wool. He has been affected by his Canaanite friends, family, and environment, so when he sees Tamar, he assumes she is a cult prostitute because she has a veil, indicating she is betrothed to the gods. The Hebrew word *qedeshah* indicates she is a cult prostitute, rather than a common prostitute, *zanah*, that would not allow her to be veiled in public. He does not recognize her as his daughter-in-law, nor does he have the means to pay for her services, since carrying money when traveling is dangerous. He promises to send a young goat to her as an expensive gift, but in her wisdom, she chooses objects that will prove his identity. She asks for and receives his signet ring, cord, and staff as a pledge until she receives her goat. His signet ring is probably a cylinder seal made of an engraved precious or semiprecious stone. This is usually attached to a cord and worn around the neck. The ring is used to seal business deals, by rolling it on a piece of soft clay to leave the distinctive design of the owner. The staff is a stick that is often carved and used for walking, a cattle prod, and weapon against wild animals. It also may be a means to identify the owner.

After their encounter, Tamar returns home, takes off her veil, and puts on her previous garments of widowhood. Judah sends Hirah with a young goat to pay his pledge and receive back his ring, cord, and staff. But Hirah doesn't find the woman and returns with the goat, reporting to Judah that he cannot find her. Note that Judah does not go himself with the goat, and fears for his reputation when she cannot be found.

After about three months (again the number three!), Judah is informed that Tamar is with child through harlotry. He self-righteously responds, "Bring her out and let her be burned!" (verse 24). He gives his order by virtue of his authority as head of the family. The normal punishment for adultery is to bring the young woman to the door of the house while the men of the city stone her to death. Punishment by burning is reserved for cases where a daughter of a priest engages in harlotry or incest (Leviticus 21:9).

As Tamar is brought out of the house to be stoned, she sends the items she's held to her father-in-law, saying, "By the man to whom these belong, I am with child"(Genesis 38:25). Then she asks him, "Please determine who's these are—the signet ring and cord, and staff" (verse 25). Judah humbly acknowledges that they are his, and says, "She has been more righteous that I, because I did not give her to Shelah my son" (verse 26). The great irony in the story is that Shelah is exonerated, while Judah is condemned.

As Tamar is giving birth, they realize she is having twins. This echoes the story of Esau and Jacob. During birth, one of them puts forth his hand and the midwife ties a scarlet thread around it, saying, "This one came out first" (verse 28). He then draws back his hand and his twin is unexpectedly born first.

"How did you break through?" the midwife asks (verse 29), and therefore, he was named Perez, meaning, "break through." Afterward, his brother is born, and they name him Zerah, meaning "shining." Once again, the one considered second becomes the first, and ultimately becomes part of the genealogy of David and Jesus.

Tamar becomes the first of four women who are included in Matthew's account of Jesus' genealogy. The other women listed are Rahab, Ruth, and the "wife of Uriah" (known to be Bathsheba). Interestingly, the genealogy excludes the famous matriarchs of Sarah, Rebekah, Rachel, and Leah. It is clear that Tamar, who is a Canaanite, joins Israel's God, as did Rahab, and becomes very significant in salvation history.

Judah, who has clearly been on the wrong path much of the time, repents of his sin in this story, and begins to change into a significant figure for God in the future. His evil act is turned by God into a positive event that fulfills His long-term plan. He becomes the redeemer figure for Tamar, and the ancestor of David and Jesus—the Redeemer of the world.

CHAPTER THIRTY-THREE

Ominous Dreams

Based on Genesis 39–41

Joseph is sold as a slave to Potiphar, whose name means "He whom Ré (the sun god) has given." He's the captain of the guard, a title that indicates he's the chief executioner, and the one in charge of the prison for royal officials.

Since Pharaoh is probably a "Hyksos" foreign Semite ruler, it's important that Potiphar be Egyptian, since his countrymen won't tolerate a foreign executioner. He is part of the royal administration, so he is no doubt a eunuch.

While Joseph is in Egypt, the Lord prospers him, and noting this, Potiphar soon elevates him to be in charge of his household. Joseph is well built and handsome, and Potiphar's wife is attracted to him. Daily she entices him, but he refuses her advances stating that his master trusts him with everything in his house. "There is no greater in this house than I," he says, "nor has he kept back anything from me but you, because you are his wife. How then can I do this great wickedness, and sin against God?" (Genesis 39:9).

She is relentless, however, and one day he's forced to run outdoors—but not before she snatches his outer garment! Standard dress for Egyptian men is a loincloth, but overseers are often portrayed also wearing a white cloth hanging from their shoulders. This is likely what she's held onto as she loudly accuses Joseph of trying to rape her.

Once again, Joseph is identified by his garment, but the most important point is his faithfulness to his master and to God.

Prison

Potiphar is furious! He throws Joseph into the royal dungeon, but doesn't execute him—probably because he does not believe his wife. Life in prison is difficult at first because, as the psalmist writes, "They hurt his feet with fetters, he was laid in irons" (Psalm 105:18). However, Joseph soon finds favor with the warden, who puts him in charge of the prison's affairs—just as he had been under Potiphar.

Dreams

Pharaoh's butler and baker offend him, and are sent to the royal prison. Then Joseph is charged with serving them by Potiphar, himself. Both the butler and the baker have dreams the same night, but do not know their meaning. The next morning, Joseph finds them both sad, so he's eager to help. He asks them, "Do not interpretations belong to God? Tell them to me" (Genesis 40:8).

The butler tells that he dreamed of a vine with three branches that budded, blossomed, and produced ripe grapes. Pharaoh's cup was in his hand, so he squeezed the grapes into his cup and gave it to the king. Joseph interprets the dream by saying that the three branches are three days in which Pharaoh will "lift up" his head and restore him to his former position (verse 13). The significant number three here corresponds to the three actions in the dream: "budded . . . blossom . . . and its clusters ripened." These, in turn, represent, "took the grapes . . . pressed them . . . placed the cup in Pharaoh's hand" (verses 10, 11).

Then Joseph requests, "But remember me when it is well with you, and please show kindness to me; make mention of me to Pharaoh, and get me out of this house" (verse 14).

The baker, encouraged by the interpretation of the butler's dream, relates his own.

He has three white baskets on his head, and in the top basket are all kinds of baked goods for Pharaoh. But birds are eating them out of the basket. Joseph interprets the dream and says three baskets are three days. Then he says that within three days, Pharaoh will "lift off" his head and he will be hung on a tree for the birds to feast on his body (verse 19). Again, the baker's dream has three elements—"basket . . . baked goods . . . birds;" and these, in turn, represent, "lift off . . . hang . . . eat" (verses 17, 19).

On the third day, Pharaoh celebrates his birthday. These occasions call for a banquet—and sometimes pardons. As part of the festivities, he restores the butler to his former position, but the baker is beheaded and hanged. Clearly, God has given Joseph the interpretation of the two dreams, because no one else could explain them. However, the butler forgets Joseph's request to remember him before Pharaoh!

More dreams

Two years later, Pharaoh has several dreams of his own. His wise men can't interpret them by using their dream books, but when the butler hears this, he remembers Joseph and his request.

Shaving his face and head to appear like an Egyptian, Joseph comes before the king. "I have had a dream, and there is no one who can interpret it, but I have heard it said of you that you can," Pharaoh says (Genesis 41:14).

"It is not in me," Joseph replies. "God will give Pharaoh an answer of peace" (verse 16).

In his first dream, seven fat cows emerge from the Nile, followed by seven skinny ones, who eat the fat ones! This is shocking, since the Nile is considered the god that gives life. The second dream reveals seven fat heads of grain being eaten by seven heads withered, thin, and blighted by the east desert wind (again three). Both of the dreams use the number seven—God's number. The fact that an east wind blights the grain is also significant, since the east is linked with God. In other words, God is the cause of all of this, so He may be glorified by fulfilling His purpose through His servant Joseph.

This time, God gives Joseph the ability to instantly interpret the dreams as seven years of plenty, followed by seven of famine. The repetition provides emphasis and indicates that this is true because the two dreams serve as two witnesses, indicating that fulfillment will be both prompt and certain. He advises Pharaoh to appoint an overseer, and to store up twenty percent every year to be used in the famine years, when the crop is meager.

Honored

Pharaoh wisely elevates Joseph to second-in-command in his kingdom, appointing him as overseer, or vizier, because "in [him] is the Spirit of God" (verse 38). He gives him his signet ring, indicating that he has full authority to sign all official documents in the name of Pharaoh. He clothes him in fine linen, and honors him publicly with a gold chain. This refers to the collar on which hung the symbol of Maat—a symbol of equality to the Pharaoh that characterizes the status of the vizier. The public ceremony places him in a second chariot, preceded by people calling out to the public to bow the knee as he passes. He also honors him as a foreigner by giving him an appropriate Egyptian name, Zaphnath-Paaneah, meaning, "The god speaks that he may live."

Then, Pharaoh honors Joseph by giving him Asenath, the daughter of the high priest of On, for a wife. She has two sons. The first is Manasseh, meaning "making forget," indicating that God has made him forget all of his trials and pain in his father's home.

The second is called Ephraim, meaning, "to bear fruit," indicating he will be fruitful in the land of his affliction.

The famine becomes severe in all of Egypt, as well as in the surrounding countries. All have to come to Joseph to buy grain and avoid starvation. In a very literal way, he is fulfilling the promise made to Abraham that, "in you all the families of the earth shall be blessed" (Genesis 12:3).

Joseph is thirty years old when he begins public service, the same age required for Hebrew priest ministry—and Jesus' age when He begins His public ministry! Joseph has been faithful to God, and He has brought him success. He is the instrument fulfilling God's covenant.

CHAPTER THIRTY-FOUR

The Famine

Based on Genesis 42–45

The great famine in Egypt also affects Canaan and the surrounding nations. When Jacob hears that Egypt has grain, he sends all of his sons, except Benjamin, to buy grain to avoid starvation. They probably join another caravan that is going to Egypt for the same reason.

Once in Egypt, they meet with Joseph, who is personally overseeing the distribution of grain. Twenty-one years have passed, and his brothers don't recognize him, since he looks like an Egyptian and speaks through an interpreter. His head is shaved, and he has no beard to avoid the lice problem so prevalent in the land. Even though Joseph recognizes them immediately, he does so through his Hebrew way of thinking—using his senses of eyesight and hearing, rather than logic. He sees they have beards and are dressed in colored woolen clothing, and he hears them speaking in Hebrew. Surely, he feels a swell of emotion, but to determine if their hearts have changed, he puts them to a test.

Spies!

Without warning, Joseph shocks them by accusing them of being foreign spies, to which they answer, "No, my lord, but your servants have come to buy food" (Genesis 42:10). Being foreigners, they are not above suspicion, since traders and merchants commonly double as spies, traveling around unnoticed.

Joseph acts as if he does not believe them and says, "No, but you have come to see the nakedness of the land" (verse 12). The brothers innocently reveal almost too much information by saying, "Your servants are twelve brothers, the sons of one man" (verse 13). Also, "the youngest is with our father today, and one is no more" (verse 13). They try to imply that spies would not all come from the same family.

Again, Joseph acts as though he does not believe them and continues accusing them of being spies. He says he will test their truthfulness by keeping them all in prison, except one, who is to return home and bring back their youngest brother. Apparently, they don't accept his proposal, because he puts them all in prison for several days.

On the third day (notice again, the importance of three), Joseph reverses his first act because of their families' need of food. He states that because he fears God, he will keep only one in prison and release the other nine, if they return with their youngest brother. This will verify their truthfulness and exempt them from being executed as spies.

The brothers talk things over in Hebrew, and soon the guilt they've carried from what they did to Joseph so long ago comes to the surface. They can't help but feel that this experience is divine retribution. Reuben reminds them of his former unsuccessful warning to not sin against the boy, and as Joseph hears their confession and regret, he is overwhelmed by his emotions. Turning away from them, he quickly exits and weeps.

When he returns, he speaks to them again, and then binds Simeon—who has the reputation of being cruel—before their very eyes!

Next, Joseph orders their sacks to be filled with grain, and for their money returned in their sacks, along with provisions for their journey. They begin their trip home with heavy hearts, and when they stop for the night, one of them discovers his payment money is in his sack! Panic strikes them as they realize he might be accused of stealing, and again, in consternation, they attribute this to divine punishment.

An unthinkable risk

Back home, they tell Jacob all that has transpired and that they must take their youngest brother Benjamin to Egypt in order to free Simeon from prison. As each man opens his sack, they find the silver they've used to pay for the grain, adding to their fears.

In anguish, Jacob says, "You have bereaved me: Joseph is no more, Simeon is no more, and you want to take Benjamin. All these things are against me" (verse 36).

Without thinking, Reuben, the firstborn, says, "Kill my two sons if I do not bring him back to you; put him in my hands. And I will bring him back to you" (verse 37).

Clearly this did not set well with Jacob. "My son shall not go down with you, for his brother is dead and he is left alone," he says (verse 38). To lose Benjamin is unthinkable, since that sorrow would surely bring him down to the grave.

Desperate measures

As time passes, their food supplies get low and Jacob is forced to ask his sons, "Go back and buy us a little food" (Genesis 43:2).

Judah instantly reminds his father that the "man solemnly warned us" that they would not see his face again unless their brother is with them (verse 3).

Jacob then accuses his sons of talking too much. "Why did you deal so wrongfully with me as to tell the man whether you had still another brother?" he asks (verse 6), and they try to justify themselves by stating that it was the man's fault for asking so many questions.

Judah speaks up and focuses on the central issue of life or death by saying, "Send the lad with me, and we will arise and go, that we may live and not die" (verse 8). He then boldly states, "I myself will be surety for him; from my hand you shall require him. If I do not bring him back to you and set him before you, then let me bear the blame forever" (verse 9).

Clearly, Judah has changed from his previous life into a man who takes responsibility and intercedes for another. This is in great contrast to Reuben, who has offered to have his two sons killed if he did not bring Benjamin back. Judah concludes, "If we had not lingered, surely by now we would have returned this second time," indicating that some time has passed as they've debated (verse 10).

Finally, Jacob decides to send Benjamin with them along with presents and double money to pay for the previous and future grain. The presents include the best of Canaan: balm, honey, spices, myrrh, pistachios, and almonds. It is interesting to note that these include some of the same products (spices, balm, and myrrh) the Ishmaelite traders were carrying when they took Joseph to Egypt as a slave. These products are the substances the Egyptians use for embalming. Honey is special to Egyptians, since it is used for sweetening food. The Pharaoh also uses honey as an offering to the gods. Almonds are common in Canaan, but rare in Egypt, and all of these are familiar to Joseph, and will remind him of his homeland.

Jacob is conformed to the idea that Benjamin must go, so he sends them off by saying, "May God Almighty give you mercy before the man, that he may release your other brother and Benjamin" (verse 14).

Seeing benjamin

When Joseph sees Benjamin, he orders his steward to slaughter an animal, for they will dine with him in his house at noon. The brothers fear retribution, because of the money they found in their sacks. Terrified that they'll become slaves and lose their donkeys, they quickly explain to the steward that each man's payment has been found in their grain sacks, and that they are returning it.

However, the steward explains that he received their money, and that their account had been paid. Then he implies that the Lord must have been the one who put their money in their sacks. However, instead of referring to their money, he calls it their "treasure." The Hebrew word for treasure is *matmown,* which means hidden treasure—implying that God is behind all this. Then, he brings out their brother Simeon who joins them at the table.

When Joseph comes in, the brothers bring their presents to him and bow before him to the ground. He asks about their welfare, and then of their father, "Is he still alive?" (verse 27).

They answer, "Your servant our father is in good health; he is still alive" (verse 28). Then they bow down and prostrate themselves, again.

When Joseph sees Benjamin, he says, "God be gracious to you, my son" (verse 29). Addressing Benjamin as "my son" is an affectionate way of greeting someone younger, but suddenly overcome by emotion, Joseph hastily withdraws and weeps. Recovering his composure, he washes his face, returns, and orders that the meal be served.

Seated in order

Joseph is placed at a separate table in front of his brothers, because eating with foreigners is considered an abomination to the Egyptians. The brothers are seated according to their age, and this amazes them. When they are served, Benjamin receives five times more than any of his older brothers. To the ancients, it is common to serve more food to the honored guest; but to serve five times more gives this much more meaning. In fact, the five portions seem to represent one portion for the offspring of each of Jacob's four wives, and one extra for being considered the firstborn, since Benjamin is the only son left of the favorite wife Rachel. Jacob had previously treated Joseph as his firstborn, but since he believes he is dead, Benjamin replaces him. The brothers appear to have no problem with this—further evidence to Joseph that his brothers have dramatically changed.

Benjamin's sack

After the meal, Joseph orders his steward to fill his brother's sacks with food, and once again, place their money on top; but in addition to the money in Benjamin's sack, the steward is ordered to add Joseph's silver cup. Stealing a ruler's cup is a serious offense, since the Egyptians believe it magically protects him against intentional poisoning.

As the brothers leave, Joseph orders his steward to overtake them and accuse them of stealing. They respond by rashly saying that if the cup is found in any man's sack, he ought to die, and the rest of them should become his slaves! In response, the steward insists that if the cup is found in any sack, *that* man will be his slave, but the rest will go free. The sacks are searched, from the oldest to the youngest, and Joseph's cup turns up in Benjamin's sack!

In utter anguish, the brothers tear their clothes as a sign of agony and mourning.

How can they tell this to their father? Not only will Benjamin become a slave in Egypt—as Joseph had—but their father also surely will not survive the loss of his last and only living son of Rachel.

A redeemer figure

Soberly they return to the city, and once before Joseph, Judah becomes the eloquent spokesman to desperately plead Benjamin's case. He acknowledges what Joseph has said about the seriousness of this incident, and how the result will cause the death of their father. He tells the whole story of how their father would not allow Benjamin to go to Egypt and how he had become surety for him. Therefore, he pleads to become the permanent substitute slave for Benjamin.

This is the third time he takes on the redeemer role for Benjamin, and this revelation surely takes Joseph by surprise! He clearly sees that Judah has drastically changed.

Tears of joy

Joseph can stand it no longer. Sending all the Egyptians away, he weeps openly and so loudly that he is heard in the house of Pharaoh. He reveals to his brothers in Hebrew that he is Joseph, and seeing their great dismay, he again states, "I am Joseph, . . . whom you sold into Egypt" (Genesis 45:4). The fact that he twice mentions his name follows the ancient Hebrew belief that you must have two witnesses to guarantee authenticity. Then he goes even further by adding information that only his brothers know, "whom you sold into Egypt."

Seeing the dismay, fear, and grief of his brothers, he quickly reassures them, "You sold me here; for God sent me before you to preserve life" (verse 5). He urges his brothers to hastily return to their father, informing him that God has made him ruler and to come quickly with his family to Egypt because there are still five more years of famine. Then he falls on Benjamin's neck and weeps, while Benjamin does the same. By turns, he kisses each brother and weeps over him too. After this, his brothers, who have been speechless, manage to regain their voices and talk with him.

When Pharaoh hears that Joseph's brothers have come, he insists that Joseph provide for their animals, and bring his father to Egypt, where he will receive the best treatment. Joseph provides them with carts, provisions for the journey, and changes of garment.

Then he gives Benjamin the enormous sum of three hundred pieces (shekels) of silver and five changes of garments. (Notice the stark contrast to the twenty shekels of silver Joseph was sold for). He also sends his father ten male donkeys loaded with the good things of Egypt, and ten female donkeys loaded with grain, bread, and food for his journey.

A happy ending

When the brothers arrive home, they tell the startling news to their father, who does not believe them at first. But when he sees the carts, his spirit revives from the shock of it all.

"It is enough," he says, finally. "Joseph my son is still alive. I will go and see him before I die" (verse 28).

Twenty-two years have passed since the seventeen-year-old Joseph has related his two dreams to his brothers and father. Now, at age thirty-nine, his story reaches its dramatic climax as he reveals his identity to his brothers. Much has happened during this period. Joseph has greatly prospered; his half-brother's characters have significantly changed for the better; and Judah has drastically grown spiritually by taking on the redeemer role for Benjamin. But most significantly, although his brothers sold him into Egypt with the intent of doing him harm, God works it all out for their good, and for His glory. The covenant promise to Abraham has been partly fulfilled when Joseph, his descendant has become a blessing to Egypt and to his family. But in addition, Judah, the son of Leah—and not the firstborn in any sense—takes on the redeemer role of the firstborn, and will later be listed in the genealogy of Christ.

CHAPTER THIRTY-FIVE

Jacob's Final Years

Based on Genesis 46 and 47

After receiving word that Joseph is still alive, and the invitation to move to Egypt, Jacob resolves to join his son. On the journey, he first pauses at Beersheba to offer sacrifices that are probably thank offerings for the good news that Joseph is still alive. He may also want to consult with God concerning his journey to Egypt in remembrance of God's revelation to Abraham that his descendants will suffer a period of affliction there.

In a night vision, God addresses him emphatically by calling, "Jacob, Jacob" (Genesis 46:2). Then, he says, "I am God, the God of your father; do not fear to go down to Egypt, for I will make of you a great nation there" (verse 3). Here God depicts Jacob as a second Abraham, who will not only go to Egypt but will also return to Canaan. He adds, "I will go down with you to Egypt, and I will also bring you up again; and Joseph will put his hand on your eyes,"—a clear indication that Joseph will bury him in Canaan (verse 4).

Jacob goes to Egypt with all his descendants, livestock, and possessions. The list of descendants numbers seventy and is structured around his two wives and their maids. This number implies that they are now a nation, since seventy is the number found in the Table of Nations in Genesis 10. It also seems to have a spiritual significance of totality because it uses the number 7. Notice that Genesis 46:26 says the number of his descendants is sixty-six, however, it does not include Jacob, Joseph, and his two sons that are already in Egypt.

An emotional reunion

Jacob sends Judah ahead to meet with Joseph and find out the way to Goshen, where they are to settle. He apparently has transferred the birthright from Benjamin to Judah, because of the role Judah has been playing.

Joseph travels by chariot to the land of Goshen, and when he meets his father, he wraps his arms around Jacob's neck and weeps for a long time. Finally, Jacob speaks to his son, "Now let me die, since I have seen your face, because you are still alive" (verse 30).

Joseph informs them that he will go to Pharaoh and tell him that his father and family have arrived. He will also state that his brothers are shepherds, and that they have brought their livestock with them. When they meet Pharaoh, and he asks their occupation, they are to say they have always kept livestock, which will allow them to settle in Goshen, apart from the Egyptians, since shepherds are considered an abomination to the native Egyptians. At this point in history, the pharaohs of Egypt are called Hyksos, foreign rulers related to the Hebrews. Goshen is part of the Nile Delta, and under Pharaoh's supervision. Settling in Goshen will help avoid hostility from the native Egyptians of the Nile valley and the evil influence of paganism.

Joseph tells Pharaoh that his father, brothers, and livestock have arrived and are in Goshen. Five of his brothers are chosen to meet the ruler, who asks them their occupation. They answer that they are shepherds who had to leave Canaan because of the famine. Pharaoh tells Joseph they should settle in Goshen, then asks if he can make them chief herdsmen of his livestock. Archaeological evidence indicates that the Egyptian herds were large and mostly herded in the Nile Delta.

When Joseph introduces his father to Pharaoh, he blesses him, and noting that Jacob is very old, he asks him his age. Jacob answers 130, but says that because of his hard life, his years are a lot less than his forefathers. The Pharaoh is amazed, since 110 years is considered the maximum lifespan for the Egyptians. Jacob concludes their encounter with another blessing—and an unusual one, at that, since he is the inferior, and Pharaoh is the superior. This significant event echoes the covenant promise to Abraham that in him, all families of the earth will be blessed.

Saved from starvation

Joseph settles his father and brothers in Egypt in the land of Ramses—a name for a later Pharaoh. This may be the result of a scribal update for the name of Goshen, or there is some evidence that the name already exists at this time. Now that they've found a place to live, Jacob provides his family with food during the severe famine.

During this time, Joseph focuses on the needs of the people by selling grain to the Canaanites and Egyptians who use up all their money to keep from starving. Joseph delivers it all to Pharaoh. Next, when there is no more money, Joseph exchanges the people's livestock for grain. The following step is to purchase all of the land of the people in exchange for food and move the people from the land to the cities, where the grain is stored, to facilitate the food distribution. Only the Egyptian priests and Joseph's family do not lose their land. Many priests belong to the royal family and have land that they received directly from the Pharaoh. In contrast to the general Egyptian population, Joseph's family cannot sell their land since they do not own it.

Then, Joseph takes Pharaoh's land and begins a tenant arrangement by distributing seed to the people to plant on the farms in exchange for one-fifth of their crops that will be given to Pharaoh. This sharecrop practice is not new in Egypt, and has occurred at other times in their history. Through Joseph's wise administration, mass starvation of Egypt and Canaan is avoided. The two dreams of his youth have reached fruition and much of the covenant promise made to Abraham to be a blessing to the nations has become a reality. Pharaoh's generosity to Joseph's family is now rewarded through the blessing that Jacob bestows on Pharaoh.

The patriarch lives another seventeen years in Egypt, and both his possessions and family increase greatly. On his deathbed, he calls Joseph and makes him promise not to bury him in Egypt, but in Canaan, with his forefathers. The promise is made with an oath, and Joseph places his hand under his father's thigh to confirm it. This symbolic gesture may be considered as pointing to future descendants, especially Christ, the promised Seed.

This makes the vow sacred and serves as a guarantee that it will be fulfilled.

CHAPTER THIRTY-SIX

Jacob's Blessings

Based on Genesis 48 and 49

Joseph is told that his father is sick, so he goes with his two sons, Manasseh and Ephraim, to his bedside. Jacob strengthens himself and sits up in bed as he recounts how God has appeared to him at Luz (Bethel) and given him the covenant promises. Now he states that Ephraim and Manasseh, who were born in Egypt, are his sons, just the same as Reuben and Simeon. Joseph's later offspring will belong to their father, and not to Jacob. Apparently, this is a way for compensating for Jacob's previous loss of Joseph and as a precaution for a fair distribution of the land of Canaan among Jacob's sons.

Jacob also recalls that when he first returned to Canaan after his time in Mesopotamia with Laban, his beloved wife Rachel died. He buried her on the way to Ephrath, also known as Bethlehem. Her grave reinforces his request to be buried in Canaan, and is a reminder to Ephraim and Manasseh that their future belongs in the Promised Land.

A crossed blessing

Jacob asks Joseph to bring Ephraim and Manasseh to him to be blessed. Joseph brings the oldest son Manasseh to Jacob's right hand and Ephraim to his left hand; however, Jacob crosses his hands, placing his right hand on Ephraim's head, and his left on Manasseh's head to bless them.

Joseph objects, but Jacob indicates that he knows what he is doing. He deliberately places the second born in the position of the firstborn—as it had been with his brother Esau and him. The right hand is the hand of strength, glory, and blessing in Scripture; so when Jacob blesses Ephraim and Manasseh, he transfers God's blessing to Joseph through his sons.

Jacob's blessing of Ephraim and Manasseh also serves as an adoption ceremony, demonstrating that he considers Joseph his firstborn and that he will get a double portion when the land of Canaan is divided among the tribes. In fact, they become the two most important tribes of the northern kingdom of Israel. The blessing is recorded in poetic form—indicating it is of utmost importance in this whole story.

Jacob now calls his sons together to give them his last will and testament. This will also include blessings and, in some cases, curses. In fact, it is really a prophecy that reveals their near and long-term futures, as well as some of their past.

He addresses them according to their birth order, and once again, all of this is in poetic form, so it will be long remembered and often repeated.

Reuben

The first son he blesses is Reuben this way:

> "Reuben, you are my firstborn,
> My might and the beginning of my strength,
> The excellency of dignity and the excellency of power.
> Unstable as water, you shall not excel,
> Because you went up to your father's bed;
> Then you defiled it—
> He went up to my couch" (Genesis 49:3, 4).

Notice that Reuben is first characterized by five positive terms: "firstborn," "my might," "beginning of my strength," "excellency of dignity," and "excellency of power." These are followed by five negative terms: "unstable," "shall not excel," "went up to your father's bed," "you defiled," and "went up to my couch." Here, Jacob is referring to the shameful incident when Reuben slept with Bilhah, his father's concubine (Genesis 35:22). Although he was destined for excellency, his character ruined all that. No significant person emerges from his tribe, and ultimately, it disappears from later history.

Simeon and Levi

Simeon and Levi receive curses, instead of blessings. Jacob addresses them this way:

> "Simeon and Levi are brothers;
> Instruments of cruelty are in their dwelling place.
> Let not my soul enter their council;
> Let not my honor be united to their assembly;
> For in their anger they slew a man,

And in their self-will they hamstrung an ox.
Cursed be their anger, for it is fierce;
And their wrath, for it is cruel!
I will divide them in Jacob
And scatter them in Israel" (Genesis 49:5–7).

These two brothers are cursed together, in an apparent association that is traced to their murder of the men of Shechem (Genesis 34:25–39) and an act of cruelty to an animal. Their curse indicates they will be scattered throughout Israel, and none of their descendants will inherit land in Canaan as a separate tribe.

For a time, Simeon *does* inherit a portion within the tribe of Judah, but later his tribe name disappears, as it is absorbed. Similarly, Levi's tribe will receive no land of its own, but will be scattered throughout Canaan. However, when the Levites refuse to worship the golden calf at Sinai, God will reward them by making them priests and instructors of the Law. Then they will be given forty-eight cities to live in and be a blessing to the whole nation by providing religious services away from the tabernacle.

Judah

The blessing on Judah is longer than any of his brothers, except for Joseph—an indication of his great importance. Jacob says of him,

"Judah, you are he whom your brothers shall praise;
Your hand shall be on the neck of your enemies;
Your father's children shall bow down before you.
Judah is a lion's whelp;
From the prey, my son, you have gone up.
He bows down, he lies down as a lion;
And as a lion, who shall rouse him?
The scepter shall not depart from Judah,
Nor a lawgiver from between his feet,
Until Shiloh comes;
And to Him shall be the obedience of the people.
Binding his donkey to the vine,
And his donkey's colt to the choice vine,
He washed his garments in wine,
And his clothes in the blood of grapes.
His eyes are darker than wine,
And his teeth whiter than milk" (Genesis 49:8–12).

Judah's blessing grants him supremacy, power, rulership, and wealth. The Messiah will come through his descendants because of his significant three-time role as a redeemer figure: first, when his brothers want to kill Joseph; second, when Jacob won't allow Benjamin to be taken to Egypt; and finally, when Benjamin is imprisoned after Joseph's silver cup was found in his grain sack. The name Judah means "the praised one," indicating that even his relatives will praise him.

He is linked with a lion and a star—both symbols of rulership. Jacob says, "The scepter shall not depart from Judah . . . until Shiloh comes," (verse 10), but although the majority of commentators believe Shiloh is a personal name referring to the Messiah, their explanations seem unconvincing. Instead, the answer may come from the context of Genesis 38 with the story of Judah and his three sons, Er, Onan, and Shelah.

Er marries Tamar, but the Lord kills him for his wickedness before he has any children. Judah then instructs his son Onan to takes Tamar in a levirate marriage (remarrying within the family for the purpose of continuing the family line), but he refuses to fulfill his redeemer role to keep the family name alive, and God kills him too.

Judah sends Tamar home until his youngest son Shelah is old enough for a levirate marriage with her, but when that time comes, he doesn't fulfill his obligation.

Taking matter into her own hands, Tamar resolves the situation by disguising herself as a temple prostitute and having an encounter with her father-in-law, Judah. As a result, a child is born that carries on the family name, and is ultimately included in the genealogy of Jesus.

Now it's important to note that in Judah's time, the Hebrew language is composed entirely of consonants. In fact, vowels were only added about two thousand, years later, around 600 AD. This explains why the same names in the Old Testament are spelled with different vowels in certain scriptural passages.

Since the consonants of Shiloh and Shelah are the same, a strong possibility exists that both words refer to the same person. If this is so, Shelah—a redeemer figure linked with the genealogy of the Messiah—is the origin of the word Shiloh in Genesis 49:10.

The last two verses of Jacob's blessing on Judah make reference to a donkey being bound to a vine. The donkey is a reference to the Messiah's rulership, since He will follow Jewish custom in riding a lowly donkey during His triumphal entry into Jerusalem. This custom follows Solomon's example of riding his father's mule to signify that he is the anointed one. The vine the donkey is tied to is the grapevine that symbolizes abundance and peace during the Messiah's ultimate rule.

Zebulun

The sixth son is Zebulun, who is listed before his brother Issachar, Jacob's fifth son.

This is probably because of his preeminence over his brother through the course of history. Jacob blesses him by saying: "Zebulun shall dwell by the haven of the sea; he shall become a haven for ships, and his border shall adjoin Sidon" (verse 13).

The tribe of Zebulun is known as a business or commercial tribe, and historically, they contribute heavily to Israel's military force. Their blessing is limited to geographical considerations that relate to the sea. They do not settle by the sea, but appear to have access to it, becoming a haven for ships. This is reinforced by the mention of Sidon—a city on the northern part of Canaan, on the Mediterranean coast.

Issachar

Issachar's blessing is as follows:

"Issachar is a strong donkey,
Lying down between two burdens;
He saw that rest was good,
And that the land was pleasant;
He bowed his shoulder to bear a burden,
And became a band of slaves" (verses 14, 15).

Issachar's tribe deals principally in agriculture. Jacob refers to them metaphorically as a strong donkey, evoking the hard physical work associated with farming. He also calls them "a band of slaves," perhaps poetically, preserving the old meaning of "laborer" that later becomes linked with slavery.

Dan

Dan is the only tribe that receives two blessings. Jacob says of them:

"Dan shall judge his people
As one of the tribes of Israel.
Dan shall be a serpent by the way,
A viper by the path,
That bites the horse's heels
So that its rider shall fall backward.
I have waited for your salvation, O LORD" (verses 16–18).

The first blessing is that they will perform the important duties of a judge, and the second, is that they will be linked with the fact that he "shall be a serpent."

Samson will come from the tribe of Dan, and he will serve as a judge for Israel for many years. His cunning, as of a serpent, echoes Genesis 3 and serves to deceive his strong Philistine foes. However, in the end, he loses his own life—even as he achieves his greatest victory by killing more of his enemies that day than he had in his lifetime.

As a tribe, Dan is probably the first to introduce idol worship into Israel, and this may be the reason why they are omitted in the description of the 144,000 saints in Revelation 7.

Included in the blessing on Dan, Jacob says, "I have waited for your salvation, O Lord!" (Genesis 49:18). This is not only a prayer for himself, but also for his descendants, that they may receive the same help from God. This is the only moment in the entire text of the blessings that Jacob addresses God personally by the name of Lord (Yahweh). The whole statement, which appears with the blessing on Dan, is located in the center of the blessings on his sons. Five blessings are given before and five are yet to come. This literary construction provides a passionate prayer within prophecies, similar to what Daniel does in chapter 9, when he addresses God as Yahweh in his prayer.

Gad

Next, the tribe of Gad receives one of the shortest blessings. Jacob says, "Gad, a troop shall tramp upon him, but he shall triumph at last" (Genesis 49:19).

The blessing on Gad's tribe includes the words "troop" and "triumph" that come from the same Hebrew root transliterated as *gaw-dad*. This word gives this blessing the essential meaning that an attacking force will attack him, but he will win in the end. The focus is on war, since they will be men of war, trained in battle. They will fight the Ammonites, Arameans, Assyrians, and Moabites—and win.

Asher

In the blessing on Asher there is a shift from war to happiness and prosperity. Jacob says, "Bread from Asher shall be rich, and he shall yield royal dainties" (verse 20).

The name Asher means "happy." His tribe will settle in the fertile lands of northern Israel on the Mediterranean coast, where grain and oil are produced in abundance. With ample food and no war, life will be comfortable and happy.

Naphtali

The blessing for Naphtali is brief: "Naphtali is a deer let loose; he uses beautiful words" (verse 21).

The reference to "a deer let loose" is likely a reference to Barak's swift raid on King Jabin, when Sisera is killed in Judges 4. The "beautiful words" may refer to Barak's poetic skills when he joins Deborah in singing their victory song.

Joseph

The blessing on Joseph is naturally the longest blessing of all of Jacob's sons.

> "Joseph is a fruitful bough,
> A fruitful bough by a well;
> His branches run over the wall.
> The archers have bitterly grieved him,
> Shot at him and hated him.
> But his bow remained in strength,
> And the arms of his hands were made strong
> By the hands of the Mighty God of Jacob
> (From there is the Shepherd, the Stone of Israel),
> By the God of your father who will help you,
> And by the Almighty who will bless you
> With blessings of heaven above,
> Blessings of the deep that lies beneath,
> Blessings of the breasts and of the womb.
> The blessings of your father
> Have excelled the blessings of my ancestors,
> Up to the utmost bound of the everlasting hills.
> They shall be on the head of Joseph,
> And on the crown of the head of him who was separate from his brothers"
> (Genesis 49:22–26).

Notice that the name Joseph appears at the beginning and end of the blessing. This double mention appears to be related to his double blessing through his two sons. The prophetic blessing is arranged into three sections: fruitful bough by the well, the archers (bows) versus his bow, and multiple blessings.

The blessing begins with reference to "well" and "wall" that is apparently linked—in typical Hebrew style—to the previous story of Hagar, Sarah's Egyptian maidservant. Hagar and, later, Joseph, are driven from home and suffer grave difficulties, but in both cases, God intervenes. Hagar is in the wilderness with her son, and they are dying of thirst, when the angel of the Lord speaks to her and opens her eyes to a well of water. In Joseph's case, he is thrown in a dry well, instead of being killed as most of his brothers desired, only to be sold into slavery in Egypt. Later, Hagar gives birth to Ishmael, and in Joseph's case, he becomes a great ruler in Egypt. Ironically, Hagar's success (the birth of Ishmael) contributes to Joseph's success, the *Ishmaelites* take him to Egypt!

The "fruitful bough" appears to be a reference to Joseph's offspring. Its parallel, "his branches run over the wall" seem to be linked with the well Joseph's brothers put him in, while the "run over" reference suggests his climbing up as he's taken out and sold to the Ishmaelites.

The reference to "archers" alludes to Ishmael (in this case, his descendants) as an archer, who ironically rescues Joseph from his brothers (the archers). The plural "archers" (with their bows) in their hatred for Joseph is contrasted with the singular "his bow" that represents Joseph, who receives strength from the strong hands of the Lord.

Reference to "the Shepherd, the Stone of Israel" refers to the Lord, who protects and cares for His own; and "the Stone" reminds us of Jacob's pillow at Bethel, when he understands that the Lord is with him.

The last section of the Jacob's blessing on Joseph focuses on God's blessings. The first is a blessing from the "Almighty" that has the connotation of protection, and the next ones relate to the cosmic blessing that includes both heaven and earth.

The "heaven above" and the "deep that lies beneath" contain the promise of water from rain and springs, and the blessing of the beasts with their multiplication is linked with "womb." Rachel's womb is opened by God to give birth to Joseph and the descendants that follow him.

The final blessing demonstrates the superiority of Joseph's blessing above that of his ancestors and that of his two sons. It applies to the royal destiny of Joseph, who excels over his father and brothers. In fact, it is an allusion to Joseph's dream of the grain sheaves bowing down to him. His distinction above them includes both a moral and spiritual superiority. He serves as a type of the coming Messiah.

Benjamin

The final blessing is for Rachel's youngest son Benjamin. It seems to be in contrast to what is known about him as a boy. "Benjamin is a ravenous wolf; in the morning he shall devour the prey, and at night he shall divide the spoil" (verse 27).

This description becomes a predictive historical reality of his tribe's military activities. They will distinguish themselves as archers, left-handed slingers, and fighters against Amalek and other enemies. The tribe will settle just west of the Jordan River, at the crucial point where the Hebrews cross the Jordan as they invade Canaan following their forty years in the wilderness. Benjamin is the only son of Jacob that is not born in Mesopotamia but in Canaan, not far from Bethlehem where Jesus is born, giving the tribe close Messianic ties.

The chapter ends by mentioning that these sons are the twelve tribes, bringing into view the future of all of Israel. Then Jacob charges them to bury him in Canaan in the field of Machpelah that Abraham had bought for a burial place. This is where Abraham, Sarah, and Isaac are buried, and where Jacob buries Leah.

After Jacob finishes his charge to his family, "he drew his feet up into the bed and breathed his last, and was gathered to his people" (verse 33).

At the age of 147 Jacob, the faithful patriarch, dies surrounded by his family. He has lived a rather difficult life, and has changed from a liar and a fugitive to one who wrestles with God and is rewarded with the new name of Israel, reflecting his transformed character. His name is passed on to his posterity as their national name.

In the description of the New Jerusalem in Revelation 21, the foundations of the walls of the city are adorned with twelve precious stones, representing his twelve sons and tribes—the eternal legacy of Jacob, the revered patriarch.

CHAPTER THIRTY-SEVEN

True Forgiveness

Based on Genesis 50

When Jacob dies, Joseph's initial response is to fall on his father's face, weeping and kissing him. Once the emotional shock passes, he orders his servants, the mortuary priests, to embalm him. This is an Egyptian practice and not a Hebrew one, but it serves the purpose of preserving the body until it can be taken to Canaan and buried.

As a courtesy to the reader, I will warn you that the following paragraph, describing the embalming process is very graphic. You may skip it if you like.

The process of embalming lasts for forty days and is very expensive. The brain is first extracted through the nostrils by using a crooked piece of metal. Then the skull is thoroughly cleaned inside by rinsing it with drugs. With a sharp knife, an opening is made in the left side to remove the organs and intestines. The organs are then placed in separate jars, and the abdomen is purified with palm wine, pleasant aromas from plants, and spices. Then the opening is sewed up, and the body is soaked for many days in a mineral salt of hydrated sodium carbonate. Finally, the body is washed, wrapped in a linen shroud, smeared with gum, and painted to appear with the natural features of the deceased.

Jacob's final journey

Both Jacob's family and the Egyptians mourn, indicating that the Egyptians have a great esteem for Joseph and consider Jacob a visiting dignitary. The mourning lasts for seventy days—forty days for embalming, plus an additional thirty. After the embalming is complete, Joseph asks Pharaoh if he can bury his father in Canaan since he already has a grave there, and Joseph has taken an oath to bury him there. Pharaoh grants his request, and a large entourage of Jacob's family and leading Egyptian court officials is assembled to accompany him on the journey. A military escort of chariots and horsemen is organized to escort them through the desert.

They do not take the closest route to the burial site but take the one the Hebrews will take many years later when they cross the Jordan River into Canaan. This makes the return of Jacob to the Promised Land a type of the return of the Hebrews after the exodus.

After crossing the Jordan, they arrive at the threshing floor of Atad for a special mourning period within Canaan. The threshing floor is a large open area for trampling out the grain by oxen. It serves well to accommodate a large group as the entourage halts for seven days of mourning. The Egyptian mourners tear their garments, beat their breasts, put dust on their heads, and chant funeral hymns accompanied with tambourines. All of this greatly impresses the local inhabitants so that they called the place Abel-mizraim, "The Meadow of Egypt." The name is a play on the Hebrew words, "mourning," *ebel,* and "meadow" *abel,* both having the same consonants, and *mizraim* is the Hebrew word for Egypt.

Worries of revenge

After Jacob's death, Joseph's brothers become worried that he secretly hates them and will seek revenge for the evil way they treated him when he was younger. It is almost inevitable that a family member will seek revenge on their siblings and their families for their mistreatment. But out of respect for the patriarch, this usually happens only after his demise. So they send messengers to him saying that Jacob had told them before his death to tell Joseph, "I beg you, please forgive the trespass of the servants of the God of your father" (Genesis 50:17).

This comes as a great shock to Joseph, and he begins to weep in sorrow for their fear. Encouraged by this emotional display, his brothers cautiously enter the room and bow low to the ground before him, declaring, "Behold, we are your servants" (verse 18).

Their request for forgiveness comes many decades after they treated him so cruelly in his youth. Jealous of his coat of many colors, and angry after hearing his dreams, they intended to kill him! Ultimately, they resolved to be rid of their brother by selling him to traders. These, in turn, sell him into Egyptian slavery.

Joseph responds, "Do not be afraid, for am I in the place of God? But as for you, you meant evil against me; but God meant it for good, in order to bring it about as it is this day, to save many people alive" (verse 21). He clearly sees that even though evil was directed toward him. God has used it for good and saved many lives through his work in Egypt during the seven-year famine. God has saved and increased his family, too, and brought them considerable prosperity.

In spite of what his brothers have done, Joseph begs them to not be afraid of him for he will forgive and treat them well. As part of his forgiveness, he vows to provide for their physical needs.

The responsibility of forgiveness

The concept of forgiveness that Joseph exemplifies has many significant features that our present-day forgiveness lacks. The Hebrew word used here for forgiveness is *nasa*. It appears over 650 times in the Old Testament, and carries a very wide range of meanings, such as, "lift up," "raise high," "pardon," "bear," "exalt," "restore," and "support." Most Hebrew lexicons relate the concept of forgiveness to derived meanings, such as "take away" or "remove."

Often, this verb is used with nonreligious meanings such as "lift up one's head" or "lift up one's eyes." Isaiah 46:7 speaks of those who take their own crafted god in a time of panic or siege, lift it up to their shoulders, and carry it.

The subject for this verb can either be God or man. Isaiah 53:4 states the following about the Suffering Servant, "He has borne [literally, 'took up'] our griefs and carried our sorrows."

Joseph's promise to his brothers is far more than a mere promise to provide for them and their little ones in the future. It means that he will *lift them up*, helping to restore them to good standing before God and man. This is exactly what God does for sinners though Christ for those who rebel against Him! In the process of forgiveness, He restores us ultimately to God and to the position we had before sin.

In that same way, when we forgive those who wrong us, we have the tremendous responsibility to "lift up" and restore them as well to God and their fellow men.

Joseph lives out his final years in Egypt, and in one respect, he lives in exile from the Promised Land. He also lives to see his great-grandchildren from both his sons, Ephraim and Manasseh. But since Joseph is the penultimate son of Jacob, he requires his older brothers to take an oath to bury his bones in Canaan.

At the age of 110, he dies and is embalmed. This is considered an ideal length of life for the Egyptians, who on the average die between forty and fifty years of age. He outlives his father by fifty-four years.

A summary of Genesis

The book of Genesis ends with the death of Joseph and the assurance that he will return to the Promised Land. Genesis begins with Adam and Eve in Eden, who are created without sin but who are tempted and fall. The book ends with Joseph as a redeemer figure, foreshadowing Christ, by providing forgiveness, redemption, and restoration for his brothers—as well as an assurance of return to the Promised Land.

Joseph is the most important human figure in Genesis, since his story takes up about one-third of the entire book. He breaks the vicious cycle of sin with its hatred, retaliation, and blood vengeance, by choosing to forgive, redeem, and restore his undeserving brothers. In this way, he serves as a type for the Messiah, who will be the Redeemer who brings forgiveness, redemption, and restoration for the world perishing in sin, as first promised in Genesis 3:15.

CHAPTER THIRTY-EIGHT

A Redeemer Figure

In ancient Hebrew thought, when one person's life is similar to another's, they link them together. In this way, the primary role of Joseph in life prefigures the role of the Messiah, who was first referred to in Genesis 3:15. Thus, Joseph's life largely parallels and illustrates the life of Christ.

Amazing similarities

Consider these amazing similarities (and surely there are many more):

- Joseph was greatly beloved by his father—just as Christ was by His heavenly Father.
- Jacob considered Joseph his firstborn—just as Christ was considered the firstborn of the Father.
- Joseph's dreams predicted his future exaltation—just as Christ prophesied He would be exalted.
- Joseph's brothers were envious of him—much as the Jewish leaders envied Christ.
- Joseph's brothers plotted his murder—much as the scribes, Pharisees, and Sadducees did with Christ.
- Joseph was sold for pieces of silver—just as Judas sold Jesus for pieces of silver.
- Joseph's brothers flattered themselves into believing they would no longer be troubled with him and his dreams, since they'd eliminated all possibility of their fulfillment. The Jewish leaders also believed they had eliminated Jesus and the threat He represented, once they had crucified Him.
- Joseph's brothers and the enemies of Christ were both overruled by God to bring about the very thing they plotted to hinder.
- Joseph was strongly tempted in Potiphar's house—Christ was

strongly tempted in the wilderness.

- Potiphar's wife falsely accused Joseph—just as the Jewish leaders falsely accused Christ.
- Joseph, the innocent, was thrown in prison with two criminals—just as Christ, the innocent, was crucified between two thieves.
- Joseph predicted good fortune for one criminal but not the other—just as Christ told one thief that he would be with Him in His kingdom, and did not say this to the other.
- Joseph acknowledged he had received dream interpretations from God, while Christ received His knowledge of the future from His Father.
- Joseph was exalted to his high position of prime minister at the age of thirty—just as Christ began His public ministry at the age of thirty.
- Joseph saved Egypt and the surrounding lands from the great famine—while Christ saved sinful man through His incarnation, life, death, and resurrection.
- Pharaoh clothed Joseph in fine linen—similar to the one-piece linen robe Christ wore.
- Joseph was given Pharaoh's signet ring to execute his authority in Egypt—just as Christ received all authority to fulfill the will of His Father.
- After Jacob died, Joseph's brothers came to him asking for forgiveness. He forgave them—even as Christ forgave those who crucified Him.

To complete his forgiveness, Joseph restored his brothers by providing for them and their families—just as Jesus Christ forgives and restores sinners.

CHAPTER THIRTY-NINE

A Baby in the Bulrushes

Based on Exodus 1 and 2

The beginning of Exodus is similar to the end of Genesis by stating that Israel now has seventy members in Egypt. This number is significant because it comes from the Table of Nations in Genesis 10 that represents the seventy nations of the world. It indicates that the covenant promise to Abraham to become a great nation is being fulfilled.

The Hebrews are apparently multiplying in a supernatural manner, since the five verbs used to describe their increase are: *"were fruitful," "increased* abundantly," *"multiplied," "grew* exceedingly mighty," and "the land was *filled"* (Exodus 1:7). The number five in biblical thought stands for full growth, because it is used to indicate the five-month period of growth from the planting of grain until the harvest. Applying this to the increase of population, indicates strong growth and maturity.

A new and cruel ruler

At this time, a new Pharaoh rises to power in Egypt and begins a new dynasty of native Egyptian rulers that largely do not know Joseph. This is a different line from the Semitic foreign rulers (Hyksos), who are related to Joseph.

The new Pharaoh worries that the Hebrews, who are so numerous, may join his enemies and revolt against him. He proposes a clever political idea to control the growth of the Hebrews through hard labor in his huge construction projects. After enslaving them, he sets taskmasters over them that probably include both Egyptians and Hebrews. Much of their work is the making of bricks. These bricks for a large building are over a foot long, about half a foot wide, and perhaps six inches thick. Brick makers have a very dirty job, working under perpetually muddy and miserable conditions. Quotas are routinely assigned but probably vary with the number of individuals assigned to a crew. Crews operate by division of labor with tasks such as: breaking up straw, hauling mud and water, shaping the bricks by hand or molds, setting the bricks out to dry in the sun, and later hauling them to the building site.

Killing schemes

Although slavery is designed to break the Hebrews' physical strength and retard their proliferation, their affliction only seems to make them multiply. Therefore, Pharaoh mandates the midwives to kill every male that is born as the Hebrew women give birth on the birthstool (called *oben* or, literally, "two stones.") They are used to support the mother's weight as she gives birth by sitting, crouching, or kneeling on them.

Killing the males and making the women and girls household slaves is a common pagan practice to control one's enemies in the ancient world. Pharaoh's latest plan does not work, since the midwives are Hebrews, who fear God. They give the excuse that the Hebrew women are not like the Egyptian women because they are "lively," or vigorous, giving birth before the midwives arrive, resulting in little demand for the services of the midwives.

Since the population growth cannot be controlled by the midwives, Pharaoh invents a new plan by making a decree to all of his people to drown every newborn Hebrew male in the Nile. In the midst of all of this, Amram, from the tribe of Levi, marries Jochebed (his aunt) who gives birth to a son named Moses, and conceal him for his first three months. Once again, the important number three appears here.

However, hiding baby Moses becomes impossible, so Jochebed sorrow-fully makes a basket of reeds, waterproofs it with pitch and asphalt, and places baby Moses in it. The waterproofing of the basket links this story with the building of Noah's ark. She places her precious baby in the sacred Nile among the bulrushes—an odd way of fulfilling Pharaoh's command, if not his intent!

A gift from the Nile?

Pharaoh's daughter arrives to bathe in the river. Since the Egyptians consider the Nile River a god, this bathing is probably a type of ritual cleansing she believes will impart fruitfulness and long life.

Suddenly, her attention is drawn to the basket and she orders her maid to retrieve it.

On opening it, she finds a Hebrew boy whose cries awaken her compassion and sympathies, and she decides to keep him. Surely, she is not surprised when a Hebrew girl (Moses' sister, Miriam) appears and asks if she needs a woman to nurse the child. She answers by saying she'll gladly pay a wet nurse her wages.

The princess names the child Moses, meaning "son" (*mes* or *mesu* in Egyptian). However, his Hebrew name Mosheh, means "to draw out" referring to the princess's words, "I drew him out of the water" (Exodus 2:10). In both languages, the names are linked with either a relationship (son) or experience that the baby (drawn out of the water) is associated with. The implication is that she believes the baby is a sacred gift from her river god.

From the biblical and historical data available, it appears that the Egyptian princess that adopts Moses is probably Hatshepsut. If this is the case, Moses probably grows up and lives under Thutmose I (1525–1508 BC), Thutmose II (1508–1504 BC), and Queen Hatshepsut (1504–1482 BC). Hatshepsut is the only legitimate child of Thutmose I. She marries her half-brother Thutmose II in order that he might legitimately succeed his father on the throne. This illegitimate marriage to Thutmose II fails to produce a male heir, so when Thutmose II dies, the powerful Egyptian priests in a sudden coup crown an illegitimate son of Thutmose II, who is only a boy, and too young to reign. Hatshepsut becomes the ruling regent for twenty-two years, and her reign is both peaceful and prosperous.

Moses' temper flares

After considerable time with his mother, Moses is taken to the palace and adopted by Hatshepsut. He receives the best education in the world from Egyptian priests and military leaders. His training would include the following areas: literature, scribal arts, speech, argumentation, military leadership, and probably foreign languages.

It appears clear that Moses never bowed to the Egyptian gods, for Hebrews 11 indicates his loyalty is to his people and his God. At the age of forty, he takes matters into his own hands and kills an Egyptian who is beating a Hebrew, then buries him in the sand. He must have had some doubts about his actions, because he looks both ways to see if anyone is observing before committing murder. Moses' military training leads him to believe that freedom for his people must come by force.

Just one day later, he sees two Hebrews fighting, and as he reprimands them, the guilty one sneers, "Do you intend to kill me as you killed the Egyptian?" (Exodus 2:14). Fearing Pharaoh would hear about this, he flees the long distance from Egypt to Midian. The flight would have certainly been very dangerous, since Egypt's eastern border is guarded by a system of manned towers, each in sight of the next.

Banished

When Pharaoh learns about the murder, he is furious. His anger is probably not so much against the death of the Egyptian as it is to deal with the revelation that Moses is acting as a friend and probable champion of his sworn enemy, the oppressed Hebrews.

When Moses arrives in Midian, he is in the land of the Midianites, who are descendants of Abraham through Keturah. He sits down beside a well, echoing the story where the fugitive Jacob sits by a well and meets Rachel, who becomes his wife. At this well, seven daughters of Reuel (also known as Jethro, the priest of Midian) come to draw water for their father's flocks.

Male shepherds come and drive the women away, but Moses defends them and waters their flocks single-handedly. Returning home, their father is surprised at their early arrival. They say, "An Egyptian delivered us from the hand of the shepherds, and he also drew enough water for us and watered our flock" (verse 19). They initially believe Moses is an Egyptian because he wears their clothes and has a shaved head and no beard (since the Egyptians shave their head and facial hair to avoid lice). Reuel tells them to be hospitable and call him to eat food with them.

Moses settles down in Midian and is given Reuel's daughter Zipporah (meaning "bird") in marriage. He lives with them for forty years, tending his father-in-law's flocks. A son is born that Moses names Gershom (meaning "banishment"), reflecting his loneliness as an alien in a foreign land.

God works out His plan

During Moses' period in Midian, the king of Egypt dies and is apparently replaced by Amenhotep II, who is very cruel and severely oppresses the Hebrews. God hears their groaning and remembers His covenant with Abraham, Isaac, and Jacob. Simultaneous with the Egyptian oppression, He grooms Moses to lead His people out of Egypt. What a drastic change has occurred to this man who is originally chosen to be the next Pharaoh. However, Moses has many lessons yet to learn!

CHAPTER FORTY

Humbled for Service

Based on Exodus 3 and 4

Moses wrongly assumes God will liberate the Hebrews by force, and by killing the Egyptian, he demonstrates he isn't ready for his great work. He hasn't learned enough patience and obedience to temper his actions, so for forty years he lives amid the solitude of the mountains and desert, learning much as a shepherd. Self-denial and discipline are developed under harsh conditions and bring out tender care for his sheep. These lessons also make him longsuffering—so much so that the Bible says he's "very humble, more than all men who were on the face of the earth" (Numbers 12:3).

A burning bush

While tending his father-in-law's sheep near Mount Horeb (also called Mount Sinai), Moses suddenly notices an unusual sight—a blazing bush that doesn't burn up! As he draws near, God calls out from the fire, "Moses, Moses!" (Exodus 3:4). Great emphasis is given by God to his importance by repeating his name twice.

He answers, "Here I am" (verse 4). God then orders him to remove his sandals in a gesture of reverence, for the ground he stands on is holy. Moses immediately obeys and hides his face for fear of seeing God and losing his life!

The fact that God speaks from a mere bush (in Hebrew, a thorn bush) seems to indicate that God chooses something small and insignificant to see Moses' attitude toward such things before He invests him with a great task for insignificant slave people. God also seems to communicate to Moses that He is powerful, being able to perform a miracle of burning a bush without consuming it. God is presenting Himself here as the God of light and fire that consumes and purifies.

"I have surely seen the oppression of My people who are in Egypt, and have heard their cry because of their taskmasters, for I know their sorrows," He says. "So I have come down to deliver them out of the hand of the Egyptians, and to bring them up from that land to a good and large land, to a land flowing with milk and honey" (verses 7, 8).

A timid leader, a mighty God

Moses, the self-assured man who would deliver his people by force now shows timidity, asking how he should respond when his people ask who God is.

"I AM WHO I AM," God responds. "You shall say . . . , 'I AM has sent me,' " then adds, "They will heed your voice" (verses 14, 18). This is later echoed in Jesus' numerous "I am" statements that reveal who He is.*

Moses reacts by saying, "Who am I that I . . . that I . . . ?" (verse 11).

Moses' emphatic "I" is immediately countered with God's emphatic "I" that is reinforced with, "I will certainly be with you" (verse 12).

"I AM" comes from the Hebrew verbal root "to be" and expresses God's true nature—the eternal present, self-existing, and personal One. Technically it is not a name, but a title. God does not present Himself with a personal name, but something that describes Him. To the ancients, when somebody calls your name, it means that they have control over you. Thus, humans do not have a personal name for God, since they can't control Him. Instead of a personal name, God reveals enough about Himself so that people can identify who He is and what He stands for, but not have control over Him.

When God appears (a theophany) at the burning bush, it is partly to direct Moses' attention to the plight of the Hebrews in Egypt. This is followed by the revelation that God has personally "come down" from heaven to deliver (literally, "snatch") them from a place of restriction and deprivation to a place that is wide and free—a place of plenty (verse 8). The land of Canaan is spacious because several nations (six are mentioned) live there. It is described from a pastoral lifestyle as "a land flowing with milk and honey" (verse 8). Milk is the product of sheep and goats and honey represents a natural resource, along with the nectar of the vine.

Pharaoh's resistance predicted

God tells Moses that he is to gather the elders of Israel and inform them that He will bring them out of the affliction of Egypt to the land of

---

* In the New Testament, Jesus says of Himself, "I am the bread of life," "I am the vine," "I am the light of the world," and "I say to you, before Abraham was, I am" (John 6:35; 15:5; 8:12, 58), etc.

Canaan. They will believe him and then the elders are to go with him to Pharaoh and ask to go three days into the wilderness to sacrifice to their God. However, Pharaoh will not let them go, so God will strike them with wonders until he changes his mind. On their exit from Egypt, the women are to ask their Egyptian neighbors for articles of silver, gold, and clothing to put on their children—a payment for their many years of slave labor!

Miracle signs

After God promises to be with Moses in leading his people out of Egypt, he still has fears, since he had to flee Egypt to save his life. Even though they are not now actively seeking to kill him, he knows that he is not likely to be absolved of all guilt in this matter. He reacts by supposing the people will say, "The LORD has not appeared to you" (Exodus 4:1). In Moses' mind, the people have no basis for trusting him, since his plan of liberating them by force did not work out. Obviously, he feels he needs more assurance that all will work out.

The Lord answers by providing Moses with three miracles as signs that will give him authority in the eyes of Israel's elders and before Pharaoh. The real authority that is displayed however, is not of Moses, but of the Lord Himself.

With the first of these signs the Lord asks him, "What is that in your hand?" (verse 2).

Moses says, "A rod,"—his own shepherd's rod (verse 2).

The Lord says, "Cast it on the ground" and it becomes a snake (verse 3). In fear, Moses flees from it!

Then the Lord says, "Reach out your hand and take it by the tail" (verse 4). Moses hesitantly obeys, and it becomes a rod again!

Moses knows that you only grab a poisonous snake just behind its head so it won't bite you, but the Lord wants to increase his trust in Him by telling him to pick it up by its tail. Surely this brings to his mind the story of the serpent in the Garden of Eden. It also brings the thought that snakes are worshiped in Egypt, and the cobra symbol (called a Uraeus) is featured in Pharaoh's crown. Taking the snake by the tail carries the implication that the Lord has complete power and authority over Pharaoh. Moses' staff or rod is what will be used in all of the plagues on Pharaoh and Egypt, and it surely has similarities with the affliction caused by the Egyptian slave masters' rod on the backs of the Hebrew laborers.

The Lord moves immediately to the second sign in which He has Moses place his hand inside his garment, next to his chest, and when he takes it out, it is covered with leprosy! Next, God tells him to put his hand into his garment once again, and immediately it is normal and healed.

Leprosy in Leviticus is generally considered to be different types of skin diseases that, in some cases, can cause the skin to become white as snow. However, leprosy can also affect houses and garments, appearing in the form of mildew and mold. Leprosy is closely connected with divine judgment in the Old Testament, but it appears to only be related here to a sign that the Lord gives Moses.

The Lord has yet a third sign to present. By giving Moses three signs, He is clearly communicating that the authentications given by these signs are extremely significant. If his people do not believe the first two signs, Moses is to take water from the Nile and it will turn to blood as he pours it out on dry ground. To the Egyptians, the Nile and its water are divine, and considered the source of all life, since it waters the crops and causes food to grow. This sign is repeated later, in the first plague to fall on Egypt. It is a reminder to them of when the Nile flowed with the blood of innocent Hebrew male infants at Pharaoh's command.

The use of the word "sign" to the ancient literal thinkers is designed to demonstrate far more than the effect or phenomenon produced by the "sign" itself. The purpose of the first two signs is designed first for Moses' benefit to establish his credibility as God's messenger and deliverer. For the Hebrews, the first two signs are to establish Moses' legitimacy before the elders as one sent by God with a reliable message. The third "sign" is not mentioned as a sign in the Bible, but when performed as a plague, it is proof of the powerful presence of God.

Moses' excuses

Even though the Lord has given Moses convincing evidence that He will bless his mission, Moses describes himself as being slow of speech and tongue. This counters the later words of Acts 7:22 that he was "mighty in words and deeds"—perhaps indicating what he ultimately became.

The Lord answers, "Who has made man's mouth?" (Exodus 4:11) and assures him that He will be with his mouth and teach him what to say.

Moses still objects saying, "Please send by the hand of whomever else You may send" (verse 13).

This displeases the Lord, and He says, "Is not Aaron the Levite your brother? I know that he can speak well . . . you shall speak to him and put words in his mouth. And I will be with your mouth and with his mouth, and I will teach you what you shall do. So he shall be your spokesman to the people. And he himself shall be as a mouth for you, and you shall be to him as God. And you shall take this rod in your hand, with which you shall do the signs" (verses 14–17).

Moses was trained in oratory in Egypt, but it has been forty years since he left.

Apparently, his Egyptian has become rusty from misuse, so it is not surprising that the Lord chooses Aaron to be his spokesman, since he lives in Egypt. However, the Lord promises to be with both men—with Moses as he speaks to Aaron what the Lord has revealed to him and with Aaron that he might communicate clearly and persuasively the Lord's message that he receives from Moses.

Moses humbly goes to his father-in-law Jethro and asks permission to return to Egypt to see if his brethren are still alive, but he does not mention that the Lord asked him to lead his people out of Egypt. Permission is given, and Moses takes his staff and places his wife and sons on a donkey for the long journey. When he arrives in Egypt, he is to perform the miracles before Pharaoh as he was instructed. Then he is to relate to Pharaoh the words of the Lord that "Israel is my son, My firstborn," let him go out of Egypt to serve Me (verse 22). "But if you refuse to let him go, indeed I will kill your son, your firstborn" (verse 23).

Declaring Israel to be His firstborn son is a very bold statement by the Lord, since Pharaoh considers himself to be the firstborn son of the highest Egyptian god, Amen-Ra. Then the threat is added to kill Pharaoh's firstborn son if he does not let the Hebrews go out of Egypt.

A very serious matter

On the way to Egypt, as they stop to camp, the Lord meets Moses and "[seeks] to kill him," since he has not circumcised his son (verse 24). As a result of this fearful threat on Moses' life, Zipporah takes a flint stone and circumcises her son, and says, "Surely you are a husband of blood to me" (verse 25). Moses knew the divine instruction given to Abraham of circumcision and failed to follow it, while his wife who is a descendant of Abraham through Ishmael apparently did not see the necessity of it. The words she says to her husband are clearly an expression of reproach. They express that she performs the rite grudgingly, not from a desire to follow the Lord's instructions but of necessity, to save her husband's life. When she says, you are a husband of blood, she appears to be saying you are a poor husband, since I have to shed blood of our son to comply with your national religious custom.

Most of us find it hard to understand why the Lord "sought to kill" Moses. However, in the context of what the Lord commissions him to do, in their literal way of thinking, it makes sense. Moses is called to be the religious leader, representing the gospel about his Lord to his own people, to Pharaoh, and to the entire Egyptian nation. He is to tell Pharaoh that his firstborn son will be killed if he doesn't let Israel leave, and when that happens, all the firstborn Egyptian sons will also die. Moreover, when the Passover is instituted, the firstborn of the Israelites will die if they don't follow the Lord's instructions to the letter. This situation is a real life-or-death matter that depends on following the Lord's instructions meticulously.

Therefore, to impress the significance of this mission that involves the possible death of so many, the Lord shows the seriousness of it all through His threat to kill Moses at the encampment.

Moses has not realized how important it is to follow the instruction the Lord gave in His covenant with Abraham, along with His promise for Israel's liberation.

His brother's help

As Moses is traveling to Egypt, the Lord says to Aaron, "Go into the wilderness to meet Moses" (verse 27). They meet at Horeb (Sinai), the mountain of God, where Moses tells of his mission and all the signs that he is to give.

Once in Egypt, they gather the elders of Israel and Aaron informs them of all the words the Lord has spoken to Moses. Then Aaron performs the signs before the people, and they believe, bow their heads, and worship the Lord.

Moses, the reluctant leader for the Lord, has finally accepted the divine commission.

He needed to be humbled to accept the Lord's leading, but in the humbling process, he has been personally established.

The Lord has also established His own authority before His people, and has given confirmation that He will fulfill His covenant promise to liberate His people and bring them back to the Promised Land.

CHAPTER FORTY-ONE

Second Thoughts

Based on Exodus 5 and 6

Moses and Aaron obey the Lord's instructions by arranging an audience with Pharaoh. Standing before him with the elders of Israel, they boldly demand the release of their people by using the words of the Lord, "Let My people go, that they may hold a feast to Me in the wilderness" (Exodus 5:1).

Moses is apparently confident of success with Pharaoh, since the elders of his people have responded well to what the Lord intends to do. He clearly pits his God against Pharaoh—the Egyptian god.

However, Pharaoh finds the request absurd and scoffs at the bold demand with, "Who is the LORD, that I should obey His voice to let Israel go? I do not know the LORD, nor will I let Israel go" (verse 2). This response is quite normal, since he has no experience with the Lord and clearly believes he is superior to any foreign god.

Moses and Aaron are taken aback by Pharaoh's response, so they rephrase their demand in somewhat milder terms. "Please let us go three days' journey into the desert and sacrifice to the LORD our God," they ask, "lest He fall upon us with pestilence or with the sword" (verse 3). Their rationale for going three days journey (three again!) outside of Egypt is based on the fact that sacrificing animals is offensive to the Egyptians.* If they don't sacrifice as the Lord commands, it may result in the Lord bringing pestilence or the sword upon them.

Harsher conditions

Pharaoh is unmoved by any threats of divine judgment and believes instead that the Hebrews are lazy or too idle. Since they are many, they may

---

* See Exodus 8:26. Many animals were considered sacred by the Egyptians. To sacrifice them would be an outrageous insult.

be plotting a revolt against him. He calls them "people of the land" (verse 5), apparently an expression of disdain for being uneducated, common people. He then proceeds to order his Egyptian superintendents (the task masters) and Hebrew foremen (the officers) to no longer supply straw for brickmaking while not allowing a reduction in their previous quotas.

It may seem strange today for us to think of adding straw to bricks. However, chopped straw holds the bricks together, increasing the strength of the bricks many times over and avoiding breakage. This is due partly to the straw itself and partly to the chemical reaction of the decaying vegetable matter upon the brick mixture, resulting in the release of humic acid. The straw they use is good-quality, chopped straw, but now they have to search for poor quality straw that is really stubble, blown by the wind.

The brick-making process starts with drawing water from a pool, mixing mud with a hoe, and transporting the mud in jars to the brickmakers, who form the bricks in wooden molds. Then they are fired, while a foreman with a stick in his hand supervises them and tries to enforce production levels.

When a brickmaking crew fails to meet its quota, the foreman is beaten with the customary form of corporal punishment by the Egyptian superintendent. The method of punishment is extremely painful, since the soles of their bare feet are beaten. Repeated beatings of this sort often result in death.

Since the Hebrew foremen are being beaten because they can't meet their quotas, they go to Pharaoh stating that the fault for their lack of straw lies with the Egyptian superintendents. Apparently, the foremen do not know that their lack of straw is a result of the request to Pharaoh by Moses and Aaron. Pharaoh responds saying, "You are idle! Idle! Therefore you say, 'Let us go and sacrifice to the LORD.' Therefore go now and work; for no straw shall be given you, yet you shall deliver the quota of bricks" (verse 17).

As the Hebrew foremen leave Pharaoh, they meet Moses and Aaron, who are apparently deliberately stationed there, waiting to deal with Pharaoh's expected rebuttal. Instead, they receive the full heat of the foremens' anger as they say, "You have made us abhorrent [literally "a stench"] in the sight of Pharaoh and his servants, to put a sword in their hand to kill us" (verse 21).

Second thoughts

Moses goes to the Lord with second thoughts about his appointed task and boldly says, "LORD, why have You brought trouble on this people? Why is it You sent me? For since I came to Pharaoh to speak in Your name, he has done evil to this people; neither have You delivered Your people at all" (verses 22, 23).

The Lord answers, "Now you shall see what I will do to Pharaoh. For with a strong hand he will let them go, and with a strong hand he will drive them out of his land." The work of the Lord to reveal His power, authority, and plan has just begun with the two encounters that Moses and Aaron had with Pharaoh.

To Moses, it appears there is a serious deterioration of the already bad situation the Hebrews find themselves in. What he does not know is that what has transpired is the Lord's preparation for what is to come. The Lord is revealing the true nature of Pharaoh's heart by creating circumstances in which he is forced to choose between obeying or to turning against the Lord. The Lord will completely reveal Himself to a haughty and ignorant Pharaoh who thinks he is the supreme ruler.

The Lord speaks to Moses and once again repeats He is the I AM. He reveals how He has already been the I AM when He says: "I appeared to Abraham," "I have also established My covenant with them," "I have also heard the groaning of the children of Israel," and "I have remembered My covenant" (Exodus 6:3–5).

Next, He uses His favored number by giving Moses *seven promises* using the significant I AM. First, He will fulfill His promise of redemption: "I will bring you out," "I will rescue you," and "I will redeem you" (verse 6). Next, He promises to adopt Israel: "I will take you as my people and I will be your God" (verse 7). Finally, He focuses on His promise of the land: "I will bring you into the land" and "I will give it to you" (verse 8).

Again, the Lord commands Moses to tell Pharaoh to let His people go out of the land. Moses responds, "The children of Israel have not heeded me. How then shall Pharaoh heed me, for I am of uncircumcised lips?" (verse 12) meaning that he is "slow of speech" as he has declared earlier. The expression "uncircumcised" is also used in Scripture for "uncircumcised ears" meaning that they do not hear and an "uncircumcised heart" that does not understand.

To further show that it is not Moses and Aaron, but the I AM that is liberating Israel, a long section is given that is related to the genealogy of Moses and Aaron. They are shown to *not* descend from the firstborn. Moses is not even the firstborn of his father. His calling is a gift of grace and not based on birth or status. Once again, this section ends with the Lord stating that He is the I AM and that Moses is to speak again to Pharaoh all that He tells him to.

Facing rebuff from Pharaoh and criticism from the Hebrew foremen, Moses has second thoughts about his task of leading the liberation of his people. The Lord, however, makes it clear that He is doing it, and not Moses, by repeatedly stating, "I AM the Lord."

CHAPTER FORTY-TWO

The Gospel to the Egyptians

Based on Exodus 7–11

When we read the stories of the Old Testament, it is easy to think that God is heavy-handed with everyone other than His people. Many Christians avoid the Old Testament because they cannot reconcile a loving God with One who orders the destruction of whole nations. But a closer look reveals the same God that Jonah spoke of when he said, "I know that You are a gracious and merciful God, slow to anger and abundant in lovingkindness, One who relents from doing harm" (Jonah 4:2).

In order for God to be just in dealing with the Egyptians, He must first present to them in our way of thinking—the gospel. The good news of who God is, and His salvation, is so foreign to the Egyptian way of thinking that God has to start by revealing Himself in a manner that they will understand in their context.

In the Egyptian mind, a god is completely different from the Hebrew God. They understand a god mainly in terms of a power that humans have to constantly deal with and fear. They have no conception of a holy God that is loving, merciful, and interested in the welfare of humans. They are polytheists that believe in more than two thousand gods.

These gods are essentially everything in nature.

Among their numerous gods is one that is the supreme god, the head of the pantheon of lesser gods. Pharaoh is regarded as a human god because he is considered the son of the supreme god. In their way of thinking, when humans are created by the gods, they have little value, since they are created to be slaves—to the point of having to feed the gods!

God's self-revelation

God starts the process of self-revelation by establishing Moses as His representative before Pharaoh, and Aaron as his prophet. Pharaoh's power is only human, even though he classifies himself as god. He will consider Moses as a human inferior and part of the slaves. However, the reality will be that he has God's authority and power, which will make him appear as "God" (Exodus 7:1) to Pharaoh.

God tells Moses to go before Pharaoh and tell him to send Israel out of his land. He will not comply, so God will warn him of His power to multiply His signs and wonders in the land. This display of divine power is designed to attract the attention of all of Egypt, winning their respect. God adds that He will bring His armies (His people) out of Egypt by judgments, or plagues.

After Moses and Aaron make their request to Pharaoh, he demands validation of their credentials, so their rod is thrown down and it becomes a snake. The word for snake in Hebrew is *tannin* and apparently portrays that it is a *monstrous* snake, since it is also translated as dragon or crocodile, elsewhere. Pharaoh's sorcerers and magicians are called in, and they throw down their rods, making them appear to become serpents.

However, as evidence of God's greater power and superiority, Aaron's rod swallows up the others, resulting in the loss of their rods!

A revelation

Ten is a complete number for the secular ancients, so God uses ten plagues as judgments on the Egyptian deities (Exodus 12:12; Numbers 33:4). This results in God establishing Himself as the only true God—a complete revelation of the gospel.

Just as Jesus came to liberate us from slavery to sin and death, God is trying to draw the Egyptians to Him and liberate them from spiritual bondage and eternal death. Step by step, Pharaoh and the Egyptians have the opportunity to either accept or reject Him.

Bible commentators spend too much time trying to explain the plagues away as simply natural disasters, so it is important to understand each of the plagues in a theological context. The ancients lived in nature and thought far more concretely than we do today, so God chooses to reveal Himself through literal aspects of nature.

The first nine plagues are arranged into three groups with each group consisting of three plagues. All of the plagues are arranged in ascending severity. The first three plagues are irritants, the second three are destructive, and the final three are fatal.

Organizing into threes is very significant in Scripture, since it emphasizes completeness and importance.

The first plague of each of the three groups (the first, fourth, and seventh plagues) begins with a warning to Pharaoh early in the morning. The second plague of each group (the second, fifth, and eighth plagues) is also introduced by a warning but is delivered at the palace. However, the last plague of each group (the third, sixth, and ninth plagues) begins without any warning.

The triplet grouping brings out the aim of the plagues and their sequence. The first plague of each triplet brings out God's *purpose* for bringing the plague. The initial plague states, "By this you shall know that I am the LORD" (Exodus 7:17), revealing that Pharaoh will come to know just *who God is,* and what His name signifies.

The first plague of the second group states, "That you may know that I am the LORD in the midst of the land" (Exodus 8:22), revealing that *God is present,* providing and guiding the land.

The first plague of the third group says, "That you may know that there is none like me in all the earth" (Exodus 9:14), revealing *the force and scope* of God's power.

It is especially important to point out that each plague results in the obvious destruction of an Egyptian god. As they continue, these false gods are systematically destroyed in ascending order of their importance and power.

The tenth plague stands apart from the others because it is a supreme blow to the leadership and authority structure of Egypt. It also delivers the fatal blow to the religious structure of the land by causing the death of the human equivalent of the head of their pantheon of gods.

Gradual growth

Real spiritual growth normally comes gradually, as we've already seen in the lives of the patriarchs. Although many commentators imply that the plagues may come a week apart, there is no clear biblical evidence to that effect. More likely, this will be a gradual process, since the people need time to absorb the spiritual significance of each plague.

God always takes the necessary time to reveal Himself.

The ancient Egyptians have a difficult time trying to live with all their gods, since they are both cruel and demanding. God longs to establish Himself as the one and only true God—the Great I AM—who supplies all their needs. He provides spiritual liberation from paganism, and through their difficulties, they gain both knowledge of Him and of true religion. He offers them a much more intimate and loving relationship than they could possibly have had before.

CHAPTER FORTY-THREE

The Plagues—Part 1

Based on Exodus 7 and 8

God seeks to free the Egyptians from bondage to false gods by systematically eliminating each deity with a plague, establishing Himself as the only true God. Before the first plague, the Lord tells Moses to take his rod and go to Pharaoh in the morning as he goes to the bank of the Nile with his servants. Probably Pharaoh performs some sort of religious ritual or worship every morning at the Nile. Moses is to intercept Pharaoh at the Nile that will be the exact place where the Lord's miracle is to occur. He is to tell Pharaoh that the Lord has sent him with the request, saying, "Let My people go, that they may serve Me in the wilderness" (Exodus 7:16). But to this point, Pharaoh has not heeded the request.

Therefore, the Lord says, "By this you shall know that I am the LORD. Behold, I will strike the waters which are in the river with the rod that is in my hand, and they shall be turned to blood. And the fish that are in the river shall die, the river shall stink, and the Egyptians will loathe to drink the water of the river" (verses 17, 18).

Pharaoh previously stated that he did not know the Lord, however, now he will begin to know Him with the first plague. This first sign or wonder will begin to wreak havoc on Egypt and its religion, and begin to reveal God's true religion.

Notice the word used for God is Yahweh, the personal God, who is revealing Himself through His mighty acts. It is the Lord that is responsible for the miracle, since He says, "*I* will strike the waters which are in the river with the rod that is in *my* hand" (emphasis added).

The Lord speaks to Moses to tell Aaron to stretch his rod over the waters of Egypt and they will become blood. The waters are designated as streams (according to the Greek historian, Herodirus, there are seven streams, likely in the eastern Delta region of the Nile), the rivers (apparently the canals that fertilize the fields), the ponds (left from the spring flooding), and the pools (artificially made to store water for later use). The number of different waters that are mentioned are four, indicating that this covers all the areas that contain water from the Nile.

Psalm 78:43 states that the plagues occurred in the field of Zoan—the ancient Tanis, that is in the eastern Delta region where Pharaoh may have been in temporary residence, since royal palaces were located in various parts of the nation.

Water turns into blood

When the rod strikes the water of the Nile it turns into blood. The rod that is originally Moses' shepherd rod is now the rod of the Lord. Contrary to popular theories on whether the waters turned to blood, or just became red in color, perhaps from an algae bloom, it is important to note that in the Old Testament the word blood is only used for the blood of humans or animals and never for anything that appears to have the color of blood.

The Egyptian god targeted is the obese Hapi, a personification of the Nile's flooding that brings prosperity to the land. For the Egyptians, the Nile god is the source of fertility and blessing, it has now become the agent of frustration and death as the fish die and stink.

The drinking water is turned into blood, even in the buckets of wood and pitchers of stones, forcing the people to dig in the sand for seven days to get filtered drinking water. The plague appears to last for seven days—rather than the idea that the plagues occur seven days apart. In fact, the nature of the various plagues and the time intervals noted by Moses seem to indicate that the plagues last about six months, from late summer to early spring.

Through their enchantments, Pharaoh's magicians imitate the plague by doing the same. However, had they had confidence in their own miracles, they might have attempted to turn the blood into water, instead of making matters worse! Pharaoh's heart is unmoved and hardened so that he turns and goes into his house.

Smitten with frogs

The Lord again speaks to Moses to go to Pharaoh and say, "Let My people go, that they may serve Me" (Exodus 8:1). If he refuses, Moses is told for the first time to warn Pharaoh of the consequences that will personally "smite" him, and his household. The Lord says, "I will smite all your territory with frogs. So the river shall bring forth frogs abundantly, which shall go up and come into your house, into your bedroom, on your bed, into the houses of your servants, on your people, into your ovens, and into your kneading bowls. And the frogs shall come up on you, on your people, and on all your servants" (verses 2–4).

Those affected are listed by order of rank, first Pharaoh is mentioned, then his government servants—followed by the ordinary Egyptians. The frogs will invade their most private chambers, even their beds. They will overrun their kitchens, their kneading bowls, and even their ovens!

The second plague discredits the frog-headed goddess, Heket, who assisted with childbirth and was thought to have creative power, since she assisted her husband Khnum in bringing men into being. This makes the goddess appear both ridiculous and vicious, since she is tormenting her own people who are religiously devoted to her. The religious beliefs of the Egyptians oblige them to respect the creatures they now loath, hate, and would otherwise destroy.

Aaron stretches out his hand over the waters, and frogs come up over the land. Soon the clammy creatures are crawling all over Pharaoh's palace, his kitchens, his bedroom and all over him! Their incessant croaking is so great that it becomes a roar! Pharaoh's magicians do the same with their magic but only appear to add to the frog infestation, since they apparently cannot remove the plague.

With this second plague, Pharaoh for the first time is concerned. He summons Moses and Aaron and says, "Entreat the Lord that He may take away the frogs from me and my people; and I will let the people go, that they may sacrifice to the Lord" (verse 8). At this point, Pharaoh clearly understands that it is the Lord causing the plague and not Moses or Aaron. He realizes that the Lord is stronger than his frog god.

As soon as Pharaoh asks Moses and Aaron to pray that the Lord remove the plague, Moses gives him the opportunity to set the time for it. Pharaoh decides it will be the next day, Moses prays, and the plague is taken away at the specified time. The frogs die en masse, are gathered into heaps, and their putrid carcasses pollute the air with their stench!

However, once again, Pharaoh hardens his heart and does not let the people go.

Dust becomes lice

The third plague begins without warning to Pharaoh or his magicians. It is directed to Geb, the god of the earth. Aaron is told to use his rod to strike the dust so that it may become lice throughout Egypt.

Interpreters are divided as to what type of insect is referred to, since the Hebrew word is used only in this context. Among the insects suggested and used by different translations are: gnats, mosquitoes, ticks, and lice.

The magicians attempt to duplicate the plague but can produce no insects. They perceive that the Lord is powerfully present in their land where their own gods should display their greatest strength. It is significant that the magicians can't duplicate the third plague, since the number three is so important in Scripture. God uses it for Himself with Three Persons of the Godhead, Jesus uses it for His three temptations, the years of His ministry, and the number of days He is in the tomb. If the magicians could imitate the third plague, it would make them think that they are equivalent to the Hebrew God.

After the magicians failed to imitate the third plague, they exclaim to Pharaoh, "This is the finger of God" (verse 18). By this statement, they recognize that it is the God of the Hebrews that is present and powerful in their land and their own gods are not able to measure up to His power. It is the first step in their beginning to recognize the God of the Israelites. The Lord is using the gentlest hand possible, since the first three plagues are light ones that serve mostly as irritants. But instead of changing his mind, Pharaoh's heart only becomes harder.

Hardening of Pharaoh's heart

The hardening of Pharaoh's heart is often difficult for us to understand, especially when it is attributed to God. Why did God harden Pharaoh's heart? Did He not give him free will?

In order to understand this matter, we must look at the information Exodus provides. Ten times it states that Pharaoh hardened his own heart. Four of these times the Hebrew word *chazaq*, "to make firm" is used (Exodus 7:13, 22; 8:19; 9:35). Five times the Hebrew word *kabad*, "to make heavy" is used (Exodus 7:14; 8:15, 32; 9:7, 34). One time the Hebrew word *qashah*, "to make hard" is used (Exodus 13:15). Pharaoh first hardened his heart when he paid no attention to the Lord's request to let Israel go. His refusal was not limited to plagues that the magicians imitated but included the third plague where the magicians stated, "This is the finger of God."

He hardened his heart again after the fourth and fifth plagues even though informed that the plagues only affected the Egyptians and not the Israelites. After the seventh plague, he is forced to confess, "I have sinned" (Exodus 9:27) but breaks his promise to let Israel go by hardening his heart again.

The Bible mentions ten times that God hardened Pharaoh's heart. Eight of these statements use the Hebrew word, *chazaq*, "to make firm" (Exodus

4:21; 9:12; 10:20, 27; 11:10; 14:4, 8, 17). In Exodus 7:3, the Hebrew word, *qashah*, "to make hard" is used. In Exodus 10:1, the Hebrew word *kabad*, "to make heavy" is used. The same three Hebrew words are used when Pharaoh hardened his own heart and when God hardened his heart. The hardening of Pharaoh's heart is mentioned twenty times with Pharaoh doing it ten times and God causing it ten times. When God hardens Pharaoh's heart, He is not forcing him to do it by taking away his free will. What God is doing is providing a situation where Pharaoh has to make a decision to either accept God's request or reject it. When he rejects it, it is his own decision, and not God's.

Through the first three plagues, God has begun to reveal Himself. By the end of the third plague the magicians have come to realize that God has taken over the realm of their gods. Even Pharaoh has come to the realization after the second plague that only God can take the plague away. In our terminology, God has begun the process of revealing the gospel to Pharaoh and the Egyptians.

The Lord applies increasing pressure on Pharaoh to accept or reject Him, but in no way does He violate Pharaoh's free will. As Bible commentators have wisely pointed out, the substance of Pharaoh's heart reacts to the chastening of God. The same sun that melts wax hardens clay!

CHAPTER FORTY-FOUR

The Plagues—Part 2

Based on Exodus 8–10

As the Lord continues discrediting Egypt's pagan gods, plagues four through nine are more severe than the first three, bringing devastation to the land, animals, and humans.

Biting flies

Once again, the Lord instructs Moses to rise up early in the morning and intercept Pharaoh as he's going out to the Nile, saying to him,

> Thus says the LORD: "Let My people go, that they may serve Me. Or else, if you will not let My people go, behold, I will send swarms of flies on you and your servants, on your people and into your houses. The houses of the Egyptians shall be full of swarms of flies, and also the ground on which they stand. And in that day I will set apart the land of Goshen, in which My people dwell, that no swarms of flies shall be there, in order that you may know that I am the LORD in the midst of the land."(Exodus 8:20–22).

Now as we know, flies multiply quickly and greatly, and so the Egyptians, in their literal thinking, worshiped Uatchit, the fly god of fertility. In fact, Egyptian queens commonly wear a golden fly necklace, hoping to produce male offspring for the Pharaoh.

Although the flies in this plague are not specifically designated in the Hebrew text, the ancient Greek translation made by the descendants of those who lived in Egypt calls them "dog flies." These are large and venomous flies that often fasten themselves to the human body—particularly to the edges of the eyelids!

Because a sharp distinction is made between the Lord's people and

Pharaoh's people, it is clear that this plague will cause the Egyptians to suffer but spare the Israelites from calamity. The purpose of this distinction is to show that the Lord, who is Israel's God, has invaded Uatchit's domain in Egypt. The ancient Near Easterners believe that the gods possess no power except in their own territory, making the gods geographical. However, this is not so, and the innocent are spared while the guilty are afflicted because the Lord is in their midst.

Moses announces the fourth plague in advance, giving Pharaoh time to repent. He and his court are singled out as the first victims of this plague because of the responsibility they bear for their stubbornness. When the plague comes, Pharaoh says to Moses and Aaron, "Go, sacrifice to your God in the land" (Exodus 8:25). However, Moses knows that animal sacrifice in Egypt will cause an uprising, since bulls, especially, were revered as gods! Immediately, Moses responds, "It is not right to do so, for we would be sacrificing the abomination of the Egyptians to the LORD our God. If we sacrifice the abomination of the Egyptians before their eyes, then will they not stone us? We will go three days' journey into the wilderness and sacrifice to the LORD our God as He will command us" (verses 26, 27).

Pharaoh is desperate, and responds, "I will let you go, that you may sacrifice to the LORD your God in the wilderness; only you shall not go very far away. Intercede for me" (verse 28).

Pharaoh's response emphasizes his importance by saying, "I will let you go." However, Moses responds in kind by saying, "Indeed I am going out from you, and I will entreat the LORD. . . . But let Pharaoh not deal deceitfully anymore in not letting the people go to sacrifice to the LORD" (verse 29).

Moses then prays to the Lord and the plague is removed, but Pharaoh hardens his heart and again refuses to let the Hebrews go.

Diseased cattle

Again, Moses is to go to Pharaoh with the same request from the Lord to let His people go, and if he refuses, the hand of the Lord will be on his cattle. This will be more severe because the hand of the Lord is heavier than His finger, mentioned with the third plague.

The previous plagues have affected the people; however, this plague will affect their property. Only recently have the Egyptians begun to use camels and horses, and camels, in particular, are luxury animals. God warns them that any animals left in the open field will die, including cattle, horses, donkeys, camels, oxen, and sheep. This plague probably targets Hathor, the sacred cow goddess of love and protection, and although the particular disease is not stated, many believe it to be anthrax.

The disease affects the Egyptian animals but not those of the Hebrews, and for the first time, Pharaoh is curious whether the animals of the Israelites are affected. But finding out the truth doesn't alter his decision, and he hardens his heart once again.

Sores

The sixth plague, like the third, comes unannounced and probably targets Isis, the goddess of medicine. Moses and Aaron take handfuls of ashes from a furnace, then Moses scatters them toward heaven in the presence of Pharaoh, and they turn to fine dust. Suddenly, sores break out on both man and beast.

For the first time the health and lives of humans are affected and endangered, indicating the increased intensity of the plagues; and although the exact nature of these sores is not clear, most translations call them boils.

Some Egyptian ritual texts refer to the scattering of ashes as a means of ending pestilence; however, here the ashes are *causing* the misery! The magicians, who are always near Pharaoh, are so severely affected that they cannot stand before Moses and quickly leave.

For the first time the Bible mentions that the Lord hardens Pharaoh's heart, resulting in him not heeding the request of Moses and Aaron. This will be stated several times as the severity of the plagues increase.

Hail and fire

The next three plagues are far more severe, having the potential to kill! The Lord instructs Moses to rise up early and stand before Pharaoh. Once again, he is to repeat the Lord's message to let His people go.

To underscore the theological significance of the next plagues, Moses gives a long message that includes the following points:

1. The Lord will send His remaining plagues on Egypt so that all will know that there is no one like Him on the earth.
2. The Lord reminds them that the previous plagues might have cut them off from the earth, had not the Lord spared them to herald His power and name throughout the earth.
3. Pharaoh has exalted himself against the Lord's people by not letting them go.
4. The Lord will send a violent hailstorm as they have never experienced.
5. The Lord is providing a means to escape the effects of the next plague if they will heed His words.

This plague probably targets Nut, the goddess of the sky, and when Moses stretches out his rod toward heaven, the Lord sends violent thunder and hail, mixed with fire (lightning) as they have never seen before.

This storm reveals the Lord's power to the Egyptians, since they only think in terms of power when they refer to any god. When the heavy hail strikes all the land of Egypt, anything that is the field, whether man or beast, herb or tree, is destroyed. Only the Egyptians that heed Moses' warning to leave the open field with their livestock are spared. Obviously, any storm comes as a complete surprise to the Egyptians, since the annual rainfall in upper Egypt is one inch, and often none at all. Only in the land of Goshen where the Israelites are, there is no hail.

The hail destroys the flax and barley harvests, indicating that it is January or February. Flax is used for linen garments and the barley for beer, horse feed, and bread for the poor. The wheat and spelt crop are not hurt because they are harvested in late March or early April.

Pharaoh sends for Moses and Aaron and says, "I have sinned this time. The Lord is righteous, and my people and I are wicked. Entreat the Lord, that there may be no more mighty thundering and hail, for it is enough. I will let you go, and you shall stay no longer" (Exodus 9:27, 28).

Moses responds, "As soon as I have gone out of the city, I will spread out my hands to the LORD; the thunder will cease, and there will be no more hail, that you may know that the earth is the LORD's." However, Moses adds, "But as for you and your servants, I know that you will not yet fear the LORD God" (verses 29, 30).

As soon as Moses goes out of the city and prays to the Lord, the thunder, hail, and rain cease, but Pharaoh hardens his heart and does not let the Israelites go.

Locusts

In the introduction to the eighth plague, God tells Moses about Pharaoh, "I have hardened his heart and the hearts of his servants, that I may show these signs of Mine before him" (Exodus 10:1). Notice that God uses the first person pronoun twice in the same sentence, clearly emphasizing that *He* is doing this. The Lord does this to make plain that He is the God in control in Egypt and that His mighty acts reveal it. Additionally, He has still another objective: to show Israel in that He authenticates Himself through His mighty acts, and that this must be taught to all future generations.

Once again, Moses and Aaron go before Pharaoh, asking how long will he refuse to humble himself before the Lord, and refuse to let the Hebrews serve the Lord. They warn him that if he refuses, the next day will bring a swarm of locusts that will devastate the land of Egypt. After making their announcement, Moses and Aaron turn their backs on Pharaoh and dramatically walk out!

The eighth plague probably targets Serapis, the god of protection against locusts—or perhaps Seth, the god of storms. Pharaoh's servants say to him, "How long shall this man be a snare to us? Let the men go, that they may serve the LORD their God. Do you not yet know that Egypt is destroyed?" (verse 7).

The Egyptians have already lost most of their cattle, nearly all their crops, and are trying to avoid a worse calamity. So Pharaoh summons Moses and Aaron back and says half-heartedly, "Go, serve the LORD your God" (verse 8). However, his command is immediately qualified by his question, "Who are the ones that are going?" (verse 8).

Moses responds, "We will go with our young and our old; with our sons and our daughters, with our flocks and our herds we will go, for we must hold a feast to the LORD" (verse 9).

Quickly, Pharaoh snarls, "The LORD had better be with you when I let you and your little ones go! Beware, for evil is ahead of you" (verse 10). Then he changes his mind and says, "Not so! Go now, you who are men, and serve the LORD, for that is what you desired" (verse 11). Then, in a fit of anger, he drives them out of his presence.

The Lord now commands Moses to call down the locust plague that brings widespread devastation to everything green in the land. The locusts fly in on an east wind, which in Scripture is always brought on by the Lord. Since the wind is from the east, the locusts are blown in from northern Arabia, and they completely cover the land so that none of it can be seen. They devour green crops, plants, and leaves—then they chew even harder materials, such as reeds, twigs, and tree bark. Fruits, such as figs, pomegranates, mulberries, grapes, and dates are all ravaged.

Since a single locust can consume the equivalent of its own weight each day, it probably takes only about half an hour to turn this fertile region into a desert, making the starvation of the Egyptians a distinct probability.

Pharaoh hastily calls Moses and Aaron back to the palace and says, "I have sinned against the LORD your God and against you. Now therefore, please forgive my sin only this once, and entreat the LORD your God, that He may take away from me this death only" (verses 16, 17).

Once more, Moses leaves Pharaoh and prays to the Lord who brings a strong west wind that blows the locusts into the Red Sea. The west wind is literally "a sea wind" that comes from the Mediterranean, and the Israelites, for whom the Bible is written, commonly use "the sea" as a synonym for "west."

However, the Lord hardens Pharaoh's heart, he does not let the Hebrews go.

Darkness

The ninth plague begins without warning as the Lord instructs Moses, saying, "Stretch out your hand toward heaven, that there may be darkness over the land of Egypt, darkness which may even be felt." As a result, an amazing, thick blackness blankets Egypt for three days. No light can penetrate this darkness, and the people are gripped with terror. They cannot see each other, and don't dare move. They are truly paralyzed by this eerie calamity!

This plague probably targets the sun god, Amon-Ra, who is considered the divine father of Pharaoh and the chief god. The darkness deals a deathblow to Egypt's core belief, since the sun's rays are Egypt's source of creative life. However, by contrast, the Israelites have light in their houses.

After three days of total darkness, Pharaoh makes a sudden and desperate call for Moses. In the darkness, he says, "Go, serve the Lord; only let your flocks and your herds be kept back. Let your little ones also go with you" (verse 24).

But Moses refuses Pharaoh's compromise with the unmistakable words, "Our livestock also shall go with us; not a hoof shall be left behind. For we must take some of them to serve the Lord our God, and even we do not know with what we must serve the Lord until we arrive there" (verse 26). This festival is brand new and has not been defined, so they will naturally need their livestock for any sort of sacrifice that might be required.

The Lord hardens Pharaoh's heart and he does not let them go. He seems to have had enough, and rudely says, "Get away from me! Take heed to yourself and see my face no more! For in the day you see my face you shall die!" (verse 28).

But Moses calmly responds, "You have spoken well. I will never see your face again" (verse 29).

The Lord has presented Himself step by step as the true God by discrediting the pagan Egyptian gods. He has consistently brought Pharaoh to the point of deciding whether he will accept the Lord and let His people go, or reject Him and not let them go.

The plagues have brought increasing pressure on Pharaoh: The first three serving as irritants, the second three bringing destruction, and the last three bringing loss of life. The plagues have also strengthened the current generation of Israelites' faith in the Lord as they see His mighty acts. They serve to help substantiate the faith of future generations, as well, since they will hear what the Lord has done in the past.

CHAPTER FORTY-FIVE

Blood on the Doorposts

Based on Exodus 11 and 12

The first nine plagues discredit the Egyptian gods. They are divine judgments, designed to be redemptive for the Egyptians and awaken their desire for salvation. They also serve to mature the faith of the Israelites in preparation for the Exodus. As they observe the consequences of rejecting the Lord, God's people marvel at His protection. In fact, Scripture records that at least half of the plagues didn't affect them, and now the Lord prepares them for the tenth plague by instituting the Passover.

The final plague

As an introduction to the tenth plague the Lord tells Moses, "I will bring one more plague on Pharaoh and on Egypt. Afterward he will let you go from here. When he lets you go, he will surely drive you out of here altogether. Speak now in the hearing of the people, and let every man ask from his neighbor and every woman from her neighbor, articles of silver and articles of gold" (Exodus 11:1, 2).

The Lord adds that at midnight, He will go into the midst of Egypt and all the firstborn in Egypt will die, from the firstborn of Pharaoh even to the lowly firstborn of the female servant who is behind the handmill. The handmill consists of two stones: a lower stone with a concave surface and an upper loaf-shaped stone. Grain is ground into flour by placing it on the lower stone, then rubbing the upper stone over it.

However, God gives His people a special promise, by saying, "Against none of the children of Israel shall a dog move its tongue, against man or beast, that you may know that the LORD does make a difference between the Egyptians and Israel" (verse 7). The Hebrew word, "move" means "to cut into," "to sharpen," or "to bring to a point" and alludes to the fact that when a dog growls, it points its tongue. The message clearly is that no injury will come to the Israelites or their animals. To the Egyptians, the fact their firstborn will die at about midnight is significant, since to them it is not the beginning of a new day, but the darkest and most formidable part of the night.

The Egyptians consider Pharaoh a deity, and the tenth plague is directed at him. In the ninth plague "his father," the sun god, was targeted. Now his son, who will probably be the heir to the throne, will die with the firstborn. This is a final blow to Pharaoh's person, his kingship, and his divinity. It is divine judgment against all the firstborn in Egypt, including man and beast. The beasts are included because this judgment is also against the Egyptians gods, who are generally animals. The Lord is contrasting Himself with these gods because He identifies Himself as, "I am the Lord."

Passover instructions

The Lord now gives instruction concerning the Passover, beginning with the calendar. The month in which the Passover falls is to be called the first month of the year, giving the idea of a new beginning, as it was after the Flood. This month will mark their new beginning as a people—saved and redeemed from bondage by the Lord. This can be compared to the new life a Christian receives when they are born again.

The Passover month begins in either late March or April and is called *abib* in Hebrew, meaning "ear month," since the grain (barley) is in the ear stage. This spring-to-spring calendar is used only as a religious calendar. Their civil calendar runs from fall to fall and begins in either September or October.

On the tenth day of the month, preparations begin for the Passover as every man chooses a one-year-old lamb or kid from his flock as a sacrifice for his household. Their understanding of a one-year-old animal is any animal younger than twelve months of age.

Usually, the Israelites prefer a lamb, but a young goat is also acceptable. The lamb is to be a male without any defect because it typifies the Messiah. It is to be kept separate until the fourteenth of the month, when the all Israel takes their animal and kills it at twilight.

The fourteenth day clearly shows this is linked with the Lord, because it is a multiple of seven—the Lord's number. The word "twilight" in Hebrew is literally "between the two evenings," and has been interpreted in two different ways.

Some say the "first evening" begins with sunset, and the "second evening" begins with the end of twilight. Deuteronomy 16:6 appears to support this view by saying, "You shall sacrifice the Passover at twilight, at the going down of the sun, at the time you came out of Egypt."

Others have interpreted the "first evening" as beginning about three o'clock in the afternoon (when the sun begins to visibly decline from its zenith) and the "second evening" as the sun begins to set. Texts such as Leviticus 23:5 and Numbers 9:3 seem to support this second interpretation with the Passover being on the fourteenth of the month.

If the animal is killed after sunset, Passover would fall on the fifteenth of the month. The prevailing custom in Jesus' time agrees with this interpretation, since the Passover lambs were slain late in the afternoon, about the same time the "Lamb of God" dies.

Saved by the blood

In order to be saved from the plague, some of the animal's blood is put on the two door doorposts and lintel (the horizontal board above the door) of the house. It is applied with hyssop, a gray-green marjoram plant associated with purification. Hyssop is a small plant with a pungent, fragrant scent that tastes similar to peppermint. Its thick, hairy leaves and branches are well adapted for holding the blood that serves as the visible sign to the destroying angel to pass the residence. However, its real meaning is that blood represents the purification of the sinner by the blood of the Messiah, who dies in place of the family's firstborn.

The lamb

The lamb must be roasted whole in fire and eaten with unleavened bread and bitter herbs. The bread must be unleavened because yeast causes fermentation—a logical symbol of impurity and moral corruption. The bitter herbs of Egypt are not clearly defined but may include chicory, thistle, endive, horseradish, cress, or a bitter lettuce. These herbs are to remind the participants of the bondage and bitter suffering in Egypt. The meal must be eaten "with a belt on your waist, your sandals on your feet, and your staff in your hand. So you shall eat it in haste" (Exodus 12:11). In addition, God instructs that none of the meat is to be eaten raw (since the pagans often eat raw flesh at their sacrificial meals) and any meat not eaten by morning must be burned with fire.

The ritual of the Passover

The Hebrew word *pesah* means more than the English translation, "Passover," meaning that the destroying angel "passes over" the house. The blood on the doorposts and lintel is seen as *purifying* the doorway of a house so the Lord can enter and abide with His children.

The Passover is to become a memorial for the Israelites throughout successive generations—obviously until the Messiah Himself dies in their place. It is to be followed by the seven-day Feast of Unleavened Bread commemorating the haste in which they leave Egypt without taking any leaven.

Leaven is generally produced from the barley content of dough that ferments and serves as yeast. A small amount of this dough is kept as a starter to ferment the next batch. When there is no starter dough, it takes between seven to twelve days to reach the required level of fermentation.

Those who did not eliminate leaven from their household during this week must be cut off from Israel. This includes the stranger and native of the land. A stranger is a non-Israelite who lives with the Hebrews, either temporarily or permanently. The native of the land is a Canaanite who considers Canaan his homeland.

A worship assembly is to be held on the first and seventh days of the feast. No regular work is performed on these days, except for the preparation of food.

The divine regulation of who can participate in the Passover meal states that it is limited to those who are circumcised. No foreigner, sojourner, or hired servant shall eat it. However, a man's servant who has been bought with money can, if he has been circumcised. In addition, if a stranger who lives with you wants to participate, he must be circumcised first.

At midnight on the day marked for the Passover, the Lord strikes all the firstborn in the land of Egypt and Pharaoh is aroused from sleep along, with his servants and all the Egyptians. A great sound of mourning rises throughout Egypt as parents discover their firstborn are dead. Mourning in Egypt is mostly expressed by women who wail inconsolably with disheveled hair, gesturing with upraised arms, and beating their breasts repeatedly.

Immediately Pharaoh calls for Moses and Aaron during the night and says, "Rise, go out from among my people, both you and the children of Israel. And go, serve the Lord as you have said. Also take your flocks and your herds, as you have said, and be gone; and bless me also" (verses 31, 32).

Pharaoh has just blurted out five commands, three of which mean go! Clearly his pride has been crushed, but he has *not* accepted Israel's God, even though his gods have been totally discredited.

Egyptian payment

Before leaving, the Israelites ask the Egyptians for articles of silver, gold, and clothing—and they gladly give them anything they want. As slaves, the Hebrews don't have good clothing; and since they are going to a special festival, they naturally need good apparel to appear before the Lord.

One cannot underestimate their desire to be rid of the people whose God has brought about so much suffering. As the Egyptians give them costly gifts, they are really only paying them for their years of slave labor; and since God gives His people favor, "they plundered the Egyptians" (verse 36).

Years of sojourn

According to Exodus 12:40, the Hebrews come out of Egypt 430 years after going into it. By comparing Galatians 3:17 and Genesis 15:13, it's evident that this period includes the time from Abram's call to leave Haran until Jacob moved to Egypt 215 years later, plus another 215 years until the Exodus.

In the time of Moses, Canaan is considered part of the Egyptian empire, so it is not unusual for the author of that period to include Canaan as part of Egypt. Genesis 15:16 states that "in the fourth generation they shall return," making it impossible for them to have been in slavery for the full 430 years.

This leads to another question about when the Exodus occurred. The subject is far too extensive to deal with in this chapter, but some scriptural evidence seems to make this reasonably clear. In 1 Kings 6:1, the Bible says, "In the four hundred and eightieth year after the children of Israel had come out of the land of Egypt, in the fourth year of Solomon's reign over Israel." This is about 970 BC, so working backwards, the date for the Exodus would be about 1450 BC.

Judges 11:26 states, "While Israel dwelt in Heshbon and its villages, in Aroer and its villages, and in all the cities along the banks of the Arnon, for three hundred years, why did you not recover them within that time?" The time referred to is somewhere around 1100 BC, and adding three hundred years to that would place the Exodus in round numbers of 1400 BC. or more. At the time of the tenth plague, the Lord has clearly revealed that He is the God ruling in Egypt, displacing the Egyptian gods in their own land. He has given Pharaoh, his servants, and the population in general the clear opportunity to accept the true God over the period of the ten plagues. Most do not accept the Lord as their new God, but a "mixed multitude" appear to and exit Egypt with the Israelites.

God has established the memorial of the Passover. It serves as a special commemorative feast to the Lord for the deliverance from bondage from slavery and sin. It points forward to the saving and cleansing blood of the Messiah, who will be the salvation and substitute for every sinner who accepts Him.

CHAPTER FORTY-SIX

Crossing the Red Sea

Based on Exodus 13–15

The tenth plague has killed the Egyptian firstborn while the Hebrew first-born are observing the Passover. The Hebrews have been liberated from Egyptian bondage and are being led to the promised land "flowing with milk and honey" (Exodus 13:4).

A special consecration

As the Hebrews begin observing the Feast of Unleavened Bread, the Lord informs Moses that all the firstborn of man and beast must be conse-crated to Him as His special property. They will be adopted and dedicated to His service.

This consecration is to be observed annually, to impress on them that they belong to the Lord by His saving grace. It is the means of keeping the experience of the exodus alive.

The Lord says to His people, "It shall be as a sign to you on your hand and as a memorial between your eyes, that the LORD's law may be in your mouth; for with a strong hand the LORD has brought you out of Egypt" (verse 9). The purpose of this statement is to impress on the minds of the people for generations to come of how the Lord miraculously brought them out of bondage of Egyptian slavery.

Much later in Israelite history, the Jews begin a literal tradition of binding portions of the Sinai law on their left arms and foreheads. They call these *tephillim*, or phylacteries. These consist of small pouches made from the skin of clean animals that are sewn to straps, then tied onto the foreheads and left arms of males who have reached the age of thirteen. Four strips of parchment inscribed with Exodus 13:2–10 and 13:11–16, along with Deuteronomy 6:4–9 and 11:13–21 are placed in the four compartments of the forehead phylactery. The arm phylactery has one pouch containing all four passages. It is clear that God never instructs them to do this; the use of phylacteries is strictly based in Jewish tradition.

All firstborn males, are to be redeemed, or bought back for a price that in Numbers 18:16 is five shekels, or about two ounces of silver. The redemption price of firstborn males and the firstborn of animals are one of the means of supporting the priests. The firstborn of clean animals are not to be redeemed, because they are holy, and devoted to the Lord to be used as sacrifices in thanksgiving to the Lord.

The firstborn of a donkey (an unclean animal) is not approved for sacrifice, so it must be redeemed by a clean animal—a lamb.

A strange route

As Israel travels away from Egypt, the Lord does not lead them north along the Mediterranean coast (the shortest route at about 160 miles) to Canaan. This route is heavily fortified, and will most certainly mean that the Hebrews will to have to fight the Philistines—something that will likely discourage them.

The first leg of their journey takes them from Goshen to Ramses, and as they leave Egypt for Succoth, the Scripture says they are about six hundred thousand men on foot, along with women, children, and a "mixed multitude" of Egyptians who choose to cast their fate with God's people (Exodus 12:38). The Hebrews are organized in military style by tribe and are called "the armies of the LORD" (verse 41). They also carry Joseph's mummified bones with them to bury in Canaan, since he required them to swear to do so.

On their journey from Succoth, they encamp at Etham, a location that has not been definitively identified. While traveling, the Lord leads them by day with a pillar of cloud that turns to a pillar of fire by night. This "pillar" has a base width that is large enough to cover the people from the intense heat of the sun, and give them light and warmth by night. The pillar of cloud and fire is just another name for the angel of the Lord, since Exodus 14:19 and 23:20–33 equate the two together. Wherever the Hebrews travel, the Lord is always present.

The people have generally traveled southeasterly, and in another day's journey in the same direction, they will be beyond the eastern border of Egypt. However, the Lord curiously directs them to change to a southwesterly course that places the Red Sea between them and their destination. They are to camp before Pi Hahiroth, between Migdol and the Red Sea, opposite Baal Zephon. Migdol means "tower" or "fortress," and is probably one of the Egyptian fortresses on their eastern border.

God sets a trap

Pharaoh assumes they are hopelessly lost in the desert among the mountains and near the sea. Once again, Pharaoh is sorry he ever let his slaves go, and now he seizes on this opportunity to capture and return them to bondage.

He makes ready his own chariot, his soldiers, and six hundred more chariots to pursue them, thinking he will trap them. Archaeologists have discovered two chariots from this period. They are open at the rear, and are encircled by a rim that is about two-and-a-half feet above the standing board. They have two wheels, a tongue, and are drawn by two small horses. Ancient historians indicate that two men—a warrior and a charioteer, probably man them. The Bible also indicates that there are captains over each of the chariots.

These may be officers who have command over the chariots, or they may be the drivers of the chariots, and called captains because they determine where the chariot will go.

Pharaoh overtakes the Hebrews as they camp by the Red Sea. They are trapped by water in front of them, high mountains beside them, and the Egyptian army behind them. Totally unprepared for battle, their situation appears hopeless, and immediately they cry out to the Lord, then fire three questions at Moses. "Because there were no graves in Egypt, have you taken us away to die in the wilderness? Why have you so dealt with us, to bring us up out of Egypt? Is this not the word that we told you in Egypt, saying, 'Let us alone that we may serve the Egyptians'? For it would have been better for us to serve the Egyptians than that we should die in the wilderness" (Exodus 14:11, 12).

Moses patiently responds with three directives: "Do not be afraid. Stand still, and see the salvation of the LORD, which He will accomplish for you today. For the Egyptians whom you see today, you shall see again no more forever. The LORD will fight for you, and you shall hold your peace" (verses 13, 14). They are to "see," indicating they are to witness what the Lord is going to do through the eyes of faith. Two things are clear from Moses' response: First, the battle is the Lord's; second, judgment will come swiftly upon the Egyptians.

Scripture is clear that when there is silence, it means that divine judgment is falling on the wicked, and the people are to stand in silence (or awe) of the magnitude of that judgment. This is quite clear in Psalm 46:10 and Revelation 8:1. Those who belong to the Lord are to be still—not meaning inactivity, but calm quiet as the Lord acts.

Now the Lord asks Moses, who apparently has cried out to Him, "Why do you cry to Me? Tell the children of Israel to go forward. But lift up your rod, and stretch out your hand over the sea and divide it. And the children of Israel shall go on dry ground through the midst of the sea. And I indeed will harden the hearts of the Egyptians, and they shall follow them. So I will gain honor over Pharaoh and over all his army, his chariots, and his horsemen. Then the Egyptians shall know that I am the LORD, when I have gained honor for Myself over Pharaoh, his chariots, and his horsemen" (verses 15–18).

The pillar of cloud—referred interchangeably as "the Angel of God," indicating Jesus—now reverses direction and settles between Pharaoh's camp and the Hebrews. This results in dense darkness for the Egyptians, and light of day for the Hebrews, so that no one can come near the other all night. The parallel to the ninth Egyptian plague is unmistakable!

God lets Moses know that even though He will win the battle for them, he must take the initiative by stretching out his hand over the sea, and that the Hebrews must march forward into the seabed before it becomes dry land for them. Again, we must not miss the parallel to the crossing of the Jordan River later on, when the priests are instructed to step into the water before it parts and the Hebrews enter the Promised Land.

As Moses stretches his rod over the sea, God sends a strong east wind that divides the waters into two huge walls and dries the land in between. This miracle allows the Hebrews to walk through the Red Sea on dry ground.

All of Pharaoh's horses, chariots, and cavalrymen pursue them until the morning watch—between 2:00 A.M. and 6:00 A.M.—when the Lord troubles the army by making the chariot wheels to come off or break. The ancient Greek version translates it by stating it as clogging their chariot wheels, making forward movement extremely difficult.

Finally, the Egyptians say, "Let us flee from the face of Israel, for the LORD fights for them against the Egyptians" (verse 25).

As they try to flee back to the shore, the Lord instructs Moses to once again stretch out his hand over the sea and let the water return to its normal position engulfing and drowning Pharaoh and the *entire* Egyptian army.

As the morning dawns, the dead bodies of the Egyptians are washed up on the shore.

This apparently indicates that when the east wind ceases, a westerly wind brings the waters together and blows the dead bodies to the eastern shore, where the Hebrews can see them! At this point, Israel has become totally free from Egyptian influence. The Lord has indisputably revealed that He is the only true God, since He has gained honor for Himself over Pharaoh and his army.

The song of Moses

After the crossing of the Red Sea and the defeat of Pharaoh and his army, the story of the marvelous victory is put into poetic form and sung by the Hebrews. When something is put into poetic form, it is considered very important, and should be remembered. Singing fixes it in one's mind and serves as a very important means of expressing the concepts and emotions of the poetry.

The Bible identifies this song as the Song of Moses, but his sister, Miriam, leads the women in song, playing a tambourine or hand drum as accompaniment. The hand drum consists of a large wooden hoop with two skins. The instrument is beaten by hand and is usually played by women. It was often used to accompany joyful singing and dancing, probably to accentuate the beat.

Religious dancing is quite common in the Bible; it is an outward expression of holy joy that is entered into with the same spirit as songs of praise. It is clearly an act of worship. Men always dance separately from women, and in the song of Moses, Miriam and the women probably sing and dance antiphonally.

An analysis of the song indicates that the Lord is both the subject and the object of this psalm. The divine name appears ten times. He is incomparable to any of the gods on earth and any beings for whom divinity is claimed. He is called a "man of war" whom Pharaoh's entire military force could not threaten, since they sank to the bottom of the sea "like a stone," "like lead," and were "as still as a stone" (Exodus 15:3, 5, 10, 16).

After the description of the overthrow of the Egyptian forces, there is the prophetic description of the Lord's entrance into the Promised Land. He will bring further victories, settlement, and the Lord's sovereign presence to Jerusalem (Zion) in fulfillment of His covenant promises.

Notice the parallels

The whole story is a conclusion of the greatness of the Lord. He has presented the gospel to Pharaoh and his people by clearly revealing Himself and His mighty acts; but most of them have rejected Him. He has discredited the Egyptian gods, and finally, in the tenth plague, He has inflicted the final blow to Pharaoh, who believes he is a god.

However, Pharaoh rises up again when it looks like the Lord has led Israel into a trap in the wilderness. He believes that he has won, because he is sure that he will re-enslave the Hebrews. However, the Lord clearly outsmarts Pharaoh, and ends his final uprising.

Please notice how the Bible re-tells this story in Revelation 20. Like

Pharaoh, Satan will march with the wicked against the righteous, thinking he can overtake them with sheer numbers and power. However, like the Egyptians, Satan and his followers will be destroyed—not in the waters of the Red Sea—but in the lake of fire.

CHAPTER FORTY-SEVEN

A Patient God

Based on Exodus 15–18

The ancients attributed everything that happened on earth to the gods. All conflicts are between them; therefore, the most powerful deity is considered the true one. The Lord has revealed Himself as the true God to His people by defeating the Egyptian gods during the plagues, by freeing them in the Exodus, and by drowning Pharaoh's army in the Red Sea. But He does not reveal His traits as a Holy God until the Israelites journey to Sinai.

Water

They travel three days into the wilderness desert area of Shur without finding water.

Normally, they carry drinking water in leather pouches; but a march of three days exhausts their supply and clearly puts their cattle in peril, since they need to be watered regularly. Through this, the Lord tests them, and begins to develop their faith as newborn followers.

Reaching Marah (which means "bitter"), they find water, but it is undrinkable.

Immediately they complain to Moses, "What shall we drink?" (Exodus 15:24), and Moses cries out to the Lord, who shows him a tree to throw into the water to make it sweet. We don't know what species of tree or how it sweetens the water, but we do know that the Lord makes it suitable for drinking.

The verb "to show" is from the verbal root "to teach or instruct." It is from the same root as the noun, "Torah" or "law." What seems to be clear is that this is imagery of the tree of life found in Genesis 2—in part of the Torah—that makes humans healthy and whole both physically, mentally, and spiritually. Revelation 22:2 also follows this tree of life imagery by saying, "The leaves of the tree were for the healing of the nations." The imagery goes beyond this because good water is provided for them and their animals.

This imagery is reminiscent of the river that flows out of Eden in Genesis 2 and provides water for all. What the Lord is trying to teach them is that He is the One who provides for all of their needs—just as He did in Eden.

Continuing this tree of life imagery, the Lord gives them an ordinance by promising that He will put none of the diseases on them that He has put on the Egyptians if they follow Him and do what is right. The diseases refer to the plagues. He will heal them as He healed the water, and keep them free from both physical and moral evil.

The Hebrews next camp at Elim, located about seven miles to the south where the Lord provides a plentiful supply of water, luxuriant groves of tamarisk, acacias, and palms, and thick, tall grass for the cattle. There are twelve wells of water and seventy palm trees—the exact numbers of the twelve tribes and the seventy persons who arrived in Egypt with Jacob. Again, this imagery is not lost on the Hebrews. They understand that He is showing what He will do, if they will follow and obey Him.

Bread from heaven

The next stop is the Wilderness of Sin that is between Elim and Sinai, and the Bible says that they arrive one month after leaving Egypt. This indicates that they apparently stay for a number of days in other places that are not mentioned in Scripture.

Immediately, they begin complaining to Moses, saying, "Oh, that we had died by the hand of the LORD in the land of Egypt, when we sat by the pots of meat and when we ate bread to the full! For you have brought us out into this wilderness to kill this whole assembly with hunger" (Exodus 16:3). Obviously, the newness of freedom has worn off and the realities of life in the wilderness have set in. Seven times in a few verses of Exodus 16, the complaint verb or noun is mentioned in quick succession. They clearly exaggerate how good things were in Egypt, saying they had plenty of meat and bread! Their lack of gratitude makes it sound like they prefer hardship, slavery, and task masters over the Lord's many miracles!

The patience and kindness of the Lord is remarkable toward His newly adopted children. In response, He says to Moses, "Behold, I will rain bread from heaven for you. And the people shall go out and gather a certain quota every day, that I may test them, whether they will walk in My law or not. And it shall be on the sixth day that they shall prepare what they bring in, and it shall be twice as much as they gather daily" (verses 4, 5).

This statement appears to use the imagery of the two trees in the Garden of Eden.

Adam and Eve had to choose between them, and now the Hebrews must choose between following the Lord's directions or going their own way. The fact that they are to gather enough for each day, and a double amount for Sabbath is a test to see whether they will follow the Lord's instructions.

The Lord tells Moses He hears the complaints of the Hebrews, and that they are to look toward the wilderness and see His glory as the glory of His presence shining especially bright. His cloud is always the visible sign of His presence, but they have taken their sight off the Lord and focused on themselves. This is a theophany—a visible manifestation of the Lord—to demonstrate to them that He is really with them, and knows their situation. He supplies their needs with quail meat that evening, and in the morning, the ground is covered with manna, which they grind into bread-like food.

The quail are a migratory bird that fly in great numbers in the spring from Sudan to northern regions, returning in the fall. Because of their long flight over the Red Sea, they land exhausted on the shores of the Sinai Peninsula and are easily caught. This game bird is about ten inches long and belongs to the same order as pheasants, partridges, and grouse.

In the morning when the dew evaporates, the Hebrews find a small round white substance resembling coriander seeds covering the ground. This foodstuff tastes like wafers or cakes made with honey, and when the people see it, they have no idea what it is, and say, "manna," which means, "What is it?" The "m" of the Hebrew word manna is an interrogative pronoun, meaning "What?"

Once again, the Lord has listened to their complaints and patiently provided "food from heaven." For the first five days of the week they are to gather one omer, or about two quarts, for each person in their tent. On Friday they are to gather double that amount, since no manna will fall on Sabbath. According to Numbers 11:8, the manna may be ground in a mill, crushed in a mortar, boiled in a pot, or baked into cakes.

One omer a day is sufficient to supply all the daily needs of an individual, and no more must be stored, except on Friday. Any manna they try to keep for more than a day will spoil and become wormy.

In addition, Moses instructs the Hebrews, "This is the thing which the LORD has commanded: 'Fill an omer with it, to be kept for your generations, that they may see the bread with which I fed you in the wilderness, when I brought you out of the land of Egypt' " (verse 32). Then he tells Aaron, "Take a pot and put an omer of manna in it, and lay it up before the LORD, to be kept for your generations" (verse 33). This manna is to be stored "before the Testimony," not the future ark of the covenant, but the two tables of stone containing the Ten Commandments, which preceded the ark.

More water troubles

The Hebrews now journey on to Rephidim but once again, there is no water. They complain to Moses and are so dissatisfied with him that they're almost ready to stone him! Moses gives this location two fitting names: Massah, meaning "temptation" or "testing," and Meribah, meaning "murmuring" or "quarreling," since they are both testing and quarreling with the Lord. By using two names, he sets up two witnesses against the people and how horrible they make this place through their actions.

Finally, he answers, saying, "Why do you contend with me? Why do you tempt the LORD?" (Exodus 17:2). In this way he states that they may have a right to question his leadership; however, in reality they are setting themselves against the Lord, who provides for their needs.

His words fall on deaf ears, and the people continue complaining, saying, "Why is it you have brought us up out of Egypt, to kill us and our children and our livestock with thirst?" (verse 3). However, by saying this, they are really questioning whether God is really with them, since He doesn't appear to be meeting their most basic needs.

All of this contention is too much for Moses. He takes it to the Lord, who instructs him to go before the people with some of the elders and strike the rock at Horeb (or Sinai) with his rod. He adds that He will stand before him at the rock.

Once again, the Lord in His patience provides for the Hebrew's physical needs even after they attack Him and Moses, His representative. They seem incapable of remembering that He continually gives them visible evidence of His presence with the pillar of cloud.

The first attack

While camping at Rephidim, the Hebrews are attacked for the first time by Amalek, a desert king from the south of Canaan. He is the son of Esau's oldest son Eliphaz, and since he is a relative, he should not feel that the Hebrews are any threat to his people's interests.

This attack angers the Lord for two reasons: First, Amalek and his people fail to recognize the known plan of the Lord in His covenant with Jacob and his descendants. Second, in their war against Israel, they target the sick, the aged, and the tired ones who lag behind the line of march (see Deuteronomy 25:17–19).

The Amalekites are the first nation to attack Israel after their freedom from the Egyptians, and this attack appears to be permitted by the Lord because of the fierce complaining against Moses and God for the lack of water at Rephidim.

Moses calls Joshua, his assistant and military leader, and instructs him, "Choose us some men and go out, fight with Amalek. Tomorrow I will stand on the top of the hill with the rod of God in my hand" (Exodus 17:8). Notice it is the "rod of God" (*Elohim*—the God of power), having switched from Yahweh (the Lord), His personal title. Moses clearly knows that the victory comes from the Lord in warfare.

Moses now takes Aaron and Hur to the top of the hill, and when he holds up his hand to heaven (indicating it is God who is winning the battle) they prevail; when he lowers it, Amalek prevails. As his hands grow weary, Moses sits on a rock and Aaron and Hur lift his hands until Amalek is defeated. Hur is the son of Caleb who later is one of the two spies who bring a good report after spying out Canaan.

After the battle, the Lord instructs Moses, "Write this for a memorial in the book and recount it in the hearing of Joshua, that I will utterly blot out the remembrance of Amalek from under heaven" (verse 14).

Recording the victory over Amalek in a book serves as a perpetual memorial of God's victory over this Canaanite king and a clear judgment on this relative of the Hebrews who refused to respond to the grace of God, brutally attacking His people, instead.

Moses now builds an altar in recognition of the Lord's victory and names it The Lord Is My Banner. Altars are built to offer sacrifices, so he probably offers a sacrifice of thanksgiving, saying, "Because the LORD has sworn: the LORD will have war with Amalek from generation to generation" (verse 16). Once again, the Lord's presence provides for the needs of the Hebrews when there is a crisis.

A new judicial system

When God first calls him to lead His people out of captivity, Moses initially travels with his family until he realizes the dangers they will face. For their safety, he sends them back to his father-in-law Jethro (also known as Reuel), a priest in Midian. The Midianites are descendants of Abraham through Keturah, his second wife after the death of Sarah.

However, Jethro now takes Moses' wife Zipporah and her sons Gershom and Eliezer to the Israelite camp in the wilderness.

When Jethro arrives at Sinai, the mountain of God, Moses goes out to meet him and greets him in the usual Oriental style by bowing and kissing him. Moses then informs Jethro of all that the Lord has done in delivering them from Egypt.

Jethro rejoices and brings a burnt offering and other sacrifices to God. Then Aaron comes with the elders and they all sit down for a communal thanksgiving meal—a banquet with the Lord as the Guest of honor.

The next day Jethro observes Moses sitting as a judge for the people, while the people stand all day. By the evening, Moses and the people are exhausted. Since he is the only judge and the people have to wait patiently to present their case to him, Jethro proposes a solution, creating four administrative levels:

1. Moses will be the advocate before God.
2. Moses will assume a general teaching role.
3. An appeal court system will be established.
4. Moses will serve as the supreme court judge on complex and difficult cases.

Jethro's recommendations are accepted, and Moses chooses able men to be rulers over groups of thousands, hundreds, fifties, and tens. Civil cases are handled by others, while Moses deals with very difficult or religious cases.

As we see by their stories, the patience of the Lord toward His stubborn and complaining people is an amazing divine revelation of His person. Instead of continually punishing Israel for their complaints, He supplies their needs and protects them, ever attempting to grow their faith and reveal His holiness to them. Even Moses has to grow administratively and God patiently accomplishes it through Jethro's counsel.

CHAPTER FORTY-EIGHT

Covenant at Sinai

Based on Exodus 19

Perhaps most of us fail to understand the Ten Commandments because we fail to see that God longs to form a personal relationship with His people—a task that Jesus later fulfills. In fact, part of Christ's mission was to show His people who the Father really is. He says, "He who has seen Me has seen the Father" (John 14:9).

To be able to understand the Ten Commandments we must first understand the broader concept of the covenant. What better way to establish a personal relationship than to come to His people in person? As God does this, He reveals Himself, and His character, attributes, and person to them in a way they can understand a being of such power and love. These personal appearances in the Bible are called theophanies, and His appearance to them on Mount Sinai is a prime example.

As the Bible gives the broad picture of the Creation story in Genesis 1, then gives more details in Genesis 2, we first get the broad picture of the Ten Commandment story in Exodus 19 and 20, followed by more details later on in subsequent chapters.

One plan for every generation

It is June, the third month after leaving Egypt, and the Israelites come to Mount Sinai, where the Lord renews the covenant He made with Abraham, Isaac, and Jacob. In our terminology, this covenant is the plan of salvation.

Centuries before, the Lord promises Abraham three things: seed (Genesis 12:2), land (Genesis 12:1), and that he and his descendants will be a blessing to all the earth (Genesis 12:2, 3). This is essentially His communication to Adam and Eve in the Garden of Eden: seed (Genesis 1:28), land (Genesis 2:8), and that they will be a blessing to the earth (Genesis 2:15).

Moses is familiar with this land, since it is where the Lord revealed

Himself in the burning bush. As he goes up the mountain, the Lord speaks to him, saying, "Thus you shall say to the house of Jacob, and tell the children of Israel: 'You have seen what I did to the Egyptians, and how I bore you on eagles' wings and brought you to Myself. Now therefore, if you will indeed obey My voice and keep My covenant, then you shall be a special treasure to Me above all people; for all the earth is Mine. And you shall be to Me a kingdom of priests and a holy nation.' These are the words which you shall speak to the children of Israel" (Exodus 19:6).

The Lord has treated His people tenderly and in a very special way, as a mother eagle does with her young. He has done it alone, without the help of a foreign god (Deuteronomy 32:11, 12).

The Sinai covenant is essentially the same as the one given to their forefathers, however, the words are a bit different. The Lord promises that He will make them a "kingdom of priests." Notice that a kingdom has land and seed, like the previous statements of the covenant. But now, they will also be a kingdom of priests, indicating they will be a blessing to the earth by being intermediaries between the Lord and man. Essentially, they are to be an evangelistic nation, and a "special treasure" to Him above all people. They will belong exclusively to Him as a "holy nation." The number three in the Bible indicates something of great importance—Christ spent three years in ministry, He was in the grave three days and three nights, and so on. Therefore, the fact that all this happens in the third month after leaving Egypt indicates this event has great importance and is very significant.

To be sure the Israelites comprehend His covenant message, the Lord communicates with His people in a way they will understand. Considering their pagan Egyptian background, He renews His covenant from the mountaintop, since the pagans believe their gods dwell on the tops of mountains. He renews His covenant with a display of awesome power because the pagans think the most powerful god is the chief god. He gives them a suzerainty-type covenant, most commonly used by the Hittites who live in Canaan.

This type of covenant is very different from what we are familiar with today. Instead of an agreement between two equal parties, it is an agreement between a superior (a suzerain, or Hittite king) and an inferior (a vassal, or conquered king). In like manner, God is the Divine King, and His people are vassal kings, sharing in His rulership under Him. The suzerain dictates all the terms of the covenant and the vassals may only accept or reject the terms—the same two choices we have with the divine covenant.

The Hittite suzerainty-type covenant is really a covenant of grace, because the one who will become a vassal has rebelled against the superior king and deserves to die in the thinking of the pagan world. Instead, he is given a chance to live and keep his rulership status as a vassal, if he remains loyal to his superior. The divine covenant is also a covenant of grace, since the Lord gives us eternal life and allows us to share in His rulership, if we remain loyal to Him.

Covenant elements

A suzerainty-type covenant normally has six elements, not all of which are always listed, or given in the same order:

- The preamble identifies who is making the covenant.
- The historical prologue gives the relationship history of the covenant-giver and his recipients.
- The stipulations indicate what is expected of those receiving the covenant.
- The witnesses legalize the covenant.
- The blessings and curse formula lists the blessings one receives by following the covenant, and the curses one suffers, otherwise.
- The provision for public reading provides a periodic reading to ensure the details of the covenant are not forgotten.

Notice how the covenant at Sinai (Exodus 19:3–6) lists four of the elements. The preamble (verse 3b) identifies the Lord as the covenant giver. The historical prologue (verse 4) gives the history of what the Lord did for the Israelites. The stipulations (verse 5a) indicate that the Israelites are to obey the Lord and keep His covenant. The blessings (verses 5b, 6a) promise that the Israelites will be a special people, a kingdom of priests, and a holy nation.

The Lord's covenant and promises are unconditional, since He will keep His promises even if they have to be delayed for a time. On the other hand, the divine covenant is conditional, since the fulfillment of the Lord's promises is based on one's response to His covenant. The Lord's plan of salvation (covenant) is far more marvelous than any rebellious human could ever imagine!

The people's response

Moses calls for the elders of the people and presents the words of the Lord to them. Their immediate response is, "All that the LORD has spoken we will do" (verse 8). This response appears to be sincere on the part of the

Israelites, however it indicates that they gave little consideration as to their inability to keep the divine precepts without the Lord's power.

When Moses reports to the Lord the response of the people, He answers,

"Behold, I come to you in the thick cloud, that the people may hear when I speak with you, and believe you forever. . . .

"Go to the people and consecrate them today and tomorrow, and let them wash their clothes. And let them be ready for the third day. For on the third day the LORD will come down upon Mount Sinai in the sight of all the people. You shall set bounds for the people all around, saying, 'Take heed to yourselves that you do not go up to the mountain or touch its base. Whoever touches the mountain shall surely be put to death. Not a hand shall touch him, but he shall surely be stoned or shot with an arrow; whether man or beast, he shall not live.' When the trumpet sounds long, they shall come near the mountain" (verses 9–13).

The literal washing of the clothes is an outward indication of how inner sanctification is to clean one spiritually in preparation to meeting the Lord. Already, the Lord is testing His people to see whether they will do what He instructs them to do.

On morning of the third day brings thunder, lightning, and a thick cloud. The sound of a very loud trumpet is heard, and the people tremble in fear as the Lord descends upon the top of Mount Sinai in fire and smoke, shaking the mountain greatly. Moses brings the Israelites out of the camp to the foot of the mountain to meet the Lord. He speaks with the Lord, who answers by calling him to come up the mountain. However, when Moses reaches the top, the Lord immediately says, "Away! Get down" (verse 24) and sends him back to keep the people and the priests from breaking through the boundaries around the mountain, lest they be killed. This suggests that there are those foolish ones who don't take the Lord's warning seriously!

Amazing grace

Normally the ancient kings kill a vassal that rebels and replace him. But in a suzerain-type covenant, if the rebellious one repents and remains loyal, by grace he can continue in his position.

In the same way when man rebels, God provides the plan of salvation, restoring the rebellious ones. God's covenant is truly a covenant of grace!

CHAPTER FORTY-NINE

The Ten Commandments—Part 1

Based on Exodus 20

As we begin Exodus 20, the Ten Commandments appear to interrupt the narrative.

Some have suggested that this is an uneasy insertion that is out of place in the story; however, it is entirely appropriate that the multitudes gathered at the base of Mount Sinai, all the fire and smoke, the earthquake, and the ever-louder trumpet blasts build up to God's theophany, or appearance to His people as He addresses them, personally. The Ten Commandments are a revelation of who He is to His people. (For more details see Moses' recounting of the giving of the Ten Commandments in Deuteronomy 5).

God introduces Himself

This is the first time God has appeared before His people, so He gives them His name, "I AM," in the same way He has presented Himself to the patriarchs:

To Abram, He introduces Himself as: "*I am the LORD*, who brought you out of Ur of the Chaldeans, to give you this land to inherit it" (Genesis 15:7, emphasis added).

During his dream of the ladder, He says to Jacob, "*I am the LORD God* of Abraham your father and the God of Isaac; the land on which you lie I will give to you and your descendants" (Genesis 28:13, emphasis added).

As Moses draws near the burning bush, He declares: " '*I AM WHO I AM*.' And He said, 'Thus you shall say to the children of Israel, "*I AM* has sent me to you" ' " (Exodus 3:14, emphasis added).

He also instructs Moses to address the people this way: "Therefore say to the children of Israel: '*I am the LORD*; I will bring you out from under the burdens of the Egyptians, I will rescue you from their bondage, and I will redeem you with an outstretched arm and with great judgments. I will take you as My people, and I will be your God. Then you shall know that *I am the* L*ORD* *your God* who brings you out from under the burdens of the Egyptians" (Exodus 6:6, 7, emphasis added).

Notice how He introduces Himself to the Israelites before giving them the Ten Commandments: "*I am the* L*ORD* *your God*, who brought you out of the land of Egypt, out of the house of bondage," (Exodus 20:2, emphasis added)—echoing His words in Exodus 6:7.

When the Hebrews gather around Mount Sinai in preparation for receiving the divine covenant, the appearance of the Lord is accompanied by lightning, thunder, a great earthquake, and smoke that covers the entire mountain. This causes intense fear in the hearts of the people and they retreat from the mountain, telling *Moses* to speak to them, rather than having the Lord speak to them directly.

Covenant context

To correctly understand the Ten Commandments, we must realize that they're only *one part* of the divine covenant. They are distinguished from the rest of the divine covenant by the fact that the Lord delivers them audibly to Moses and the people, and are written down later on two tablets (tables) of stone.

Exodus 20:2 demonstrates this covenant context when the first two elements of the covenant are given. First, we have the covenant *preamble*, "I am the LORD your God," stating who is giving the covenant. However, the preamble is more than just an identification of who is giving the covenant; it is a self-revelation of who He is—"the LORD" (*Yahweh),* the personal God who intimately knows them and understands all their needs. He is "your God" (Elohim)—the God of power who has not only liberated but also will now make them into a victorious nation through His strong hand.

Second, the covenant historical prologue, "who brought you out of the land of Egypt, out of the house of bondage," gives the history of the relationship between the covenant-giver and the covenant recipients.

Before God expects the Hebrews to know and keep any of His commandments, He first redeems them from Egyptian bondage. In Scripture, freedom from bondage is often used as imagery for freedom from sin. Therefore, God has saved them before He expects them to keep His commandments. *If they try to keep the commandments without recognizing they've already been redeemed, then they're earning salvation by works, and not by grace!*

The third element of the covenant is the *stipulations,* in this case, the Ten Commandments (Exodus 20:3–17). They are what the Lord expects from those who He has redeemed. In light of the fact that He has *already freed* them by grace from bondage, surely, out of gratitude, they won't want to disobey any of His commandments that will affect their relationship with Him.

Relational, not legalistic

We've inherited our understanding of law from the Greeks, who made laws very legalistic. However, God's covenant is primarily *relational,* and *not* legalistic. Our interpretation of the Ten Commandments is that they are all given in *imperative* or *command* form. However, this is somewhat of a distortion of what they really are.

We can interpret each of God's commandments negatively or positively. Since the moral law is always double-sided, it both commands and prohibits—for every moral act is simultaneously a refraining from a contrary mode of action. In light of this, notice that each of the Ten Commandments is also a promise: after having been redeemed, we promise not to commit that sin; while from God's standpoint, it is a promise that if we follow Him, we will *not even want to* sin.

Apodictic law

The Hebrew word for law is *Torah,* from the root, "to teach." The law *teaches* the realities of God's government. The Ten Commandments are often stated as being *apodictic law*—one that prohibits or requires a certain type of behavior. In modern times, this would be the type of law that a congressional body makes that states a *broad* principle that is to be applied, and *not* the narrow specifics.

It needs to be stated that the Ten Commandments are not only connected to law but also are part of the covenant. The apodictic nature and form of the Ten Commandments places them more in the category of covenant than in law. However, the first five books of the Bible often use law and covenant interchangeably.

Notice that the first four commandments affect our relationship with God; they are four in number, and therefore universal. The last six commandments deal with our relationship with God's family; they are six in number because they deal with our relationship with other humans, using the imagery of man being created on the sixth day.

Since these commandments are first given to the ancient Hebrews who have been in pagan Egyptian bondage for so many generations, they are listed *very simply.* In Matthew 22:37–39, Jesus summarizes these same Ten Commandments in two "great commandments" to the more mature: Love for the Lord and love for our neighbor or fellowman.

These commandments are emphasized as the *Lord's commandments,* because He prepares the stones, He writes them, and delivers them. He uses two tablets, using the imagery that two witnesses guarantee truth.

CHAPTER FIFTY

The Ten Commandments—Part 2

Based on Exodus 20

God's law is closely linked with His name or title—Lord (*Yahweh* in Hebrew). This name embodies His nature, person, essence, attributes, and position. It also expresses His personal covenant relationship with His people through His grace, and especially His character of love.

Greek thinking

The ancient Hebrews encompassed the whole law as one concept—the divine law is everything *Yahweh* spoke and embodied. However, our thinking today has been heavily influenced by the Greeks, who fragmented the divine law (and knowledge in general) into multiple specialized categories such as moral law, ethical law, ceremonial law, cultic law, criminal law, and so on.

Most of the Western world bases a large number of their laws on divine law, and generally, these fall under two categories. The first is the *apodictic* or general law, given by a direct command from God reflected in the Decalogue (Ten Commandments) and similar to the laws voted by congress. The second is *casuistic* or case law, which applies the principles of general law to specific situations dealt with in law courts (Exodus 20:18–23:33).

As stated earlier, the important context for the Ten Commandments is found in Exodus 20:2 where God identifies Himself as "I am the LORD." The Lord is known and identified by His acts that are revealed here by His liberating them "out of the house of bondage." Biblically, the word "redeemed" often carries the connotation of being freed physically from slavery, and then saved spiritually from sin. As a result, the Ten Commandments must be understood as the Lord's expectations, to be fulfilled in response to who He is and because of the salvation He has already provided.

No other gods

The first commandment says, "You shall have no other gods before Me" (verse 3), making it clear that He is the one and only God for His people. He alone redeemed them from slavery, and only He should be worshiped.

Recognizing and worshiping only the Lord is the foundation for building a covenant relationship with Him. It prohibits His people from associating with any other god, even though they were used to dealing with over two thousand gods during their captivity. The Egyptian religion has a plethora of gods with the strongest one as the head of the pantheon, but the Hebrews are to have only one God. But the first commandment refers to more than their background of numerous gods in Egypt. It goes back to their history in Eden, where two trees grew in the middle of the garden. The tree of life represented God, and the tree of the knowledge of good and evil represented man. If he chose to eat of the fruit of the tree of the knowledge of good and evil, he exalts himself as another God.

No carved images

Originally, the Ten Commandments were short, and Deuteronomy 4:13 calls them "ten words" in Hebrew. However, the second commandment, given in Exodus 20:4–6, is quite long and detailed, indicating it probably had to be expanded because the people had trouble observing it. It states, "You shall not make for yourself a carved image—any likeness of anything that is in heaven above, or that is in the earth beneath, or that is in the water under the earth; you shall not bow down to them nor serve them. For I, the LORD your God, am a jealous God, visiting the iniquity of the fathers upon the children to the third and fourth generations of those who hate Me, but showing mercy to thousands, to those who love Me and keep My commandments."

While the first commandment specifies *who should be worshiped,* the second gives restrictions on *how He should be worshiped.*

The first commandment already eliminates the worship of other gods, so the second commandment eliminates any images made of the Lord. This commandment clearly addresses the fact that the Hebrews have been affected by their pagan environment.

Elements from the three divisions of the universe (heaven, earth, and water under the earth) have been made into images to be worshiped, representing their Egyptian gods. These images are commonly carved from wood, are overlaid with hammered sheets of silver or gold, and clothed in the finest attire. They can also be made of gold, silver, stone, or clay.

The second commandment is concerned with how these images have been used, and the issue here is power. Images of deities are the means by which they become a present reality for the people. As a result, incantations, spells, and other magical arts can be performed on their followers.

The worshiping of images is inconsistent with how the Lord reveals Himself. He is a "jealous God" that demands exclusive devotion because of what He has done—and is doing—for His people.

Unto the third and fourth generations

The term "jealous" or "zealous" is not to be misunderstood as "envious," "suspicious," or "distrustful." It denotes that He expects complete devotion from His followers. Those who "hate" or are hostile to Him are those who defiantly worship other gods. To these, He visits "the iniquity of the fathers upon the children to the third and fourth generations."

Many have concluded this to be proof of a vengeful spirit, and that *Yahweh's* punishment of a father's sin will last for the next four generations. However, Deuteronomy 24:16 states, "Fathers shall not be put to death for their children, nor shall children be put to death for their fathers; a person shall be put to death for his own sin." Ezekiel 18:2–24 also clearly demonstrates this, when God says that a righteous son shall not bear the guilt of the father, nor a righteous father bear the guilt of his son.

So what is God referring to in "visiting the iniquity of the fathers upon the children to the third and fourth generations"? To the ancient Hebrews, this simply refers to all living members of one household, since married sons live with their father. It is common to have three, and sometimes even four-generations living under the same tent, so a man's entire family suffers from his punishment. In contrast to this one household, *Yahweh* shows mercy to thousands (generations) of those who love Him and keep His commandments. Once more, *Yahweh's* second commandment clearly demonstrates His loving nature.

We should clarify that this commandment is not directed against a pictorial *representation* of things, but rather the *worship* of them. The tabernacle has ornate representation of things that are ordered by God, and they are not to be worshiped.

The name of the Lord

The third commandment says, "You shall not take the name of the LORD your God in vain, for the LORD will not hold him guiltless who takes His name in vain" (Exodus 20:7).

This commandment is linked with how the word "Lord" is used and reverenced in worship and in all aspects of human life. The divine names,

Lord and God, are not really personal names. They are titles that identify who He is by including everything that tells something about Him, such as His attributes, essence, characteristics, and so on. "The LORD (*Yahweh*)" occurs more than sixty-eight hundred times in Scripture, and "God (*Elohim*)" about twenty-six hundred times. Sometimes *God* does not dwell in a place, but instead, His name will dwell in that place—such as the temple in 1 Kings 8:29, "My name shall be there." When we add God's "name" to this list, the impressive total suggests how important these divine names truly are.

To "take the name of the LORD in vain" carries the connotation of nothingness, falsehood, iniquity, and vanity. It drastically diminishes who He is, and His importance in worship and life.

Probably the chief purpose of this commandment is to invoke reverence for God as our Lord and Master. It is a continuation of the main thrust of the first and second commandments. Observing this commandment eliminates careless, irreverent, and profane use of His divine name. It prohibits empty ceremony and formality in worship, false swearing, and careless repetition of His name. However, it does not exclude legitimate oaths, since these are often found in the Bible.

Remember the Sabbath

The fourth commandment admonishes to, "Remember the Sabbath day, to keep it holy. Six days you shall labor and do all your work, but the seventh day is the Sabbath of the LORD your God. In it you shall do no work: you, nor your son, nor your daughter, nor your male servant, nor your female servant, nor your cattle, nor your stranger who is within your gates. For in six days the LORD made the heavens and the earth, the sea, and all that is in them, and rested the seventh day. Therefore the LORD blessed the Sabbath day and hallowed it" (Exodus 20:8–11).

This commandment is the longest of the Decalogue, probably because the Hebrews had more trouble observing it. If this is the case, it explains why so much detail is given. The commandment begins with the word "remember," expressing the sense of "remember without lapse" or "hold as a present and continuing priority."

The word "Sabbath" stems from the Hebrew verb "to rest" or "to cease." Its imagery stems from the seventh day of Creation, when God ceased His labor of the first six days of Creation, and rested on the seventh. It is to be remembered as a day set apart for holy purposes and kept free from the customary work, because it belongs exclusively to the Lord. On the Sabbath, *everybody* is to rest from work, including one's entire family, servants, cattle, and the stranger (or foreigner) who has joined the family of his own free will.

Since the Sabbath belongs to the Lord, He blesses it, makes it holy, and a day of worship. Man is created on the sixth day, and the first full day Adam spends with his Creator is the Sabbath. Since "sanctuary" is defined as God and man together, the first Sabbath becomes the beginning of a "sanctuary in time," where God and man can dwell together in time during the hours of the seventh day.

The fourth commandment is the culmination of the first three commandments. The first tells us *who* should be worshiped, the second tells us *how* He should be worshiped, the third deals with the *One* to be worshiped, and the fourth deals with *who* should worship Him, and *when*.

This commandment legally confirms the Sabbath by the use of two statements—or legal witnesses. The first statement or legal witness is that the Lord created the earth in six days but rested on the seventh. The second statement or legal witness is that He blessed and hallowed it. In ancient Hebrew thinking, the two witnesses guarantee the legality of the Sabbath and why the Lord should be worshiped.

Honoring parents

The fifth commandment is, "Honor your father and your mother, that your days may be long upon the land which the LORD your God is giving you" (verse 12). This commandment gives the principles of life in the divine covenant with the Lord. The first four commandments provide the principles guiding the Hebrews' relationship with the Lord. The last six commandments set forth the principles guiding the Hebrews' relationship with the Lord's human family, and more broadly, the covenant community.

According to the Old Testament, one's first relationship is to the Lord, the giver of life. The second most important relationship is to one's father and mother, who provide for their offspring the gift of life.

The form of the verb "to honor" emphasizes a strong action of giving weight to honor, glory, and esteem. We are to give our parents special deference by the recognition of their importance and love.

The equal status of the mother with the father is significant here, in Leviticus 19:3 the mother is even listed first. This probably stems from the custom that a male spends his first twelve years with his mother in the home and then passes to the male world of his father from then on. The mother controls the home and all its activities, while the father controls the external affairs.

This commandment is the only one that contains a direct promise—"that your days may be long upon the land which the Lord your God is giving you" (Exodus 20:12). This is a significant promise, and a lack of respect for one's parents can just as certainly mean an abrupt end to those days!

No murder

The sixth commandment states, "You shall not murder" (verse 13). In the Old Testament there are seven words for killing, but the one used here is *rasah,* and it occurs over forty times. Of the seven verbs that deal with killing, this is the one that especially involves premeditated and intentional murder of a fellow member of the Lord's covenant community. Its primary reference is religious in the context of the divine covenant, where every relationship is important. However, the verb, in some cases, makes allowances for capital punishment, manslaughter, war killing, and the slaughter of animals. In a broad sense, this commandment applies to any diminishing of the quality of life of an individual in the covenant community through continued abuse of any sort. It is also applicable to situations of anger, resentment, gossip, hatred, contempt, and influencing others to do evil and forfeit eternal life.

No adultery

The seventh commandment is short but very significant. It says, "You shall not commit adultery" (verse 14). The violation of this commandment is often linked by analogy with idol worship. The Hebrew verb is used of both men and women although in Old Testament times with male dominance, adultery is usually charged to women and not men.

Old Testament references to seventh commandment violations include sexual intercourse of a man with the wife of another man; sexual intercourse of a man with the fiancée of another man; and the sexual intercourse of a wife with a man other than her husband. In Matthew 5:27, 28, it includes adultery, fornication, and impurity of every kind in word, act, and thought.

The penalty for adultery was death by stoning or burning. This attitude toward adultery can only be fully understood in view of the fact that more than the integrity of marriage, home, and personal honor are referred to in covenantal relationship with the Lord. The integrity of the Hebrews' relationship with the Lord is at stake. In the Ancient Middle East, adultery was a crime against persons, but in the context of the divine covenant it is even more a great crime against the covenant giver.

No stealing

The eighth commandment states, "You shall not steal" (Exodus 20:15). This commandment prohibits stealing from either a person or confiscating an object. It covers such things as kidnapping and stealing intangibles like dignity, self-respect, rights, and freedom. It is best summed up as a prohibition of stealing of any kind under any circumstances. The context determines that the ultimate penalty for stealing is not the penalty of the community, but the penalty of the Lord—the loss of His presence.

No false witness

The ninth commandment says, "You shall not bear false witness against your neighbor" (verse 16). The language of this commandment connects it to the legal process of the covenant community. In the Old Testament, it is primarily connected to lying testimony in a judicial context. The fact that at least two witnesses are required to sustain a charge indicates that false testimony was a common problem. The reference to lying indicates that this commandment has a broad application of truthfulness, such as speaking evil of another, suppressing the truth, or only speaking part of the truth. As ambassadors for the Lord, the Hebrews had the important responsibility to rightly represent their God as His witnesses to the world.

No covetousness

The tenth commandment states, "You shall not covet your neighbor's house; you shall not covet your neighbor's wife, nor his male servant, nor his female servant, nor his ox, nor his donkey, nor anything that is your neighbor's" (verse 17). The idea of the Hebrew *hamad* is "to desire earnestly," "to long after," "to covet," or "to lust after" someone or something.

This commandment represents a decided advance beyond the morality of ancient law codes. Most codes deal only with the deeds and a few take into account speech, but none deal with regulating thoughts. It confirms the principle that even our thoughts are under the jurisdiction of God's law, and we are responsible for our inner attitudes. It deals with the root of all sin, since it begins with a selfish desire that if left unchecked, always results in a sinful act. The violation of this commandment is a first step that can lead to violation of any one or all the rest of the commandments, making it all encompassing, and descriptive of an attitude rather than a deed.

The commandment sets forth a comprehensive statement of the ownership of property with a list of what belongs to your neighbor: house, wife, male servant, female servant, ox, donkey, or anything that is your neighbor's. It clearly indicates that the ten elements of the Divine Decalogue are relational in respect to the Lord and His covenant community.

The full impact

To receive the full impact of Exodus 20 we need to review its context, emphasis, and result on the people. In Exodus 19, the Hebrews are instructed to gather at the base of Mount Sinai to sanctify themselves in preparation for the third day when the Lord will come down upon the mountain to meet them. On the morning of the third day, He reveals what they understand as the true God, with powerful thunder, lightning, a thick cloud, and a very loud sound of a trumpet. As He makes His appearance (theophany), He declares, "I am the LORD your God"—a self-revelation of everything His name implies.

He reveals that He is their Redeemer, and that His attributes, character, and inner person are all based on the principle of love. Through the commandments, He reveals that He loves them and expects them to love Him and His earthly family in return.

This whole self-revelation is new to them and they are afraid to meet and be close to Him. As a result, they tremble and stand afar off, clearly needing to develop an intimate relationship with their Covenant Giver. The result of their reluctance to meet the Lord is to make Moses the intermediary between the Lord and the people. This separation between the people and their God lasts until Christ comes and the people gain direct access to their Lord.

CHAPTER FIFTY-ONE

The Book of the Covenant

Based on Exodus 20–23

The Hebrews see the frightening sights that accompany the Lord's appearance on Mount Sinai, and they tremble when the Lord speaks the Ten Commandments. Then they say to Moses, "You speak with us, and we will hear; but let not God speak with us, lest we die" (Exodus 20:19). As a result, the Lord speaks to Moses, who speaks to the people, giving what is called the Book of the Covenant (Exodus 20:22–23:33). It is an enlargement and an application of the principles of the Ten Commandments to everyday life.

Images and altars

The first thing covered in the Book of the Covenant concerns the first two commandments, and especially the second, that deals with the worship of the Lord. It is an emphatic command not to make any rival god because He is the Hebrews' only God. No doubt, this is the first thing considered because of the rampant idolatry of the time and the propensity of the Hebrews to indulge in it. They have witnessed the Lord speaking from the top of Mount Sinai, but they do not see His physical form, so they must not entertain any thought of making a material image of Him.

The second thing covered in the Book of the Covenant is the altar, linked with the importance of the presence of the Lord in worship. The essential thing about the altar is that they must avoid making it into a worship object of its own, since God is the all-important One in worship. The altar is to be simple—an earthen one, or one made from uncut field stones, to avoid attracting the attention of the worshipers. The altar is only the location where the worshiper personally enters in the Lord's presence to receive a blessing.

God also directs them not to build steps up to the altar. This prohibition apparently comes because nudity and immodesty are widespread among the pagan priests as they climb and descend the steps to their altars.

Another reason for this restriction for the Hebrew worshiper is that his long garment will trail behind him as he descends, raising it up or catching on the steps and exposing his nakedness. Later, in Ezekiel 43:13–17, God gives construction details for an altar with steps—but only after ordering the priests to wear linen undershorts in Exodus 28:42. The underlying principle here is modesty in the presence of the Lord during worship.

Laws about slaves

In Exodus 21, the laws are called judgments because they deal with justice or judgment. As noted before, the Ten Commandments are classified as apodictic or general law, similar to the laws voted by a legislative body. However, the laws of the Book of the Covenant are classified as casuistic or case law, made by supreme courts, where general law is applied to specific circumstances. Generally, these laws are introduced by *if* or *when,* and conclude with *then,* based on the idea of cause and effect. God's case law for the Hebrews assumes the equality of all citizens, so punishment for crime is not hindered or magnified by class or wealth.

The first of God's judgments or ordinances deals with the issue of slavery, a common practice at this time. One usually is enslaved because of war or economic misfortune, and slaves are generally treated as possessions, rather than as human beings. They are required to perform hard labor, and often receive unmerciful beatings. Slaves have few social privileges—and even fewer rights. So it is very significant that the first of God's judgments deals with this issue in Exodus 21:1–6. Without a doubt, this indicates that slavery greatly violates the principles of the Ten Commandments in respect to human relationships, because it diminishes the dignity of man, made in the image and likeness of God.

Slave rights

While God does not totally abolish slavery at this time, in His great mercy, He takes them as they are and gently leads them to a loftier ideal. Through His judgments, He sets limits on slavery by heavily regulating it.

Hebrew slaves are to receive much more dignity and protection; and after a maximum of six years of service, they even gain their freedom! If the slave begins his enslavement as a married man, his wife is freed when he is.

Later, in Deuteronomy 15, the Hebrew slave's rights are expanded. He is to be called "brother" by his master, and when he is freed, he must be given provisions from his master's flock, threshing floor, and winepress.

This reminds them of their bondage in Egypt and that the Lord redeems that and supplies all their needs. In addition, God promises to bless the slave owner when he releases his slave in Deuteronomy 15:10, saying, "You shall surely give to him, and your heart should not be grieved when you give to him, because for this thing the LORD your God will bless you in all your works and in all to which you put your hand."

The bondservant

Since Hebrew slaves are to be treated well by their masters, it is not unusual for a significant bond to develop between them, resulting in continuous voluntary servitude. When this happens, the master must take him before the judges, who become legal witnesses of the slave's voluntary servitude. Then, in a public ceremony, the slave's master holds the slave's earlobe to the doorpost, and using an awl (a small pointed instrument for making a hole in leather or wood), pierces them with it. In their literal thinking, this permanently attaches the slave to that household.

This ceremony testifies of a changed heart, and becomes a badge of deep love for his master. In the New Testament, Paul, Timothy, James, Peter, and Jude are all called bondservants of Jesus Christ.

The Hammurabi Code

We know of several case law codes from the ancient Middle East that show similarity to biblical laws, however, they do not show equality of all citizens, or that the punishment is not affected by class or wealth.

Perhaps the best known of these is the Code of Hammurabi, a king from the First Babylonian Dynasty who lived 250 or more years before the Sinai case laws. In his code there are different degrees of punishment for slaves, citizens, and nobility. A wealthy man who kills someone suffers no penalty, however, a freeman who kills someone will. Killing a slave brings no penalty, however, if a poor man kills someone, he is put to death.

Obviously, the Lord shows His greater justice by limiting the maximum punishment for a crime to be no greater than the crime itself.

Capital punishment

Four crimes in the Hebrew society call for the death penalty: murder, striking one's parents, kidnapping, and cursing one's parents. This form of punishment is deemed necessary, since the guilty one is a threat to the wellbeing and safety of the entire community.

Humans are created in the image of God, so no amount of money or property can atone for the premeditated loss of human life. The principle governing the death penalty appears to be that leniency will encourage others to commit these crimes. Stoning by the members of the community is the usual form of execution, taking the responsibility off any single individual.

Accidental death is distinguished from intentional murder in that a place of refuge is provided for the slayer, usually at an altar, or later, at one of the cities of refuge. But for intentional murder, even if they cling to the horns of an altar, they must die.

Honoring one's parents echoes the fifth commandment, and is so important in biblical law that merely striking or cursing them is a capital offense! Many think this punishment harsh, but since parents are like God to their children until they reach the age of accountability, cursing one's parents is equal to blaspheming God Himself!

The broader meaning here is the treatment of one's parents with contempt, since this weakens the family structure and increases the possibility that the parents will not be provided with the respect, food, and protection they deserve. It is also very interesting that the law mentions the father and mother together, stressing their basic equality.

Kidnapping also carries the penalty of death. It is not a property offense, since none of those offenses carries the punishment of death. Instead, it is the theft of a human being with the design to sell him into slavery. Even *holding* them is slavery, since they are being forced to stay against their will.

Crimes of violence

There are five cases of assault and bodily injury in God's judgments that result in punishment other than death. The first case is of two men fighting, when one is injured and bedridden but later can walk. The guilty one is acquitted, but must compensate for the loss of the wounded man's time when he cannot work.

The second case is of a master striking his slave. If the slave does not die, the master is acquitted because he is judged to have struck the slave with disciplinary intentions, rather than homicidal ones. This law is considered strange by today's standards, but it must be considered alongside the law against brutality. The master has the right to restore his authority over his slave, since the slave is considered his property. However, he is not allowed to be brutal, and if he mistreats his slaves, they must be set free (see Exodus 21:26, 27).

The third case is of two men fighting and one accidentally striking a pregnant woman who gives birth prematurely. If there is no further injury beyond the premature birth, her husband proposes a fine that must be approved by the judges. However, if the woman suffers further damage, the famous law of retaliation, called the *lex talionis* by the Romans is invoked. Exodus 21:24, 25 states it as "eye for eye, tooth for tooth, hand for hand, foot for foot, burn for burn, wound for wound, stripe for stripe." This law is a stereotype formula stating that the punishment cannot be greater than the crime.

The fourth case is when a slave owner strikes his slave causing permanent injury that affects his ability to work. In this case, the slave may go free. Losing one's slave is designed to make the master think twice before he is abusive.

The fifth case is when an ox is not known to be dangerous, but gores a human. The ox is to be stoned but his owner is acquitted. If an ox is known to be dangerous and gores a man or a woman to death, then the owner is put to death, or pays a sum of money that is equal to the value of the life taken. If an ox gores another man's slave, the ox must be stoned to death, and the slave owner must be paid thirty shekels of silver—the normal price of a slave.

Property loss

If negligence results in the loss or damage to another's property, then full restitution is required. If an animal is killed, the negligent person pays to replace the animal and the dead animal is his.

Loss of oxen

If a man's ox kills another's ox, the live ox is sold with the money divided between them and half of the dead ox is given to each. If the ox is known to be dangerous and not confined, the owner shall pay for the dead ox and the dead animal shall be his.

Loss by theft

A third group of property damage is linked with stealing that echoes the eighth commandment. The punishment for theft is greater than that of negligence. Since the thief directly benefits from his robbery, there is to be a five fold restitution for stealing an ox or a sheep because these animals are involved in the livelihood of the one robbed. If a thief breaks in at night and is killed, the killer is not considered guilty; but if it happens during the day, he *is* considered guilty because there might be witnesses, or he might cry out and others might hear him. If a thief cannot make restitution for his robbery, he is to be sold into slavery as a debtor.

Grazing and fire damage

The fourth group of property damage is of two types: (1) if your livestock graze in another's field or (2) if you start a fire that burns a neighbor's field—you must pay restitution.

Damage of goods entrusted others

The fifth group of property damage deals with four classes of goods entrusted to others. It may be money or articles that a thief steals, that he must restore double when caught. If the thief is not found, then the keeper of the goods must appear before the judges to determine his guilt or innocence.

The second case deals with animals entrusted to another that have been injured or driven off by robbers and go missing. Both parties must appear before God, taking an oath to decide guilt and only God can decide culpability or innocence.

The third case is when the animal is stolen, if the one to whom the animal is entrusted is negligent, he must make restitution.

The fourth case is when the animal is killed by a wild beast, if evidence is presented, no restitution is made.

Various societal laws

If a man seduces an unengaged virgin, he shall pay her father the bride-price and she becomes his wife. If the father refuses to let them marry, then the seducer must still pay the bride-price.

A sorceress is not to be allowed to live. One who has sex with an animal shall die.

Anyone who sacrifices to a foreign god will be destroyed.

The name of foreign gods ought not even be mentioned, since they might influence someone.

You shall not mistreat or oppress a stranger, based on the fact that they were once strangers in Egypt.

If you afflict a widow or a fatherless child (the vulnerable of society), the Lord will hear their cry and cause you to die by the sword.

If you lend money to a Hebrew who is poor, you shall not charge him interest.

However, it must be noted that they did not live in a capitalistic society where interest is very important and wealth is largely concentrated in money. Wealth for the ancients was largely concentrated in goods, services, and property, not in money. The issue for them was that charging interest to their brother was a way of avoiding their responsibility to the poor.

If a day laborer pledged his outer garment as collateral against a full day's work, then the garment must be returned to him at night to serve as his blanket against the night's cold.

God shall not be blasphemed or a ruler cursed.

The firstfruits of everything is to be offered to the Lord whether it be the first of the produce of your land, your sons, or your animals. Sons are to be redeemed by a money payment, but all the others were to be offered as sacrifices to the Lord. The animals are to be with their mother for seven days before sacrificing to give her relief through suckling of her young.

In tune with the covenant purpose, they are to be a holy people. Animals killed by beasts are unclean for food because they are killed by carnivorous animals, and the blood would remain in the flesh.

Justice and neighborliness

Stemming from the ninth commandment, a false report is prohibited and they must avoid following an evil group in a false report. The Hebrews must make impartial judgments with all classes, and not just favor the poor.

They are to help their enemy when his animal goes astray or lies down under an improperly laden burden.

When called to testify between their enemy and someone else, they must not pervert judgment against their enemy. They must keep themselves from false charges and accept no bribes.

A summary statement is given to not oppress an alien, since the Hebrews were themselves aliens in Egypt.

Sacred seasons

The Hebrews must plant and harvest for six years, but on the seventh year they are to give the land a sabbatical, letting it rest with no planting or harvesting of those fields, vineyards, or olive groves. The land needs to rest like man rests on the Sabbath, supplying the poor with food, and allowing what is left over is to be food for the wild animals. In a similar way, man is to work six days and rest on the Sabbath along with his animals and all those in his house—including the alien staying with him.

Three annual feasts are to be observed. The first festival is the Feast of Unleavened Bread, celebrated for seven days, when the only bread eaten is unleavened. This occurs in the spring at the time of the beginning of the barley harvest, and commemorates the exodus from Egypt. This festival also reminds them to be thankful for the beginning of a new crop year.

The second festival is the Feast of Harvest, also called the Feast of Weeks or Pentecost. It comes at the end of the grain harvest, and commemorates the first fruits of their labor. Literally, it means, "sacred feast of sevens [weeks]" in Exodus 34:22, because it comes seven weeks after the harvest of the early grain.

The third festival is the Feast of Ingathering, also called the Feast of Tabernacles. It comes at the end of the harvest of olives and grapes in the autumn, and commemorates the wilderness wanderings.

Three times a year, all males are required to appear before the Lord God to celebrate these feasts, and women and children are to accompany them if they can.

The blood of the Lord's sacrifice is not to be offered with leavened bread, nor is the fat of His sacrifice to remain until morning.

Another law prohibits boiling a young goat in its mother's milk, apparently a reference to a pagan Canaanite practice. This is practiced today in conservative Judaism, where two sets of cooking utensils, sinks, dishes, silverware, and even cabinets are used to keep anything that has touched meat or dairy products apart.

Promises to bring Israel to the promised land

The Lord promises that He will send an Angel before the Hebrews to keep them in the way and bring them into the Promised Land. The Lord's name (His Presence) is in the Angel and if they obey Him, the Lord will open the way through all the territory of the Canaanites by cutting them off. If they serve the Lord, He will bless them with bread and water, eliminate calamities from them, and give them a full life. He will even send hornets to drive out the inhabitants of Canaan in one year, because they may become a snare to the people as they inhabit the Promised Land.

The Book of the Covenant is the Lord's means of providing the Hebrews with a permanent document of who He is and how the people are to live under His rulership. It expresses His values, the essence of His character, and the norms of His rulership. It clearly emphasizes the value of human life because we were created in His image. It not only gives the Ten Commandment, but also shows how to apply their principles to everyday life. It provides applications of these principles into criminal law. It stresses that in true justice there must be equality of all individuals with no distinction between wealth or class. In simple terms, the covenant is based on love—for God and their fellow men.

In the end, God's promises in the covenant will only be a reality, if they faithfully follow and obey Him.

CHAPTER FIFTY-TWO

The Festivals of Thanksgiving

Based on Exodus 23

God saves Israel from Egyptian bondage, and then provides His covenant to free them from their bondage to sin. However, He knows that human thankfulness is absolutely necessary for maintaining a relationship with Him, so He establishes three yearly festivals (Exodus 23:14–17). They are based on the agricultural year Israel must observe in the future, both when the sanctuary is built, and when they are in the Promised Land. These festivals are linked to both their seasonal agricultural harvests and the great historical events of their redemption history. All men are to attend every feast, along with the women and children, if possible.

The Feast of Unleavened Bread

The first is the Feast of Unleavened Bread—beginning right after the celebration of the Passover. The Passover is not mentioned in this passage of Scripture because this feast is an *agricultural festival* in which unleavened bread is also eaten. It begins on the fifteenth day of the first month of Abib on their religious calendar, which corresponds to March or April on ours, today. This is the time of spring lambing, and requires the eating of unleavened bread for seven days, from the fifteenth to the twenty-first of the month.

The first day of the feast is a festival Sabbath, a day of rest with no heavy work and a holy convocation. The last day of the feast is on the twenty-first, where everything done on day fifteen is repeated.

There are two meanings to the unleavened bread. First, it commemorates their hasty exodus from Egypt; and second, leaven must not be used in the bread because it is a symbol of sin that spreads through the whole body—just as yeast does throughout the dough. The instruction to not use leavened bread in the exodus from Egypt stems from the fact that the

Hebrews are to take dough without leaven because they don't have time to knead it and let it rise in their hasty exit.

Barley has the shortest growing season of the grains the Hebrews regularly use. It is planted in winter, and is the first grain to mature. The Hebrews are to take a sheaf of barley and wave it before the Lord on the second day of the feast in thankfulness, indicating that the Lord is responsible for sustaining their lives. In addition to the wave sheaf, a one-year-old, male lamb is to be offered as a burnt offering, along with a grain offering of two-tenths of an ephah (about seven quarts) of fine flour and a drink offering of one-fourth hin (about 2.5 pints) of wine as a sweet aroma.

The Feast of Harvest

The second festival is the Feast of Harvest (also called the Feast of Weeks.) It occurs seven weeks after the Passover (in our May or June), at the time of the grain harvest of wheat and spelt. These grains are planted in the fall, and the spring rains, called the latter rains, mature them into a plentiful harvest. Scripture says this feast is to occur fifty days after the first day of Unleavened Bread. Although they call it fifty days, it is seven weeks in our thinking, since they count from the beginning date and also add the day of the new festival to the number 49. In the same manner, a week with a new festival is stated as being eight days later, since the new festival, in their thinking, is the eighth day.

This feast lasts only one day, and in gratitude to the Lord for the harvest, two barley loaves are baked with leaven and presented before Him as gifts (Leviticus 23:17).

Accompanying the barley loaves is a whole burnt offering, consisting of seven unblemished one-year-old lambs, one young bull, two rams, and a grain offering of two-tenths of an ephah (about seven quarts) of fine flour, mixed with oil. It is baked with leaven, since this is to be a joyous occasion with no restrictions. A drink offering is also to be brought, consisting of one-fourth of a hin (about 2.5 pints) of wine. In addition, a young goat is to be sacrificed as a sin offering, and two one-year-old male lambs as a peace offering. Then a holy convocation is called and no heavy work is to be done on that day. This festival is considered the first fruits of the full harvest of the year, and celebrates all of the agricultural bounties of field, orchard, and vineyard.

The Feast of Tabernacles

The third festival is called by three different names: The Feast of Tabernacles, The Feast of Booths, and The Feast of Ingathering. It occurs in the seventh month of Tishrei and lasts for eight days, starting on the fifteenth and ending on the twenty-first.

This joyous agricultural festival comes in our October or early November, after the fall harvest of olives and grapes. The people are to make booths of tree branches and live in them during the festival. They are to be constructed like the temporary shelters that will later be erected in Canaan, enabling them to live there during the harvest and protect their fields from both humans and animals. The booths have roofs, but generally one side is left open.

A holy convocation occurs at the beginning and end of the festival, when no regular heavy work is to be performed. The great day of judgment, called the Day of Atonement has just passed, and they have received assurance that their sins are forgiven and that the Lord accepts them.

The number of animals sacrificed during the festival is extensive. On each of the first seven days, two rams and fourteen male lambs are sacrificed, along with the required grain and drink offerings. In addition, on the first day, thirteen bulls are sacrificed, twelve on the second, and one less on each of the days leading to the seven bulls sacrificed on the seventh day—a total of seventy bulls in seven days! On the eighth day, one bull, one ram, and seven male lambs are sacrificed, along with the required grain and drink offerings. In each of the days of the festival, a male goat is also sacrificed as a sin offering, along with the normal daily offerings (Numbers 29:12–38).

The Lord provides

The three great agricultural festivals of the year have their context in the self-revelation of the Lord to the Hebrews. He has literally revealed what He has done for them, what He is doing, and what He will do. These festivals reveal who He is through their literal celebrations, sacrifices, and offerings.

When the Hebrews travel to the sanctuary in the future to celebrate the three great agricultural feasts, they must leave their homes and land unprotected from thieves and invaders, trusting in God for protection. These festivals are designed to help fulfill their social needs. They also strengthen their relationship with God by reminding them of how He has redeemed them from bondage, how He provides for their salvation, and how He sustains them with a bountiful harvest. The Lord is having the Hebrews offer to Him an extensive amount of their wealth to make it plain that He is the one who provides, saves, and blesses. It is not their wisdom and hard work that makes them prosperous, and if they truly understand what He is doing for them, they will burst forth in great thanksgiving to the Lord!

CHAPTER FIFTY-THREE

Promises Fulfilled

Since the Hebrews are literal thinkers, God communicates with them in literal terms that portray the true spiritual reality. After Adam and Eve sin, God promises redemption through the seed of the woman (Genesis 3:15), and this is ultimately fulfilled through the Messiah, Jesus Christ. Each ritual, festival, and sacrifice foreshadows the Messiah, and will no longer be needed when He comes.

Pointing forward

The Lord God clothes Adam and Eve with garments of skin after they sin, graphically portraying that the Redeemer will ultimately cover their nakedness with His perfect and sinless robe of righteousness.

The sacrificial system is already functioning when Abel brings a lamb from the firstborn of his flock as a sacrifice to the Lord—representing the Messiah, who must die. As Noah comes out of the ark, he builds an altar and offers burnt offerings to the Lord in thankfulness for the salvation of his family.

The Lord calls Abram out of Ur, leads him to Canaan, and establishes His covenant with him, promising seed, land, and to make him a blessing to all people (Genesis 12:2, 3). The seed will be his descendants, but the principal One will be Christ. The land will initially be Canaan, but once God's sovereignty is established, it will ultimately be the whole earth. The blessing will be the spreading of the knowledge of the true God and His salvation for all who accept Him.

The Lord liberates His people from Egypt and leads them to Sinai, where He establishes His covenant with them. This covenant is the plan of Salvation, portraying, in a literal way, how it works by His grace and their faith.

The Lord instructs them to build a literal sanctuary for Him to dwell among them and gives detailed instructions for various offerings and rituals. Priests are established for the daily service of the sanctuary, and a High Priest is named to officiate on the Day of Atonement. Annual feasts are established, such as the Feast of Unleavened Bread (Passover), the Feast of Harvest (Pentecost), and the Feast of Ingathering (Tabernacles). But while God instructs the Hebrews to keep these feasts, He also wants them to understand that each of them point to the Messiah.

Should the feasts be observed by Christians?

Some Christians believe that the three great agricultural feasts should be observed, since they provide regulations for specific times and ways of thanksgiving to the Lord for what He's done in providing food. However, *all the sacrifices, offerings, rituals, and festivals end when the Messiah becomes their complete fulfillment.*

Animals will no longer need to be sacrificed, since Jesus Christ is the real sacrificial Lamb (1 Corinthians 11:28). Sacrifices will no longer need to be repeated, since Christ's sacrifice is once for all (Hebrews 9:28).

There will be no need for the grain, olive, and grape festivals of Unleavened Bread, the Feast of Harvest, or the Feast of Ingathering, since Christ declares, "I am the bread of life" (John 6:35) and "I am the living water" (see John 7:38). The Lord's Supper, or Communion, will replace the old feasts, and His true followers will express their extreme thankfulness through this celebration.

No longer will the wave sheaf of first fruits need to be offered, since He becomes the Wave Sheaf for the full harvest of the righteous at His resurrection.

No longer will there be need of Unleavened Bread because He offers Himself without spot to God (Hebrews 9:14).

The sanctuary will no longer be needed, because in Christ's incarnation, He is the sanctuary—both divinity and humanity dwell in His Person. In Revelation 21:22 the Lord God Almighty and the Lamb are the temple. Christ comes to dwell with His people, making God's people His true temple. He will dwell *within* them (1 Corinthians 6:19).

Fulfillment

The book of Hebrews emphasizes how Jesus Christ is the fulfillment of what was given at Sinai. No longer will there be need for human, mortal priests, because Jesus Christ is both our common priest and our High Priest, interceding for us (Hebrews 7:15–17; 8:3–5; 1 John 2:1).

No longer will there be a need for the previous covenant, because there is a new one (Hebrews 8:13), based on better promises (Hebrews 8:6).

No longer will the Law need to be read every seven years because of our forgetfulness. Instead, God's law will be in our minds, and written on our hearts in Jesus' new covenant (Hebrews 8:10).

No longer will the old sanctuary need to function with its sacrifices and services, since they are all replaced by Jesus Christ (Hebrews 9:11–28).

If it is abundantly clear that Christians should no longer offer animal sacrifices, in the same manner, it should be abundantly clear they should no longer observe the requirement of keeping the annual feasts.

All the old things of the sanctuary and festivals are but a shadow of the good things to come. Every one of God's promises *have been fulfilled* through Jesus Christ, our Savior, and our Redeemer! *Our thanksgiving and rejoicing should only be centered in Christ the Messiah, and what He has done for us.*

CHAPTER FIFTY-FOUR

The Blue Stone

Based on Exodus 24

The long narrative that began in Exodus 19 of the events at Mount Sinai is interrupted with the Ten Commandments of Exodus 20:1–17. Then it is resumed in Exodus 20:18–21, and again interrupted with the judgments of the Book of the Covenant recorded in Exodus 20:22–23:33. Finally, in Exodus 24, the narrative is again resumed and reaches its conclusion with the ratification of the covenant. After this, the Lord promises, "Behold, I send an Angel before you to keep you in the way and to bring you into the place which I have prepared" (Exodus 23:20).

Ratifying the covenant

Moses tells the people all the words of the Lord and all of the judgments, and they all answer, saying, "All the words which the LORD has said we will do" (Exodus 24:3). Then Moses writes down all the words of the Lord to preserve them. Through this act, he initiates the terms of the covenant agreement in preparation for its ratification.

Next, Moses erects an altar representing the presence of the Lord, and twelve pillars to represent the tribes in the covenant ratification. Both parties have come together to solemnly pledge their allegiance to each other through a written agreement and a sacrificial act.

Now, Moses sends young men, who apparently are firstborn, to offer burnt offerings and sacrifice peace offerings. The burnt offerings symbolize personal consecration and self-surrender, while the peace offerings signify a renewed fellowship between the Lord and His people. A portion of the peace offering is sacrificed, and the remainder serves as a meal that consummates the covenant agreement between the Lord and His people.

Half the blood of the sacrifices, representing the life of the victim, is sprinkled on the altar—a symbol that binds the Lord to the terms of the covenant. Moses reads the words of the Book of the Covenant, and again, the people say, "All that the LORD has said we will do, and be obedient" (verse 7). This public reading of the terms of the covenant is always a part of a covenant ratification or renewal. Then the other half of the sacrificial blood is sprinkled on the people, binding them to the terms of the covenant. The concept of sprinkling the blood on both parties of the covenant makes it clear that if either party breaks the covenant, the fate of the sacrificial victim will be theirs.

The blue stone

Now, the Lord says to Moses, "Come up to the LORD, you and Aaron, Nadab and Abihu, and seventy of the elders of Israel, and worship from afar. And Moses alone shall come near the LORD, but they shall not come near; nor shall the people go up with him" (verses 1, 2).

Nadab and Abihu are the two oldest sons of Aaron, and are the next in line to be high priests. The seventy elders are the representatives of the twelve tribes, and the number 70 apparently is derived from the seventy that went into Egypt in the time of Joseph, representing Israel as a nation. They may also be the elders that Jethro recommended to help Moses when the people brought cases to him for judgment.

Moses is to come near to the Lord by going farther up the mountain to be alone with Him, while the others are to stay behind. He alone is to be the mediator between the Lord and the people.

Those who go up the mountain "saw the God of Israel. And there was under His feet as it were a paved work of sapphire stone, and it was like the very heavens in its clarity" (verse 10). Since man cannot look on God directly, they apparently see the glory of His presence, similar to the manifestation of the cloud that led Israel. Notice the sapphire stone they stand on is blue and resembles "the very heavens." In fact, it is stated to have the likeness of God's throne in Ezekiel 1:26 and 10:1. This is linked with a pavement of sapphire that has been attested to have been used in biblical times as trim in royal audience chambers. It is one of the most precious stones of ancient times, and the legendary building material for the dwelling places of the gods.

The mention of the heavens, the color of the stone, and the fact that the leaders of Israel are up the mountain meeting with the Lord, link the color of the sapphire stone with the dwelling place of the Lord. Since the paved work of sapphire stone is under His feet, it indicates that it serves as the foundation of His dwelling place and government.

The leaders of Israel are with the Lord on Mount Sinai and they confirm the covenant of grace by eating and drinking in the presence of the Lord in the traditional meal that takes place at the conclusion of a treaty or covenant between two parties. This indicates that a close relationship has been established between the Lord and His people as the divine covenant is legally sealed.

The tablets of stone

Now, the Lord calls Moses to come farther up the mountain alone, so He might give him the tablets of stone containing the Ten Commandments. The Hebrew text literally reads, "I will give you tablets of the stone," and the definite article, "the" precedes the noun, "stone." Notice that the only stone that has been mentioned is the sapphire stone. This means that the Ten Commandments are carved out of the blue sapphire that makes up the Lord's standing platform and throne. It makes the tablets of stone of the Ten Commandments blue in color, and clearly links them with the Lord's throne. It indicates that the commandments are identical to the foundational principles of the Lord's government.

The Ten Commandments are recorded on the front and back of two tablets of stone (Exodus 32:15) by the finger of God. Writing them down in stone makes them as permanent and important as possible to the ancients. The fact that there are two tablets of stone serve, in their thinking, to be two witnesses—making them absolutely true.

After Moses and the leaders eat their meal on Mount Sinai, they return to the camp; but soon the Lord calls Moses to come up again to receive the Ten Commandment tablets. As Moses prepares to go up, he tells the elders to wait until he returns. Aaron and Hur will be with them, if any problems arise.

Moses and his assistant, Joshua, begin the climb, even as the glory of the Lord rests on the mountain in the form of a cloud. For six days Moses prepares to meet the Lord, then, on the seventh day, He calls Moses out of the midst of the cloud.

The glory of the Lord is now a consuming fire on top of the mountain to the Israelites, but Moses goes into the midst of the cloud, well up the mountain, into the very presence of the Lord. He stays there forty days and nights as the Lord reveals the plan of the sanctuary, along with the details of its construction and function.

The long narrative of Exodus 19–24 gives the whole story of the Lord revealing Himself in a theophany, speaking the Ten Commandments, and giving the judgments of the Book of the Covenant. The people respond, and the confirmation and ratification of the covenant is completed through the sprinkling of blood and the communal meal. The manner of the giving of the covenant, its general nature, and the procedure for its ratification are all very familiar to the Hebrews. The Lord reveals Himself and communicates His message to them in their context.

The Ten Commandments are shown to be the eternal principles that the Lord's cosmic government is based on, and because of the people's promises and the nature of the ratification of the covenant, they have the solemn responsibility to remain within the covenant terms.

When seen through the eyes of the ancients, the giving of the covenant has significant and solemn symbolic meaning. The Hebrews know from their history that cruelty, death, and alienation from the Lord followed Adam and Eve's transgression. They understand that the covenant the Lord is making at Mount Sinai is characterized by grace, love, and eternal life, but if rejected, it will result in eternal death. The covenant is designed to reunite them with the Lord.

Sanctuary parallels

Before sin enters, Adam and Eve are clothed with the light of the Lord and walk and talk with Him daily. The Garden of Eden is their first sanctuary: the land outside Eden's gates represents the sanctuary court, the garden corresponds to the Holy Place, and Eden is the equivalent of the Most Holy Place. Now, Mount Sinai is their present sanctuary. The base of the mount is their sanctuary court; the lower part of the mountain is their Holy Place, and the upper part of the mountain, where Moses is called, is the Most Holy Place.

The Garden of Eden was also the first sanctuary in time, since man was created on the sixth day, and spent the entire seventh day with his Creator. Imagery of Creation is used as Moses is up the mountain for six days, and then, on the seventh day, he goes into the cloud in the presence of the Lord, as if experiencing the time with the Lord of the Sabbath.

Moses stays up on the mountain forty days and nights, corresponding to what the Messiah will do when He fasts for that whole period. In the same manner, it seems reasonable to expect that Moses also fasts for the whole period he is with the Lord.

CHAPTER FIFTY-FIVE

God's Sanctuary and Royal Palace

Based on Exodus 25–27; 30; 36–38; and 40

While Moses is up Mount Sinai with the Lord for forty days and nights, He reveals to him the description of the sanctuary, its construction and purpose. In Exodus 25:8 He says, "And let them make me a sanctuary; that I may dwell among them." This sanctuary is more than a structure; it embodies the whole process of making the covenant a reality. Its primary function will be to unite sinful man with a holy God, since sin has separated them. All the structure, articles of furniture, clothing and function of the priests, offerings, rituals, and special services are designed to teach each aspect of the plan of salvation for sinful man *in a literal manner.*

The sanctuary

The Hebrew word for "sanctuary" is only used for Israel's sanctuary and never for a heathen temple. The Hebrew word for "dwell" means to be a permanent resident with His people. Even the alternate term for the sanctuary is "tabernacle," which stems from the Hebrew verb, "to dwell." It will be a dwelling place for the Lord in the midst of His people, rather than a building in which to congregate for corporate worship. Since the sanctuary will be portable, it will go wherever His people move. This is different from the heathen gods and temples, which are fixed in their region or country.

Precious materials

The Lord first tells Moses to instruct the people to bring a freewill offering of precious items that will be used in the building of the sanctuary. There are fourteen different items mentioned, echoing the number seven of Creation, or multiples of it. These items are: gold; silver; bronze; blue, purple, and scarlet thread; fine linen; goat hair; ram skins dyed red; badger skins; acacia wood; oil; spices; and onyx stones. These represent a catalogue of opulence: the finest metals, the finest fabrics, the finest leathers, the finest wood, the finest oil, the finest incense, and the finest semiprecious stones.

There are many interesting facts about the precious materials used by the ancients. The dyes used in the colored yarns are very expensive. In fact, it is said that one gram of pure purple dye is derived from the secretions of ten thousand murex shellfish. The dye for scarlet is derived from the eggs and bodies of insects that are dried and ground into powder to produce the bright red color. The fine linen is produced from beaten flax, containing more threads per inch than the most finely woven linen fabrics of today. The Hebrew word for "badger skins" has also been translated as "sea cows," and "seals." The acacia wood is darker and harder than oak, making it a material that wood-eating insects won't attack. The spices used for anointing oil in the tabernacle are myrrh from sap of a balsam bush; cinnamon from bark of a cinnamon tree; cane from the root of a reed plant; and cassia from the dried flowers of a cinnamon tree.

Most of these items are very expensive—not the type of items that former slaves would naturally have; so the only logical explanation is that the Hebrews receive all this wealth from the Egyptians when they flee Egypt. Many of these items have probably been originally imported from other countries.

The sanctuary

The sanctuary is portrayed to the ancient Hebrews as both a sanctuary and a royal palace. As a royal palace, it has two rooms and an outer court. The innermost room is the king's throne room and the adjacent outer room is the king's living quarters with the necessary articles of furniture. In front of the living quarters is an outer court, as the palaces or rich men would have.

As a sanctuary or tabernacle, it is also the Lord's temple, with a courtyard and two rooms known as the Holy Place and the Most Holy Place. The sanctary is holy because it is the place where the Lord's presence dwells. It is where the Hebrews will come to meet their Lord in worship, and where they will receive salvation.

The courtyard

The Lord directs Moses to make the courtyard 150 feet long and 75 feet wide. It will completely surround the Holy Place and the Most Holy Place, with half of its square footage being in front of the tabernacle, and the other half along the sides and behind the tabernacle. It will be surrounded with a fine linen curtain seven-and-a-half feet high, about half the height of the outer walls of the two rooms of the tabernacle.

The courtyard serves the tabernacle in several ways: it is a barrier to prevent unlawful approach, it is a positive line of demarcation between the world and the presence of the Lord, and it is the only entrance to approach the Lord. The opening of the sanctuary courtyard is on the east side, reflecting the east gate of the Garden of Eden where Adam and Eve came to worship the Lord after sin. It is interesting to note that the sanctuary is deliberately positioned so the people will turn their backs to the rising sun (a deliberate rejection of pagan sun worship) as they come to worship the Lord.

The Lord is always portrayed as living in the East, and there are many instances where this is revealed. It is where Venus, the "Bright and Morning Star" of Revelation 22:16, rises in the morning (representing Jesus); it is also the source of the "east wind" referred to in Hosea 13:15 as "the wind of the LORD." This east wind brings in the locust plague in Egypt, parts the Red Sea for the Hebrews, and blows hot on Jonah's head many years in the future as he sits outside of Nineveh waiting for its destruction.

Inside the courtyard is the altar of whole burnt offering where sacrifices are made to the Lord. The altar is made of acacia wood, stands at four-and-a-half feet high and is seven-and-a-half feet square. It is overlaid with bronze and has a bronze grate that divides the altar into equal lower and upper parts. At each corner of the altar are four horns that are part of the four corner posts.

To the ancients, a horn takes its meaning from animals and symbolizes power, strength, and protection. Therefore, when a man grabs the horns of the altar while fleeing from an enemy, they provide protection from danger.

For the Hebrews, the meaning of the altar stems from the story of Abel when he brings his offering to the Lord. His sacrifice foretells the death of the Messiah, bringing salvation to sinful man. It is also linked with the fact that when Adam and Eve sin and find themselves naked, the Lord clothes them with animal skins from animals that must be killed.

Between the altar and the entrance of the Holy Place is the laver used for washing the hands and feet of the priests before they serve at the altar or enter the Holy Place. Made of bronze from women's polished mirrors (Exodus 38:8), the laver guarantees the cleanliness and purity of the priests while serving in the presence of the Lord.

Later, in Solomon's Temple, it is called the "sea," and its symbolism appears to stem from the Flood story that cleansed and purified the earth for the Lord.

The Holy Place

The outer room of the sanctuary building is the Holy Place. It is rectangular in shape—thirty feet long, fifteen feet wide, and fifteen feet high. Inside the Holy Place, on the left or south side, is the seven-branched golden lampstand.

The lampstand is not cast in a form, but is hammered instead from a single block of pure gold weighing a talent (about seventy-five pounds). It is patterned after an almond tree bursting into bloom—the first tree to flower in spring. It has three branches protruding from each side, and one straight up. The tip of each branch contains a cup for oil, imitating an almond flower.

For the Hebrews it has multiple symbolic meanings. First, since its purpose is to provide light, it represents the Lord—who provides light the very first day of Creation. It also links it with the almond tree—the first to put forth blossoms in the spring. Second, the lampstand is to burn continually, symbolizing the continual light of the Lord's presence. And finally, since it is a tree, it symbolizes the tree of life that portrays God as the life-giver and sustainer.

On the right or north side of the entrance is the table of showbread, or the table of the Presence. It is three feet long, twenty-seven inches high, and one-and-a-half feet wide. It is made of acacia wood overlaid with gold, decorated with golden beading all around, and encircled by a golden border.

Four kinds of containers of pure gold are placed on the table. The first is a dish or plate where the twelve loaves of showbread are placed in two stacks of six. The second is a small pan on which pure frankincense is placed as an accompaniment offering to the bread of the Presence. The third is a pitcher for wine of the libation, or drink offering, and the final container is a bowl in which the drink offering is poured.

In the New Testament Greek of Mark 2:26, the bread is literally called "the bread of the presentation," meaning the bread presented to God that represents the twelve tribes of Israel. These twelve loaves symbolize a perpetual thank offering to God from the tribes for the blessings of life they receive daily from the Lord.

The concept of presence has more symbolism than just the presence of the twelve tribes before the Lord. There is also the reciprocal concept of the continual presence of the Lord with His people. This symbolism stems from the basic concept of the sanctuary, where the Lord and His people dwell intimately, together in each other's presence.

Later, when the tabernacle and the priesthood are established, the priests eat the twelve loaves and replace them with fresh ones. This adds to the symbolism of the Lord providing spiritual food and drink for His people.

Finally, it may refer back to the covenant meal on Mount Sinai, giving the people a weekly opportunity to reflect and reaffirm their relationship with the Lord in joyful communion.

The third item of furniture is the altar of incense, located in the western side of the Holy Place, next to the veil in front of the Most Holy Place. Although its primary function is linked with the Most Holy Place, it is placed here so the priests have daily access to it.

It is also made of acacia wood overlaid with gold, is eighteen inches square and stands three feet high. It is similar in shape to the altar of burnt offering, right down to the horns.

Twice each day, during the morning and evening prayers, incense is offered on this altar, and since it is located next to the low veil separating the Holy Place from the Most Holy Place, the incense ascends over the curtain into the presence of the Lord. The smoke from the burning of the incense hovers over the Most Holy Place and serves to mask the Lord's presence from human eyes.

On the Day of Atonement, the blood from the special sacrifice of the day is put on the horns of the altar of incense as part of the ceremony, making both the blood and the altar symbols of cleansing.

Because Scripture links the daily burning of the incense with the morning and evening devotionals, it symbolizes the prayers of the saints; and since the incense and smoke are both linked with the Lord's dwelling place in the Most Holy Place, they also symbolize His presence.

The Most Holy Place

The Most Holy Place is the compartment of the sanctuary located to the west of the Holy Place. Its form is a cube, since its length, breadth, and height are each fifteen feet.

The only article of furniture in this compartment is the ark of the covenant that is made of acacia wood overlaid with gold inside and out, being about three-and-three-quarters feet long, and about two-and-one-quarter feet wide and high. The cover is called the mercy seat, where one seeks and obtains divine mercy. Atonement is made here on the yearly Day of Atonement. Around the top of the mercy seat is a crown of gold. Inside the ark are the two tablets of the Ten Commandments. They are called the Testimony, and serve as the foundational principles of the Lord's government.

On the top are two golden cherubim with their wings stretched out over the mercy seat. Their bodies are turned toward each other with their faces bowed down toward the mercy seat. The position of their faces symbolizes the reverence of the heavenly host for the law of the Lord, and the plan of redemption that the mercy seat symbolizes.

In the thinking of the ancients, the sanctuary with the Lord as its Divine Being should reflect His central role by mapping His sanctuary into zones of progressive holiness. Remember that the court completely surrounds the two compartments of the sanctuary. With this in mind, the altar of whole burnt offering is located in the exact center of the eastern part of the court and symbolizes how the Lord achieves redemption for sinful man. The ark of the Testimony is located in the exact center of the western part of the court in the exact center of the Most Holy Place. It portrays the place of the Lord's presence in the midst of His people, and the holiest part of the whole sanctuary.

Looking at the sanctuary from man's standpoint, the closer he gets to the divine, the holier the ground. The courtyard is the closest a common Hebrew can physically come to where the Lord dwells. Then, only the priests may enter the next holier space—the Holy Place. Finally, the Most Holy Place is strictly restricted to only the high priest, who may enter the abode of the Lord once a year.

The sanctuary is also depicted as a royal palace because the Lord has a dual role of both Redeemer and King. The Most Holy Place is the throne room of His royal palace. The only article of furniture here is the ark of the Testimony that has no back above the mercy seat, or arms on the sides, as a human throne would have. The Bible explains the Lord's throne well with these words, "heaven is My throne, and the earth is My footstool" (Isaiah 66:1). His throne is cosmic, with the earth being the lower part of it and serving as the footstool. A person seeking mercy from a king comes and bows down at his feet to plead for mercy.

In the typical ancient Near Eastern manner, the throne is protected by guards that are depicted here as the two covering cherubim. The curtains of the Most Holy Place that surround the ark have cherubim portrayed on them as well.

The Holy Place with its articles of furniture is the living quarters of the king. Since it is a royal palace, the finest materials are used and the articles of furniture are made of, or overlaid, with pure gold. The golden lampstand is its source of light. The table of showbread has food and drink, but unlike heathen temples, no food or drink is ever provided for the Lord. Naturally, both the Holy and Most Holy Places must smell good, so the air is pleasantly scented with the spices and perfumes that come from the altar of incense.

The court is the only entrance, giving the palace both protection and control over who is allowed into the presence of the King. It has a place to wash hands and feet so that no one who is dirty enters the palace or sees the King. It also offers the people an opportunity to bring gifts, such as one of their own animals for the King.

For the ancients to understand their Lord, His sanctuary is described in very literal, everyday terms. The sanctuary is His house in the midst of His people; He has come to permanently dwell with them. This is the Lord's way of expressing His desire to reunite them to Him after the separation caused by sin.

As their Lord God, He is their Ruler in the form of both their King and their Lord. Spiritually, He saves them by providing a remedy for their sins as they are reunited with their Lord.

As their Lord and King, He is their Ruler. This is why His sanctuary is so aptly pictured as a residence, a sanctuary, and a palace.

CHAPTER FIFTY-SIX

Representing the Messiah

Based on Exodus 28

The common priest and the high priest of Israel both represent the Messiah and His roles in the sanctuary, and God uses them to communicate the process of salvation to these literal-thinking ancients.

Only Aaron and his four sons Nadab, Abihu, Eleazar, and Ithamar are to serve as priests in the sanctuary. Aaron is the high priest and his sons are common priests. A hereditary succession of future generations of priests stemming from Aaron is established, and thus the lineage will strictly be from the tribe of Levi, and more specifically, through Aaron. These priests are some of the few in Israel that are literate, serving as teachers of the divine law.

Special garments to be worn only by priests enhance their symbolic role, and are only to be worn when they are on duty in the sanctuary. Priests have certain rights and responsibilities that no other Hebrew has. A portion of the sacrifices is set aside as food for them. They cannot own land or perform nonpriestly functions. They are held to a higher standard and expected to provide an example to the people that corresponds to their position.

The common priest's role and garments

The priest is a common Levite man—just as the Messiah will be human through His incarnation. Priests are set apart for holy service to the Lord— just as the Messiah's holy service will bring about salvation.

The clothing of the common priests is linen, like the high priest's, but of somewhat inferior quality. They are first clothed with linen trousers or undergarments that reach from the waist to the knee. Then a one-piece linen tunic is worn over the trousers, covering his entire body from the neck to about the feet. The tunic has long sleeves that reach to the wrists—just as the white, one-piece linen robe the Messiah will wear.

The priest wears a sash or girdle of white twined linen around his waist, and a white linen turban on his head, its color representing the purity needed to serve in the tabernacle.

The common priest's work corresponds to the Messiah's work on earth. He's the spiritual leader serving as intermediary between sinners and God—just as the Messiah will be the intermediary between sinners and God.

The priest's religious rituals deal with sacrifices and offerings that portray forgiveness for sin and its transfer from the sinner to the sanctuary. In turn, the Messiah will pay the penalty for sin and forgive the sinner, transferring his sins to the heavenly sanctuary.

The priests teach the people the Lord's statutes, judgments, and His law, while the Messiah will teach the principles of God's kingdom.

The priests also teach how to live healthfully, avoid disease, and have a long life—while the Messiah will heal the sick and provide eternal life.

The high priest's role and garments

The high priest represents what the Messiah will do in heaven as the intermediary between sinners and God in the final eradication of sin. His colored clothing and duties portray the roles of the Messiah in carrying out the Plan of Redemption.

Scripture first describes the most sacred ephod—a two-part vest covering the chest and back, held together by a girdle. It is hung on each shoulder by a strap on which is mounted an onyx stone. One stone has the names of the six younger sons of Israel engraved on it, while the other stone has the names of the six older sons (Exodus 28:10).

The ephod is made of fine linen with gold thread and blue, purple, and scarlet yarns, reflecting the same colors as the sanctuary curtains. Gold represents the Messiah's kingly role, blue represents His heavenly role, purple represents His royal role, and scarlet represents His sacrificial role as king of the Jews. Wrapped around the ephod is a girdle or sash with the same colors of the ephod.

The breastplate of judgment

The breastplate is a piece of linen that utilizes the same colors as the ephod and the sanctuary curtains. It is a single piece of fabric folded over to make about a nine-inch square that Scripture calls a span (or one half of a cubit). It is attached at the top to the shoulder straps of the ephod and at the bottom to the back of the ephod with a blue cord. The ephod is probably the most significant piece of clothing for the high priest because it holds the breastplate.

This fabric contains twelve attached gems in four rows of three. The first-row gems are a sardius, a topaz, and an emerald. The second-row gems are a turquoise, a sapphire, and a diamond. The third-row gems are a jacinth, an agate, and an amethyst; and the fourth row is made up of a beryl, an onyx, and a jasper.

Most of the colors of these gems from antiquity cannot be determined with certainty today, however, we do know that these stones are engraved with the names of the twelve tribes. Since the breastplate is square, it may reflect the later encampment in the wilderness being a hollow square with three tribes camped on each of the four sides.

A literal Hebrew translation for breastplate is "ornament." When the ancient Hebrews viewed their high priest with this ornament and its twelve semiprecious stones, they were no doubt stunned and awed by its beauty. However, as they contemplated its beauty, they suddenly realized that the gems symbolized them!

As slaves in Egypt, they never considered themselves valuable, beautiful, or important. In the Hebrew mind, the fact that the twelve tribes are represented both on the shoulders and the breastplate of the high priest is a strong indication of their importance to God!

Since the high priest represents the Messiah, the onyx stones on his shoulder symbolize that His people are His main responsibility and concern. When they are again pictured over His heart, it proves that He loves them, that they are very precious to Him, and that He has an intimate relationship with them. In other words, His whole life, work, and being are forever and inseparably intertwined with His people. As their spiritual leader, He restores them back to their Lord and brings them health, strength, and fullness of life, both spiritually and physically.

The Urim and the Thummin

The breastplate is called the "breastplate of judgment" because it has the Urim and Thummin stones, used to get an answer or judgment from the Lord (Exodus 28:15, 29, 30).

The Urim and Thummin, which in Hebrew may mean "lights" and "perfections," are placed in the breastplate, and Scripture makes reference to them seven and five times, respectively.

The Bible does not describe them in detail. However, in New Testament times, the Jewish historian, Flavius Josephus, refers to shining stones on the breastplate of the high priest that appear to be used to get a yes or no answer from the Lord. If the Urim shines, it is considered to be a yes answer; and if the answer is no, some sort of indication comes from the Thummin.

Remember, the people are just beginning to mature in their new faith, so the Lord needs to use simple, familiar, methods that are common in the ancient Middle East. This process will be in place for a period until their spiritual growth increases beyond the need of having the Lord make the decisions for them.

The robe

Underneath the ephod is a long, sleeveless blue robe that is the foundational garment of the high priest. It reaches below the knees almost to the ankles, and is apparently woven without a seam because it is to be put on by slipping it over the head. The opening at the top has a reinforcement to avoid tearing or fraying. It has no sleeves, so there are slits to put the arms through. At the bottom of the garment, a reinforcing hem is attached with blue, purple, and scarlet embroidered pomegranates, alternating with golden bells, that hang as tassels. These bells produce a sound that indicates to the people that the high priest is performing his duties within the Most Holy Place and has not died while in the presence of the Lord.

This valuable, seamless robe corresponds to Jesus' seamless robe and spiritually depicts the robe of Christ's righteousness given to the sinner. The colors represent Christ's roles, linked with heaven and His kingship.

The turban

On the high priest's head is a linen turban or miter, from which hangs a golden plate over the forehead engraved with the words "HOLINESS TO THE LORD" (verse 36). The golden plate is attached to the turban with a blue cord, again, reflecting heaven. The engraving on the plate indicates that the high priest is set apart to the Lord, and therefore holy. In the same manner, he represents all of Israel as being set apart to the Lord, and therefore, also holy.

The tunic

Under the robe, is a tunic of linen with a variegated pattern of colors from the sanctuary curtains. It is a shirt-like garment, similar to a long coat, with a sash or girdle to tie around the waist. Since it is under the robe, it is not seen by the public.

The undergarment

Unlike the common people, the priests are also required to wear an under garment of plain linen to avoid what Scripture calls "uncovering their nakedness" when on the altar steps. It reaches from the waist to just above their knees.

Set apart

Clearly, the high priest is set apart to the Lord on earth, just as the Messiah is set apart in both the heavenly and earthly realms as the divine/human Redeemer of mankind. The Messiah accomplishes the restoration of sinful mankind back to the Lord, changing their status from sinful to holy.

The supreme function of the high priest is to perform the ritual cleansing of the earthly sanctuary. Meanwhile, the Messiah in His ministry will ultimately cleanse His cosmic sanctuary by eradicating all sin from the universe, once and for all!

CHAPTER FIFTY-SEVEN

The "Miracle" of the Golden Calf

Based on Exodus 32

Moses climbs Mount Sinai and stays there for forty days and nights, which the people take as a negative omen hearkens back to the fact that it rained for forty days and nights at the time of the Flood. Finally, they approach Aaron, the high priest, saying, "Make us gods that shall go before us; for as for this Moses . . . we do not know what has become of him" (Exodus 32:1).

Moses is their sole contact with the Lord, and the mediator of His power and guidance. For all they know, he may be dead or has deserted them. With him gone, they believe their contact with the Lord is lost, and they feel the need for a replacement mediator to fill the role of "going before them." Because of their background in Egypt, they want a *visible god* who will lead them quickly to the Promised Land.

Because of their urgency, and fearing for his life, Aaron demands their golden earrings, given them by the Egyptians, hoping they will balk at giving up their treasured possessions. However, they're all too willing, and now he feels compelled to fashion the gold into a molded calf.

Compromise

When the people see the golden calf, they cry, "This is your god, O Israel, that brought you out of the land of Egypt!" (verse 4). When Aaron sees it, he compromises by building an altar before it, and declaring a feast the next day *to the Lord!*

This calf idol is not unfamiliar, since they observed the pagan worship of Apis, the bull, in Egypt. In their minds, the bull represents the true God and is a symbol of virility, strength, and fertility. Pagans in the region believe that most deities ride on animals, and if it is interpreted in this way, the bull or calf serves as the pedestal for the Lord, similar to the molten sea of Solomon's temple in the future that will be mounted on oxen.

However, this mixing of pagan and true worship, this spirit of compromise, is an abomination to the Lord, and will plague God's people for many years—as it still often does, today.

Worship of this calf is clearly in defiance of the Lord's second commandment. He has been trying to wean them away from a physical image of Him and help them accept an invisible One, by faith. But the people make burnt offerings and peace offerings to their golden calf, and sit down to eat and drink in a communion meal with their god. After their meal, they rise up to "play"—a Hebrew verb that has the connotation of drunkenness, immoral orgies, and sexual play!

From the original context of trying to replace Moses as the people's mediator between them and their Lord, this story is not so much an abandonment of the Lord for other gods. It is more an account of transferring the center of authority of faith in the Lord from Moses, and the covenant laws and symbols he has announced, to a calf, without laws and symbols beyond itself. The calf is to be the representative of the same God whose invisibility is compromised by a forbidden image.

The irony of this foolish action of Israel is shown in Psalm 106:19, 20:

They made a calf in Horeb,
And worshiped the molded image.
Thus they changed their glory [meaning the Lord—manifested through
   a cloud]
Into the image of an ox that eats grass.

Mediation needed

The Lord instructs Moses to go down immediately from the mountain because "your people" (Exodus 32:7) have corrupted themselves by making a molded calf, have worshiped and sacrificed to it, and have declared it is their god that brought them out of Egypt.

Notice that the Lord does not declare the Hebrews "My people" as he did in Exodus 3:10, but essentially gives them over to Moses, since they have abandoned Him. He is ready to leave them and make Moses and his descendants into a great nation.

In his role as the divinely appointed mediator, Moses instantly appeals to the Lord, reminding Him of His covenantal relationship with His people at the exodus. He appeals to the Lord to keep His name honorable before the Egyptians and to remember His patriarchal promises.

As a result of Moses' appeal, the Lord relents of what He said He would do to the people. The Lord does not change His character or purpose, but

244 | THROUGH THE EYES OF THE ANCIENTS

He does change the course of events when the situation changes, or when the attitude of His people changes.

Shattered stones

Descending the mountain with the Ten Commandments in his arms, he meets up with Joshua, who has awaited him for weeks. Again, the tablets are two in number and are called the Testimony—indicating they are two witnesses. They're made of stone and contain the Lord's handwriting, and are therefore very important.

As they near the bottom of the mountain, Joshua exclaims he hears the noise of war in the camp, but Moses answers correctly (using poetry to indicate its importance) that this is not the shout of victory or defeat, but the sound of singing and dancing at the riotous orgy celebrating the golden calf.

Soon they can see what is taking place, and Moses' abhorrence of the situation is so great that he throws the two tablets to the ground, shattering them. This is in great contrast to his reaction when the Lord was ready to abandon His people because of their rebellion.

The breaking of the two tablets of the Testimony has great significance. It symbolizes that the Hebrews have broken the divine covenant and shattered the relationship between them and their Lord. Just recently, at Mount Sinai, they have all declared, "All that the LORD has spoken we will do" (Exodus 19:8).

Moses then takes the calf and burns it, grinds it to powder, scatters it over water, and forces all the Hebrews to drink it—effectively turning the instrument of their sin into the instrument of their punishment. In doing this, he also completely destroys their idol, showing that it is absolutely nothing.

The "miracle" calf

As Moses confronts his brother Aaron, he does some quick thinking to extricate himself as an accomplice in the people's reveling. He actually tries to justify his lack of leadership by blaming the people. He says they demand gods to lead them since Moses hasn't returned—quickly adding that he throws their golden earrings into the fire, and out comes this calf! (What a miracle *that* would have been!)

Standing at the entrance of the camp, Moses calls all those who choose to be on the Lord's side to come to him, and the sons of Levi bravely come forward. Firm action is necessary to crush the rebellion, so Moses gives the order to destroy the rebellious ones—who undoubtedly include some close relatives of the Levites. About three thousand, men die that day, and then Moses says to the sons of Levi, "Consecrate yourselves today to the LORD, that He may bestow on you a blessing this day, for every man has opposed his son and his brother" (Exodus 32:29).

Moses now returns to the Lord, stating that the people have committed a great sin and made themselves a god of gold. Yet he pleads for the Lord to forgive them, but if not, he requests that He blot out his name from the book He has written—the Book of Life.

The Lord answers,

"Whoever has sinned against Me, I will blot him out of My book. Now therefore, go, lead the people to the place of which I have spoken to you. Behold, My Angel shall go before you. Nevertheless, in the day when I visit for punishment, I will visit punishment upon them for their sin" (verses 33, 34).

Moses, like Christ, is willing to surrender his life, even eternally, if that will atone for their sin. But were the Lord to permit this offense to go unpunished, His people would have yielded more readily to idolatry in the future. As their loving Protector, He removes the defiant ones, lest they lead others to ruin.

Major contrasts

The episode of the golden calf brings out some major contrasts. The Hebrews have been liberated from abject slavery, and through a tremendous miracle have been brought out of Egypt in the exodus. They have been brought to Mount Sinai, the mountain of God, to receive the personal revelation of the Lord. He has revealed Himself through the plan of salvation by giving the covenant, and at the end, the people have solemnly promised that all the Lord has said, they will do. But when Moses is up Mount Sinai for forty days and nights, they think *he* is their leader. He brought them out of Egypt, instead of the Lord.

They repudiate what they have promised, ask for a god, worship it, and celebrate in pagan fashion.

By contrast, Moses does all that the Lord asks him to do, and even requests that his name be blotted out of the Lord's Book of Life for eternity if it will serve to atone for Israel's terrible sin. By further contrast, Aaron is unfaithful in his role and sides with the people in their rebellion.

CHAPTER FIFTY-EIGHT

Divine Covenant: Singular or Plural?

Most Christians don't understand the Lord's covenant, but since it is the plan of salvation, it *must* be understood!

A covenant is generally understood as an agreement between two equal partners; but this is not so with the Lord's covenant, since it is based on the ancient Hittite, suzerainty-type of covenant. The Lord elaborates the whole plan of salvation, and the people can either accept or reject it—they *cannot negotiate any of the terms, or modify it in any way.*

A deeply flawed idea

As Christians we know we must overcome sin, and most of us believe we need the Lord's help for us to do this. However, this idea is both deeply flawed and unworkable. We quickly find we cannot succeed, and then either try harder and fail again or give up altogether. I came close to that myself when I was a young man, but more on that, later.

Some speak of two divine orders, or dispensations—one of law, and one of grace. Others say the Lord had a covenant of works in the Old Testament and a covenant of grace in the New Testament.

So what is the reality?

The "old" covenant

After Israel's exodus from Egypt, the Lord enters into a covenant relationship with them at Mount Sinai—one that will save them from sin and restore their relationship with Him. In Exodus 24:1–3, the Lord calls Moses up Mount Sinai to worship Him, and when Moses tells the people all the words of the Lord, they respond, "All the words which the LORD has said we will do" (verse 3).

Sacrifices are offered to the Lord to ratify the covenant, legally binding them to each other. The Lord is now their God, and they are His people. Because they're bound to each other, half of the sacrificial blood is sprinkled on the people, and half on the altar, symbolizing that if either party breaks the covenant, the sacrificial victim's fate will be theirs.

Although the Lord's covenant is based on divine grace, the people in their weakness try to keep it by their own strength and soon break it by worshiping a golden calf. It now becomes known as the "old" covenant of works—because they tried to keep it in their own strength.

Hebrews 8:13 refers to this covenant when it says that the Lord "made the first old" (KJV). The Greek word for "old" here does not mean *old in time* but *old in quality,* since it is *useless for salvation.* However, the Lord did not make His first covenant useless—*the people did.* They perverted it by trying to keep the law by their own strength.

The "new" covenant

In Jeremiah 31:31–34, the Lord promises He will make a new covenant with Israel and Judah. The word "new" here has the connotation in Hebrew of *freshness, renewal, or restoration.* It does not have the concept of new in time, but *new in quality.*

The ancient Greek translation of Jeremiah 31, quoted in Hebrews 8:8–12, clearly shows that the "new" is really new in quality, not chronologically.

In addition, this covenant will not be written on tablets of stone again, separate from the people; instead, it will be written on their hearts and minds *by the Lord Himself.* The Lord will accomplish this task, making it a work of divine grace, rather than human effort.

The Lord does it

Is the covenant singular or plural? The Lord never deceives humans by giving something that will not work. He always gives the same covenant to sinful man down through time—so it is one in content. However, human reception of the covenant makes it essentially two different covenants. For the people, one covenant is of works when they try to keep it in their own strength. But it is a covenant of grace when, by faith, they allow the Lord to write His law on their minds and hearts.

When David sinned with Bathsheba, he didn't ask the Lord to *help him* do this or that. He asked Him to "cleanse me," and "restore me." The Lord had to do that. Most of us don't understand this concept. We pray, "Lord, help me overcome sin," as if we were doing part of it and God is only helping.

But the Lord doesn't help. He does it. Our only part is to constantly choose whether or not to allow Him to *do it all.* We are saved *only* by His power and grace.

CHAPTER FIFTY-NINE

The Restoration of Relationships

Based on Exodus 33–40

The making and worshiping of the golden calf has brought on a major crises in relationships in Israel. It all begins when Moses is up Mount Sinai for forty days and nights and the Hebrews think they have either lost him, or that he has abandoned them. They decide to replace him, and then convince Aaron to make a golden calf to substitute as their mediator with the Lord.

When Moses descends from the mountain and sees what they've done, he becomes very angry, throwing down and breaking the two tablets of stone containing the Ten Commandments. The breaking of the two tablets of stone symbolize that the Hebrews have broken their promise of the divine covenant, that all that the Lord has said, they will do. Their breaking of the covenant symbolizes that their relationship with the Lord is also broken. The Lord is angry and poised to abandon them, and it is obvious that the restoration of the relationship between a rebellious people, their leader, and their Lord is a significant task. It will take initiatives and overtures from all parties to accomplish this goal. Obviously, it must initially begin with the Lord and His faithful servant, Moses.

Expelled

The Lord gives the order to leave Sinai because the sin of the golden calf has ruined the people's right to remain in His presence. This is like the expulsion of Adam and Eve from the Garden of Eden.

The Lord will not go with them to the Promised Land, but will send His Angel to accompany them. When the people hear this shocking news, they begin to mourn. Their grief is so strong that they take off their pagan ornaments they received from the Egyptians. The men in Egypt wear armlets, bracelets, and anklets as some form of amulets.

The presence of the Lord with Moses

Moses takes his tent far outside Israel's camp and calls it the tabernacle of meeting or sanctuary. This tent serves as Israel's temporary sanctuary until the permanent one is built. His move also symbolically indicates that the Lord is not dwelling with His people anymore. When Moses enters the tent, the pillar of cloud, representing the Lord's presence, descends and stands at the door as the two communicate with each other. When this happens, it evokes a spirit of worship among the people.

Moses speaks to the Lord reminding Him that he was informed to take this people to the Promised Land. However, the Lord has not told Moses whom He will send with him. The Lord has told him that He knows his name, and that Moses has found grace in His sight. This indicates an intimate relationship, and that His presence will go with him to Canaan.

But the real question Moses wants to know is what is the Lord's intention in respect to Israel. In Moses' mind, he can only have success in leading the people to the Promised Land if the Lord's presence will go with him *and* Israel, as they depart Sinai. Moses learned this lesson before. He was only able to deliver the Hebrews from Egypt because of the Lord's presence; therefore, he will only have success in leading the people to Canaan if the presence of the Lord is both with him and His people.

As a result of Moses' intercession and his close relationship with the Lord, he receives the answer from the Lord that His presence will go with *both him and the people.* Then Moses boldly asks the Lord, "Please, show me Your glory" (Exodus 33:18).

This request to see the Lord's glory while on Sinai is really a request to demonstrate more fully the promise He's just made about His presence. The revelation of the Lord's glory is a revelation of His attributes, demonstrating who He is.

The Lord says, "I will make all My goodness pass before you, and I will proclaim the name of the LORD before you. I will be gracious to whom I will be gracious, and I will have compassion on whom I will have compassion" (verse 19).

The Lord's "goodness" means His graciousness and compassion, and this is a revelation of His name (Yahweh), a proclamation of who He is. A revelation of all His name includes His attributes, characteristics, and nature. The Lord is really saying, "I am not showing you how I look, but who I am," then adds, "You cannot see My face; for no man shall see Me, and live" (verse 20).

Moses "sees" the Lord

Now the Lord tells Moses, "Here is a place by Me, and you shall stand on the rock. So it shall be, while My glory passes by, that I will put you in the cleft of the rock, and will cover you with My hand while I pass by. Then I will take away My hand, and you shall see My back; but My face shall not be seen" (verses 21–23). These precautions are given for Moses' protection.

Then, the Lord tells Moses to cut two tablets of stone, like the first ones, and that He will write the Ten Commandments on them. Since Moses broke the first tablets of stone the Lord prepared, he must now prepare the new ones.

In the morning, Moses ascends to the very top of Mount Sinai, while neither man nor animal comes near the mountain. The Lord descends in the usual cloud on the mountain with Moses, and says, "The LORD, the LORD God, merciful and gracious, longsuffering, and abounding in goodness and truth, keeping mercy for thousands, forgiving iniquity and transgression and sin, by no means clearing the guilty, visiting the iniquity of the fathers upon the children and the children's children to the third and the fourth generation" (Exodus 34:6, 7).

Notice, the Lord (Yahweh) proclaims His name twice, echoing Moses' encounter with the Lord at the burning bush, and emphasizing the reality of the Lord's presence with Moses. He is revealing Himself by expounding on the meaning of His name through a recital of His essential attributes that have been historically displayed to the Hebrews: merciful and gracious, longsuffering, abounding in goodness and truth, keeping mercy for thousands, and forgiving iniquity and transgression and sin.

This divine revelation to Moses naturally causes him to immediately bow down before the Lord and worship. Then he requests, "If now I have found grace in Your sight, O Lord, let my Lord, I pray, go among us, even though we are a stiff-necked people; and pardon our iniquity and our sin, and take us as Your inheritance" (verse 9). After asking for forgiveness, Moses is again asking for the Lord to go with him and the people.

The Lord answers Moses with the renewal of His covenant that assures that He will go with them. He promises, "Behold, I make a covenant. Before all your people I will do marvels such as have not been done in all the earth, nor in any nation; and all the people among whom you are shall see the work of the LORD. For it is an awesome thing that I will do with you. Observe what I command you this day. Behold, I am driving out from before you the Amorite and the Canaanite and the Hittite and the Perizzite and the Hivite and the Jebusite" (verses 10, 11).

With His declaration that He will renew the covenant with His people, the intimate relationship between the Lord and His people is restored. And while He promises to drive out the inhabitants of the Promised Land, He simultaneously expects His people to avoid any covenantal alliance with the pagan inhabitants, and that they will totally eliminate all their altars, sacred pillars, and wooden images connected with their pagan gods. The sacred pillars or poles are linked with the goddess Asherah. Clearly the context for all these prohibitions is the people's worship of the golden calf at Sinai.

The Lord's requirements

Next, the Lord gives a summary series of His requirements to keep them completely devoted to Him, without compromising with pagan gods or practices. They are: not to make gods of shaped metal, keep the Passover as directed, keep the Sabbath and the three yearly feasts, consider every firstborn of man or beast as the Lord's, and not to boil a kid goat in its mother's milk. If they faithfully follow all that He has stipulated, their newly established relationship with Him will be maintained.

Moses is on Mount Sinai for forty days and nights communing with the Lord, and is told to write down the words of what the Lord will do, and what He expects the His people to do. During this time, Moses neither eats nor drinks, just as he did during his last time on the mountain. Clearly, the Lord sustains his physical strength. In this respect, Moses stands as the type for Jesus, who will spend forty days and nights in the wilderness without food or drink, being tempted by Satan.

Moses' shining face

When Moses comes down from Mount Sinai, he brings the new tablets of stone containing the Ten Commandments, but does not break them, indicating that this renewed covenant between the Lord and Israel remains binding.

As he talks with Aaron and the people, the skin of his face shines so brightly that they are afraid of him. The transformation of his appearance is notable, apparently reminding the people of the theophany of the Lord at Mount Sinai. It also serves as a type for the future transfiguration of Jesus.

Moses' shining face is a reflection of the glory of the Lord and is designed to impress upon the people the significance of His divine law. As Moses gives them all the words of the Lord that were given to him on Mount Sinai, his face remains uncovered and shining—clearly linking the shining face with the commandments he is giving.

When he finishes, he puts a veil over his face at the request from the people, similar to how Christ will veil His divinity during His incarnation. Whenever Moses goes into the tent of meeting to be with the Lord he goes in without the veil, but when he comes out, he puts the veil on. This indicates the light provides divine authority to his message, and clearly restores his credibility as the mediator between the Lord and the people.

The building begins

Much progress has been made in restoration of relationships. The people have repented from their sin of making and worshiping the golden calf. Moses has been restored as the mediator between the people and their Lord and has also convinced Him to change His mind so He will accompany the people to the Promised Land. The only thing lacking is the building of the sanctuary so the Lord's presence will be visibly and constantly among them.

As preparations are being made for the construction of the sanctuary, the Lord gives instruction that work is be done on the first six days of the week. But the seventh day is the Sabbath and no work is to be done, because it is the day for worship.

Although the instructions for donating goods and labor have already been given, construction has been delayed because of the golden calf idolatry. However, the construction process begins with the gathering of the materials, followed by the Lord appointing Bezelel to be in charge, with Oholiab as his assistant.

The building instructions are given in this order: the sanctuary in general, the ark, the lampstand, the altar of incense, the altar of burnt offering, and the courtyard. Then instructions are given for making the ephod, the breastplate, and the other priestly garments, to be followed by Moses' inspection and approval of everything.

The cloud of the Lord's presence covers the sanctuary, and the glory of the Lord fills it. The Lord has moved in, symbolically living with His people. The broken covenant has been renewed and relationships have been restored. The sanctuary is ready to function as the book of Exodus ends and the book of Leviticus begins.

CHAPTER SIXTY

Salvation in Unforgettable Terms—Part 1

Based on Leviticus 1–6

The ancients thought literally, so when the Lord gives them the plan of salvation in covenant form, it is portrayed to them in that manner. Initially the covenant is delivered verbally, and later, in a show-and-tell form for literal thinkers with the establishment of the sanctuary with its compartments, sacrifices, and offerings.

The sanctuary for the ancients is the dwelling place of the Lord on earth with His people. It is a portable structure, enabling the Lord to live with them, even as they move from place to place. It is divided into three parts: the court, the Holy place, and the Most Holy Place. The sinner's progressive religious experience involves all three areas.

Having come from Egypt, the Hebrews have only a vague idea of the holiness of God and the sinfulness of man. They need to be taught the basic principles of reverence, worship, and salvation. The sanctuary, sacrificial system, and the rituals are all designed to teach the people what the coming Messiah will literally do for them as He changes them from sinners separated from the Lord to righteous individuals saved by grace. The sanctuary, with its offerings and rituals will show, in a literal way, the step-by-step process of salvation that the Messiah will achieve for them.

To begin with, they need to learn how a sinful human is to approach a holy God. They learn that they have very limited access to the Lord's house. They learn that the closest they can come to the Lord is His court, and that is with an offering that represents the Messiah and what He will do for them. Five major offerings to the Lord are listed as sacrifices: whole burnt offerings, grain offerings, peace offerings, sin offerings, and trespass offerings.

Whole burnt offerings

The basic offering for the sinner is the whole burnt offering. The beginning of Leviticus is primarily concerned with the individual whole burnt offering, rather than what is done collectively each day for the whole encampment. The individual sinner's occasional whole burnt offering consists of an animal without defect that he can afford—ranging from a bull or a male sheep or goat, to certain birds. He brings the animal to the entrance of the court, puts his hand on its head, indicating a symbolic acknowledgment of the substitution of the animal for himself. Next, the sinner takes his animal to the northern quadrant of the court and kills it, since the northern direction for the Hebrews has the connotation of judgment. Having to kill one of your own animals that you know by name, drives home the awfulness of sin.

A priest brings the animal's blood and sprinkles it all around the altar, indicating the death of the animal is the means of symbolically purging the sinner from the contamination of sin. The sinner must now skin the animal and give the hide to the priest, wash the entrails and legs of the animal, and cut it in pieces. The priest then puts the pieces on the wood of the altar and burns them completely to ashes. By this ceremony sin is symbolically transferred to the sanctuary.

Since there is no reference to any specific sin, it is assumed that this whole burnt offering is primarily to atone for the person as a sinner, rather than his sinful deeds.

That is why the animal must be completely consumed, because the penalty for sin is death. The idea behind this death is the total extermination of sin. In terms of what the Messiah will do, He becomes the substitute for the death of the sinner. In sacrificial symbolism, His life is totally consumed.

Grain offering

A grain offering is used in both a secular and religious context. In the secular context, it is a gift presented to another person, especially to one you are obligated to, or to someone you want to win favor with. It is also used for tribute paid to a nation or overlord.

In a religious context, it is a simple gift offered to the Lord that does not involve blood or atonement. It is a gift to the Lord in recognition of His lordship and His grace in giving the presenter his daily food and all the good things he enjoys.

It is made with fine wheat flour, olive oil, and frankincense with no leaven to avoid spoilage. It has several forms: uncooked flour, bread baked in an oven, bread prepared on a griddle, or bread cooked in a pan. The presenter brings the offering to a priest, who takes a small portion of it and burns it on the altar as a memorial sacrifice to the Lord, who by His grace, provides for all the sinner's needs. The remainder of the offering is given to the priests for food, that can only be eaten by them within the precincts of the sanctuary, serving as a means of support. In terms of the Messiah, He will provide the sacrifice that brings the sinner eternal life.

Peace offering

The peace offering is also known as the fellowship offering, which literally means, "to make peace" or "to be at peace." This is reflected in the greeting, "Shalom."

The animals used are a bull, a male or female sheep, or a goat. The sinner lays his hand on the head of the animal in symbolic identification and transfer of guilt. The animal is then killed at the door of the sanctuary, and its blood is sprinkled by a priest on the altar of whole burnt offering. The fat around the intestines, liver, and kidneys, as well as the kidneys, themselves, are burned on the altar of whole burnt offering.

The right breast and the right thigh is the portion given to the priest, and the remainder of the animal is given to the worshiper to eat with his family and friends. As can be observed, the main feature of this offering is the communal meal held within the sanctuary court in which the worshiper with his family, servants, friends, and the priest eat together. They celebrate the fact that there is peace between the Lord and man, and between man and man.

Sin offering

"Sin" and "sin offering" are both translated from the Hebrew, *chat-ta'th*. In some situations, "purification offering" is a better term than "sin offering."

The purpose of the sin offering is to provide a means for the repentant sinner to obtain full restoration to the Lord. In Leviticus 4, the offering is for inadvertent sins that the Hebrew lexicon defines verbally as "to commit error" or "to sin inadvertently." In some passages, the translation "wrongly," or "in error" seems to be an even better translation than "inadvertent."

If a common person sins, he is to bring a female goat to the sanctuary and lay his hand on the head of the animal, thereby identifying himself with it. The animal then becomes his substitute. He is to personally kill the animal, and the priest will smear its blood on the horns of the altar of whole burnt offering and pour the remaining blood at the altar's base.

The usual fat and kidneys of the animal will be removed and burned on the altar, indicating that the sin has been symbolically transferred to the sanctuary. The priest then eats a cooked portion of the meat—an indication that the sinner's sins have been transferred to him.

The remainder of the carcass is to be burned outside the camp in order not to pollute it. This indicates that this part of the offering ritual does not refer to the sinner, since it is done outside the camp, in what is considered the realm of evil for literal thinkers. It may indicate that this part of the animal deals with the devil's part in the sinner's sin.

Trespass offering

The trespass offering is also known as the "guilt offering" and "reparation offering." This offering is designed to deal with a particular category of sin that represents a breach of faith or a violation of something sacred.

Breach of faith would be represented in the violation of the covenant, while the violation of something sacred generally refers to desecration of sacred areas or objects that are holy to the Lord.

The three examples of sins given in Leviticus 5 are if one hears an oath and as a witness, does not reveal it; if one touches anything unclean and is unaware of it; or if one thoughtlessly swears an oath, and is unaware of it.

The guilty one is to confess his sin and bring a female lamb or goat as a trespass offering to the sanctuary. If the sin involves something wrongfully taken, the sinner is to offer a ram and make restitution of what he has taken, adding 20 percent. The sinner is to kill the animal, skin it, wash it, cut it into pieces, and extract the fat portions and the two kidneys. The priest smears the blood of the animal on the horns of the altar and offers the fat portions and kidneys on the altar of whole burnt offering. This transfers the sin to the sanctuary. Then, similar to the sin offering, he eats a portion of the meat, and burns the remainder of the carcass outside the encampment.

The sinner's spiritual journey

The sanctuary court is where the sinner's spiritual journey begins, and the altar of whole burnt offering is its religious center. An animal is killed each day in its northern part, representing judgment; its entrails and legs are washed in the southern part of the court, which is considered the favored section.

The animal is completely burned on the altar as a whole burnt offering, representing the sinner and his sinful nature. This ritual portrays the complete sacrifice and death of the future Messiah.

The animal's death symbolically pays the penalty for sin, in substitution for the death of the sinner. Through this, the sinner is saved and completely justified (or declared righteous) before the Lord. The Messiah's righteousness becomes the sinner's righteousness.

It's personal!

The sinner commits a sinful deed, becomes remorseful of it, and confesses it. He brings one of his animals to the sanctuary court, places his hand on its head, and symbolically transfers his sin to the innocent creature. Now he must personally kill it, wash its entrails and legs, and cut the animal into pieces. Giving some of the meat to the priest as food, he separates the fat portions and kidneys to be burned on the altar.

Through this ceremony, the sinner, in literal terms, transfers his sinful deed to the sanctuary. For him, the sin is completely forgiven and taken away, prefiguring the Messiah, who will be both the symbolic victim and the sanctuary, itself.

The individual sins are atoned for by both the sin and trespass offerings that are very similar in nature, ceremony, and meaning.

The grain offering does not involve the shedding of blood but is a gift to the Messiah as a tribute for what He does for the sinner.

The peace offering is an actual sacrifice that follows similar steps to the sin and trespass offerings. It is essentially an offering of thanksgiving for the peace that comes from the Messiah when He pays the penalty of death for the sinner.

Through the very literal portrayal of the different sacrifices, the sinner both comprehends and experiences salvation from his sinful nature and deeds. The result is great gratitude to the Lord, and the assurance that he is at peace with both the Lord and his fellow men.

CHAPTER SIXTY-ONE

Salvation in Unforgettable Terms—Part 2

Based on Leviticus 16

In the previous chapter, following the rituals of the sanctuary court and the Holy Place, as given in Leviticus 1–6 the common man experiences complete forgiveness from the Lord for his sinful nature and sinful deeds through the substitutionary sacrifice of the animals. His sins have been taken from him and transferred to the sanctuary. As a result, the sanctuary becomes polluted and needs to be cleansed.

The Day of Atonement

Of the traditional five books of Moses, Leviticus is the center of the Pentateuch and is considered its heart because it deals with forgiveness, salvation, transformation, and holiness. Leviticus 16 is considered the center of the book and the center of the whole Pentateuch, and consequently, the most important chapter in all of the five books. To the Hebrew mind, this indicates that *this particular chapter* is the theological center of *everything*.

Leviticus 16 describes the Day of Atonement that depicts the cleansing of the sanctuary in a literal way from the sins that have accumulated there. The chapter not only describes how the sanctuary is cleansed but also how sin is disposed of.

On the morning of the Day of Atonement, Aaron, the high priest, comes to the sanctuary with a bull as a sin offering and a ram as a burnt offering. For the ceremony, he puts on a linen tunic, linen pants, a linen sash, and a linen turban, garments similar to those of a common priest. These more common garments are used only on the Day of Atonement, since on this very solemn day, he needs to approach the Lord dressed humbly and contritely. Before putting on the clothes, he washes himself in water to be clean before functioning as the high priest, since he is a sinner himself.

The sacrifices

The congregation, represented by the leaders, brings him two goats as sin offerings and a ram for a whole burnt offering. Aaron uses the burnt offering and a sin offering to make atonement for himself and his house, that consists of all the other priests. Next, he casts lots over the two goats to determine which one is to be sacrificed as the Lord's goat, and that which is to be released into the wilderness alive. The casting of lots may have been done by placing two inscribed objects (probably made of wood) into an urn, and then drawing them out. The selection is left to the Lord.

The Lord's goat is a sin offering to Him, while its counterpart appears to also be a sin offering called the scapegoat, in Hebrew called *azazel* (literally in Hebrew, "to *azazel*," or "for *azazel*"). Both actions are part of the atonement process to completely cleanse the sanctuary and eliminate sin from it and from the encampment.

Before Aaron is prepared to make atonement for others, he must make atonement for himself and his house, by sacrificing his bull as a sin offering. Then he goes inside the veil of the Most Holy Place with incense, which produces a cloud that covers the mercy seat of the ark of the Testament, shielding him from death.

Next, he returns to the court and brings the blood of the bull into the Most Holy Place, sprinkling it on and before the mercy seat seven times. This completes the atonement for the high priest and his house.

Then, he sacrifices the Lord's goat and takes its blood into the Most Holy Place and sprinkles it on and before the mercy seat seven times. This cleanses the Most Holy Place and the Holy Place from the impurities of the forgiven sins.

Three categories of sins are cleansed in this process: sins involving physical uncleanness; sins that occur accidentally or out of ignorance; and intentional, rebellious sins. This is the only place in the Pentateuch that mentions where atonement for intentional sins is mentioned.

Next, he goes outside to cleanse the courtyard. He does this by first taking some of the blood of the bull and goat that were sin offerings and putting it on the horns of the altar of whole burnt offering, followed by burning the fat and kidneys on the altar. The remainder of the Lord's goat is taken outside the camp and burned.

What remains is to deal with the second of the two goats for which the lots were cast. The first goat was the Lord's, used as a sin offering, and it appears the second goat is also a sin offering that is not to be sacrificed but led away into the wilderness to die. To understand what this means, it must be understood through the eyes of the ancients.

Outside the camp

As noted before, a sin offering is divided into two parts, and the fat and kidneys are sacrificed on the altar of whole burnt offering (taking care of the sin of the penitent Hebrew), and the rest of the animal is burned outside the camp (this is Satan's responsibility in tempting the sinner).

This realm "outside" the camp has great significance for the ancients. When Adam and Eve sin, they are expelled from the Garden of Eden to the "outside" world—considered the realm of evil. They have to go to the east gate of Eden to worship the Lord.

When the Hebrews are camped at Mount Sinai and the Lord is to come down on the mountain to speak to them, they must remain "outside" the base of the mountain, because the mountain is considered the Lord's sanctuary.

Once the Hebrews are in the wilderness, the "mixed multitude" are camped "outside" the camp of the twelve tribes. They have committed the unpardonable sin, and during their forty-year period, these rebellious Hebrews are condemned to wander in the wilderness—just as the second goat on the Day of Atonement. They are "outside" the area of salvation, and cannot celebrate the Passover, perform circumcision, or go into the Promised Land. They have literally lost their salvation—and only their children may be saved.

When the Messiah suffers for the sin of the world, the book of Hebrews says, "Therefore Jesus also, that He might sanctify the people with His own blood, suffered *outside* the gate" (Hebrews 13:2, emphasis added). Because He suffered the fate of the sinner, He must die in what is considered the "outer" sinful world.

In the book of Revelation, the righteous are taken to heaven; but Satan (the equivalent of the scapegoat) is confined to the earth for a thousand years (Revelation 20:1–3). After the millennium, the holy city, New Jerusalem, descends from heaven (Revelation 21:2), and Satan surrounds the camp of the saints and the beloved city—again the "outside" world is depicted as evil (Revelation 20:9). In Revelation 22:14, 15, the wicked are "outside" the gates of the holy city.

The scapegoat

In the final act of cleansing the sanctuary from all sin, Aaron lays his hands on the head of the scapegoat to symbolically transfer Satan's part in the sins of the righteous and his role in originating sin. The scapegoat is then led into the wilderness (his realm) to die as a sin offering.

Many have said all the sins of the sanctuary (sins of the righteous) are placed on the scapegoat, however, if that were to be true, *Satan becomes the savior of the righteous,* and the Lord's goat (representing the Messiah) is completely *invalidated!*

At the close of the ceremony, Aaron takes off his humble linen garments and leaves them in the sanctuary. He washes his body with water and puts on his golden garments and offers the usual evening burnt offering, both for himself and for the congregation. Sin has now been atoned for, and the camp is holy and free from sin.

Salvation in symbols

The whole symbolic journey of the sinner through the sanctuary gives a theological illustration of the role of the Messiah in saving the sinner and making him holy.

The journey begins at the courtyard, the entrance of the sanctuary. First, the sinner is legally declared righteous—justified with the death of the Messiah, represented by the burnt offering and sin offering.

Second, the sinner is sanctified by the blood of the Messiah that forgives his sins and transfers them to the Holy Place. This separates him from the world and makes him belong fully to the Lord—making him holy. Through the process of sanctification, the Messiah changes him, so that he possesses the attributes of the Lord's character.

The last phase of the sinner's salvation journey through the sanctuary takes place in the Most Holy Place (called the Holy Place in Leviticus 16, but made evident by the ritual described). This is the most sacred compartment of all, because it portrays, in literal terms for the ancients, the cosmic throne of the Lord. The top of the ark of the Testimony is described as the footstool of the divine throne. This is where the sinner comes to seek mercy and salvation. The ancients understand this; in their time, the guilty one always seeks mercy at the feet of a superior, such as a king. The sinner is judged to be holy in the process, because he is considered free from sin, and holy, like his Lord. Theologically he is classified as glorified, because he reflects the attributes and character of his Lord.

CHAPTER SIXTY-TWO

Sudden Judgment

Based on Leviticus 10

Through the command of the Lord, the tabernacle is constructed and Aaron and his sons are instructed about the sanctuary duties, services, and offerings for seven days.

Then they are consecrated to the sacred office of the priesthood, and on the eighth day, they begin their ministration.

Aaron, the high priest, assisted by his sons, offers the sacrifices and offerings the Lord requires, then goes into the sanctuary with his brother Moses. When they come out, they pronounce a blessing on all the people and the glory of the Lord appears to them all. Immediately, fire comes down from heaven and ignites the wood on the altar—completely consuming the burnt offering.

Swift punishment

Not long after the inauguration, all twelve tribes of Israel meet at the entrance of the tabernacle for community worship. The prayers and praise of the people ascend to the Lord as Aaron's sons Nadab and Abihu light their censers to burn fragrant incense within the sanctuary before the Lord.

However, they do not follow instructions to take coals from the holy fire on the altar of whole burnt offering that came from the Lord and consumed the sacrifice during the inauguration. Instead they use *common fire*, and *immediately*, the fire of retribution goes out from the Lord and consumes them!

Moses reminds Aaron,

"This is what the LORD spoke, saying:
'By those who come near Me
I must be regarded as holy;

263

And before all the people
I must be glorified' " (Leviticus 10:3).

Moses' words probably come from Exodus 19:22 where the Lord said, "Let the priests who come near the LORD consecrate themselves, lest the LORD break out against them." Apparently, their dedication service before the inauguration of the sanctuary did not result in Nadab and Abihu's consecration!

All eyes are upon Aaron, who maintains his silence and does not enter into the noisy wailing that usually accompanies mourning for the ancients. He is determined to follow the procedure of the Lord that officiating priests should not be in mourning during their service in the sanctuary.

Moses calls Mishael and Elzaphan, sons of Uzziel, the uncle of Aaron, and says, "Come near, carry your brethren from before the sanctuary out of the camp" (Leviticus 10:4).

Taking care of the dead is normally the role of the immediate members of the family. However, in this situation, the brothers of the deceased are involved in priestly service, so other relatives have to carry out the dead.

Mourning customs

The mourning customs of the ancients usually include disheveled hair and torn clothing. Other signs may include shaving of the head or beard, and putting dust on your head. Moses warns Aaron and his other sons Eleazar and Ithamar, "Do not uncover your heads nor tear your clothes, lest you die, and wrath come upon all the people" (verse 6). Any of these mourning traditions could be interpreted by the people as sympathy for Nadab and Abihu, who had visibly and dramatically come under the condemnation of God. They could also cheapen the holiness of both the sanctuary and the Lord's presence, as well as the consecration of the priesthood that is referred to with the anointing oil.

Wine and strong drink

Next, the Lord permanently prohibits Aaron and his sons from drinking wine or strong drink before entering the tabernacle—indicating that Nadab and Abihu took common fire in their censers when they went into the tabernacle because they were intoxicated. Their sin was deliberate and reflected scorn for the sacred things of the Lord, thus disqualifying them for service and making them worthy of divine judgment.

The prohibition of wine and strong drink is linked to distinguishing between holy and unholy, and clean and unclean (verse 10). Everything that *is* holy (consecrated to the Lord) is clean (ritually purified). Everything that *is not* holy (common or profane) can either be clean or unclean. It is the duty of the priests to maintain these distinctions, but Nadab and Abihu, in their intoxication, were unable to make these distinctions. The duties of the priests include teaching the people the statutes of the Lord to make these distinctions.

Misunderstanding solved

Notice that Moses has called Mishael and Elzaphan, cousins of Aaron, to carry the remains of Nadab and Abihu away from the camp. In the confusion that follows, Aaron suspends the tabernacle ritual of eating the portion of the meat offering that pertains to him, but Moses warns him in forceful terms to continue the ritual. When priests eat their portion of the sin offering (purification offering) that atones for the sin of another, they bear the guilt of the sinful offerer—a foreshadowing of what the Messiah, in His priestly role, will ultimately do. In the thinking of the ancients, they understand that when the priest eats his portion of the meat of the sin offering, he is swallowing the impurities of the sin of the offerer—thus transferring the sin to himself.

Moses gives long and detailed instructions to Aaron, as well as to his sons Eleazar and Ithamar, about the sin offering and the offerings that often accompany it, saying, "Take the grain offering that remains of the offerings made by fire to the LORD, and eat it without leaven beside the altar; for it is most holy. You shall eat it in a holy place, because it is your due and your sons' due, of the sacrifices made by fire to the LORD; for so I have been commanded. The breast of the wave offering and the thigh of the heave offering you shall eat in a clean place, you, your sons, and your daughters with you; for they are your due and your sons' due, which are given from the sacrifices of peace offerings of the children of Israel. The thigh of the heave offering and the breast of the wave offering they shall bring with the offerings of fat made by fire, to offer as a wave offering before the LORD. And it shall be yours and your sons' with you, by a statute forever, as the LORD has commanded" (verses 12–15).

Moses is primarily concerned with the goat for the sin offering. In some sin offerings, the blood of the animal is taken into the Holy Place to make atonement, but in the case of this goat that is used as a sin offering, its blood *is not to be carried* into the sanctuary but put on the horns of the altar of whole burnt offering. Then some of the flesh of the goat is to be eaten by the priests and the remainder is disposed of outside the camp.

Nadab and Abihu, in their intoxication, do not follow the law and eat any of the flesh of the sin offering. As a result, there is no transfer of sin to Nadab and Abihu, or to Aaron and his sons, because they cannot make atonement for sins they do not bear by eating some of the flesh!

Moses becomes angry because none of them have eaten some of the meat, as the ritual indicates. However, Aaron responds, "If I had eaten the sin offering today, would it have been accepted in the sight of the LORD?" (verse 19). The obvious answer is no.

Nadab and Abihu have become *their own* sin offerings by bearing the responsibility for their own sins, by being burned up, and by being carried outside of the camp to be disposed of, as the law requires. Moses finally understands that there is no reason to continue the ritual in this case.

CHAPTER SIXTY-THREE

God's Incredible Economic Plan

Based on Leviticus 23; 25; and Deuteronomy 15

The Lord blesses the Hebrews with an incredible economic plan that has never been equaled—one that eliminates the serious problems that human economic systems create. It is based on the premise that the Lord will give the land to the Hebrews to use, but He still will retain the title, as the owner of the land. In this plan, which will begin in the Promised Land, the Hebrews are stewards, not owners.

Annual feasts and the number seven

In Leviticus 23, the Lord gives instruction to the Hebrews concerning the feasts, and in Leviticus 25, He instructs them on the special years in respect to the land. The interval between these events is based on the number seven, stemming from the seven-day week of Creation that ended on the Sabbath; and since they are feasts, they involve some sort of sabbatical rest.

Seven special convocations to the Lord are attached to the feasts, making them religious in nature. Two of these convocations are for the Feast of Unleavened Bread (first and last days), one is set aside for the Feast of Pentecost, another for the Feast of Trumpets, one for the Day of Atonement, and two for the Feast of Tabernacles (first and last days).

The annual cycle of these feasts begins in the spring with the Feast of Passover and is continued for a week with the Feast of Unleavened Bread. This is followed by the Feast of Pentecost, seven weeks after the Passover (although the ancients, with their system of reckoning, call it fifty days later).

Seven months after the Passover, trumpets are blown for the Feast of Trumpets, announcing the judgment of the Day of Atonement, on the tenth day. Then the Feast of Tabernacles follows in the same month.

All of the annual feasts deal with some portion of the yearly harvest: Passover marks the beginning of the grain harvest, and Pentecost marks the end. Trumpets begin the seventh month that ends with tabernacles, marking the end of the fall harvest of olives and grapes and the end of the harvest year.

The sabbatical year

The first of the special years is the sabbatical year, based on the weekly Sabbath rest. Every seventh year is designated as a sabbatical year of rest for the land, and during that year there is to be no planting or harvesting, so the land can rest and be renewed. At this point, presumably none of the ancients have any idea of why this will be good for the land, but after some time, they will see the benefits.

During the sabbatical year, they are not to plant their fields or prune their vineyards. There is also to be no normal work of harvesting or grape gathering that involves servants and storage. The concept behind this is twofold. First, just as the manna fell twice as much on the sixth day, the grape crop of the sixth year will be more plentiful because of the Lord's blessing, and there will be a surplus. Second, the natural crop of that year will be public property—to feed the poor and provide food for both domestic and wild animals. The Lord desires His people to be periodically free from continuous labor, so they might enjoy the blessing of the gift of the Promised Land. When the people observe the sabbatical year, they acknowledge His ownership of the land and demonstrate their trust in Him for their food.

Deuteronomy 15 also deals with the sabbatical year, but its concern is more with debt cancellation and the freedom of indentured slaves. A Hebrew who enters into financial difficulties, and becomes unable to continue to pay his debts is ultimately forced to sell himself to whom he is indebted. He is not a slave, in the traditional sense of being owned by his master, but becomes, instead, an indentured slave or servant who works off his debt. In the sabbatical year he is set free and his debt is canceled. The maximum length of service for an indentured slave is six years, and for most, it is far less.

The jubilee year

The second special year is called the jubilee year, and it occurs simultaneously with the seventh, or sabbatical year. This year rectifies the misfortunes of those who have gone into debt during the previous forty-eight years and who have been forced to deliver their land in a form of a lease to whomever they are indebted. At the jubilee year, their debt is canceled, and their land is returned.

The maximum number of years they can lose their land is for forty-eight years, and for most individuals, the period is far shorter. In the Hebrew's way of reckoning time, the jubilee

The fiftieth year is called the years of jubilee.

The jubilee year is based on the premise that the Lord owns the land and that through the covenant, He has given it to the Hebrews as a gift to use. Each parcel of land given to a family through the divine covenant carries the right of redemption. In essence, they are tenants who work the land and live off its increase. The land is never to be sold or permanently lost to the family or its descendants. It is to be their perpetual inheritance.

The right of redemption does not allow the one who receives the land in payment for the debt to hold back the return of the land to the original owner, whenever the debt obligation is met. Meeting the debt obligation can be done in one of three ways:

First, the debtor can raise enough money to pay off the debt. Second, a kinsman (usually a relative) can pay off the debt.

Third, at the year of jubilee, the debt is automatically canceled and the land returns to the original owner. Notice that, in the beautiful divine covenant terms, *the Lord Himself is acting as the next of kin* and restoring the property and freeing the indentured slave.

How the economic plan works

God's economic plan does not function on the basis of money, but on the value of land, goods, and services. In God's economic system, the value of services cycles every seven years, because in the seventh year, the indentured slaves go free. Land depreciates almost two percent per year, because it will revert back to the previous owner in the jubilee year. As the land depreciates, the value of goods increases. Then, when the land appreciates again, the value of goods decreases. This eliminates inflation, and prosperity is continuous as the population increases.

In today's terms, the gross national product probably increases somewhere in the range of two to six percent annually. The result is no entrenched poverty or wealth, yet there is steady prosperity. The sabbatical years are also a great blessing to the people and the land, because the land does not wear out through continuous farming.

Spiritual blessing for the people

The system of sabbatical years is a great spiritual blessing to Israel because they have to depend on the Lord to supply their needs during the time of no planting or harvesting of the sabbatical year. They also learn that God wants them to see value in their fellow men by not allowing anyone to lord over them through permanent slavery, or entrenched wealth.

Jesus appears to be making a direct reference to both the sabbatical year and the jubilee year in Luke 4:18, 19, where He quotes from Isaiah 61:1, 2. He is appointed "to preach the gospel to the poor," to "proclaim liberty to the captives." Jesus seems to take the literal freedom from indentured slavery and apply it to His anointment, to bring spiritual freedom from sin. This is similar to what the Lord did with the Hebrews, when He brought physical redemption from Egyptian slavery that also meant redemption from sin, in covenant terms.

In the same manner, Jesus is "to proclaim the acceptable year of the Lord" (Luke 4:19) as a direct reference to the year of jubilee, when after redemption from debt, one receives his land (inheritance) back. Jesus is stating that He is appointed to establish His kingdom when His people will receive their covenantal inheritance of their land.

CHAPTER SIXTY-FOUR

God's Amazing Love

Based on Numbers 1–26

The Hebrew title for the book of Numbers is "In the Wilderness." Genesis, Exodus, and Leviticus provide the history of Israel from their ancestors at Creation through the Egyptian captivity and Exodus to the sojourn at Mount Sinai. The book of Numbers begins at Sinai and follows through the forty-year trek in the wilderness to the eve of the entering of Canaan.

The title, Numbers, originates from the two censuses of Israel found in chapters 1 and 26. Chapter 1 gives the census of the Israelites that left the encampment of Mount Sinai in route to Canaan. This is a military census to determine how many men can fight under the Lord's commandership to conquer Canaan. The census numbers, the lists of Hebrew names, and an extensive amount of repetition is very boring to us moderns.

However, it was not so to the ancients because the Lord has a different message for them than what we tend to get from reading it. We will try to see some of the significance of the names, numbers, and repetition, to understand the book through the eyes of the ancients.

The mention of the names of the leaders of each tribe and the number of soldiers they can muster speaks to the pride of each entity. More importantly, they serve as a *celebration of the faithfulness of the Lord to His covenant people.*

The census of chapter 1 gives the numbers of the generation that come out of Egypt that should have gone on to settle in Canaan. However, because they rebel against the Lord, they forfeit their opportunity to settle in Canaan. All that generation must die in the wilderness.

Chapter 26 is also a military census of how many fighting men are among the Hebrews who will serve under the Lord's leadership in conquering Canaan. Their total numbers make up the next generation that will enter the Promised Land.

This census focuses on the generation for whom the book is primarily written. They must learn from the failures of their parents, and the absolute necessity for faithfulness to the Lord in spite of all the hardships of wilderness living.

The story of the experiences of the first generation is presented in two parts. Chapters 1–10 give the story of their preparation for success; chapters 11–25 provide the sad story of their numerous rebellions and unbelief, and the Lord's wrath and instances of His grace.

During the journey of the Hebrews in the wilderness, God demonstrates His incredible love and patience to His grumbling and rebellious people. He is true to His covenant promises to lead and care for them as He takes them toward the Promised Land. One of the most significant aspects of the book is that the Lord speaks to Moses, who speaks to the people. This is stated more than 150 times and in more than twenty ways. It serves as a record of the Lord's self-disclosure to Moses, who transmits this revelation to His people.

The opening words of the book, "In the Wilderness" have significance. The wilderness has been attached to a negative connotation, first, when the Messiah is tempted forty days and nights in the wilderness; and second, in that sin affects the land, and after divine judgment occurs, the land tends to become a wasteland or wilderness.

The book of Numbers begins on the first day of the second month of the second year after the exodus. It ends almost thirty-nine years later, but they are in the wilderness for forty years, if one includes the time after they leave Egypt until the beginning of this book.

First census

The first census number is 603,550 (Numbers 1:46). It is a military census that has the exact same number as that of Exodus 38:26, and it includes only men twenty years of age or older that can go to war. Women, children, and Levites are not counted, nor are the "mixed multitude" of non-Israelites or partial Israelites. The word "thousand" may not mean literally a thousand, since in Numbers 31:5 and 2 Samuel 18:1, it means a large group as a military division.

Between the two censuses one can count ten rebellions. Ten in Scripture denotes a complete secular number. These rebellions are as follows:

1. Complaints of hardships in the wilderness (Numbers 11:1–3). The Lord sends a fire that consumes some of them.
2. Complaints of no meat (Numbers 11:4–15). The Lord sends quail for a month and many die.

3. Complaints from Miriam and Aaron against Moses and his wife (Numbers 12:1, 2). The Lord strikes Miriam with leprosy.
4. Refusal of the ten spies to allow the Hebrews to enter Canaan (Numbers 13:31 to 14:4). The Lord makes the people spend forty years in the wilderness.
5. A man flagrantly violates the Sabbath by gathering sticks (Numbers 15:32–36). The Lord orders that he be stoned.
6. Rebellion of Korah, Dathan, and Abiram who claim they are holy and should be able to minister in the sanctuary as priests (Numbers 16:1–19). The ground devours them. Also fire from the Lord consumes 250 men that are offering incense as if they are priests.
7. The congregation rebels against Moses and Aaron, saying, they killed the 250 men offering incense as priests (Numbers 16:41). The Lord sends a plague that kills fourteen thousand seven hundred, of them as a sin offering.
8. People complain of no water at Kadesh (Numbers 20:2–5). The Lord tells Moses to speak to the rock and bring forth water, but in anger against the congregation, he strikes the rock and loses his chance to enter the Promised Land.
9. People complain of no food or water and that they are tired of manna (Numbers 21:4, 5). The Lord sends fiery serpents and many die.
10. People commit harlotry with the women of Moab (Numbers 25:1–3). The Lord orders the judges to kill their men that are committing immorality, and that results in the death of twenty-four thousand.

Second census

The second census number is 601,730 (Numbers 26:51). Even though the new census is taken after the plague of Numbers 25 and the ten rebellions, the number of men of the new generation are almost the same as the previous generation. There is less than a 0.3 percent decrease (1,820), clearly a very negligible sum! This demonstrates that they have received the blessing of the Lord. Many of the more rebellious tribes lose great numbers, the worst loss is to the tribe of Simeon that has lost about 63 percent of its population. Many of the more faithful tribes increase their numbers greatly—Manasseh has increased its numbers by 64 percent.

This new census is regarded as the turning point from the first generation to the second, shifting from the fathers and mothers to their sons and daughters. But they face serious questions. Will this new generation be used by the Lord to enter Canaan, conquer the land, and enjoy the land that is given to them as a gift? Will they come to the border of the land,

274 | THROUGH THE EYES OF THE ANCIENTS

send out spies, and then believe an evil report and refuse to go in? The final haunting question is: Will they believe in the Lord, obey His commands, and take up arms under the Lord's commandership, marching victoriously into the Promised Land?

This new generation is regarded as the exodus people. It is as though their parents never lived or rebelled. They are the substitute generation for the first. The story begins anew with them as if they just left Egyptian bondage and are going to the Promised Land.

Clearly, the Lord is patient with this new generation of Hebrews by not abandoning or destroying them in His judgments on their parents' multiple rebellions. His faithfulness to His covenant promises clearly reveals His amazing love and care for the second generation. If His promises can't be fulfilled to the first generation, they will be fulfilled to the next or a later generation.

CHAPTER SIXTY-FIVE

God Is Our Fortress and Strength

Based on Numbers 2–4

Communication in the Hebrew language, is both rich and varied for the ancients.

Using their five senses of sight, hearing, touch, smell, and taste, they come to know and understand something by personal experience, rather than by rational thought.

Through hearing, they understand words, thoughts, and symbols; and through sight, they experience reality, beauty, and form. Imagery of things they've experienced or understood in the past is used to understand similar new things, or experiences they encounter in the present.

The camp

In Numbers 2, the Bible portrays the Israelites as a military camp, where each tribe is numbered as a military unit and encamped separately around the sanctuary by its own banner or flag.

Judah is camped on the east side as the chief tribe, along with the tribes of Issachar and Zebulun. And since all cardinal points of the compass are based on an individual facing the east, on the right or south side, is the chief tribe of Reuben, along with Simeon and Gad. The chief tribe of Ephraim is camped on the west (or literally, in Hebrew, "the sea," since the west side of Canaan faces the Mediterranean Sea), along with Manasseh and Benjamin. On the north (or left side), is the chief tribe of Dan along with Asher and Naphtali.

This geometric pattern is also likely repeated on the breastplate of the High Priest.

By constantly carrying the symbols of the twelve tribes over his heart, He visibly portrays his love and concern for them.

The thirteenth tribe

You will notice that this chapter lists thirteen tribes, even though Joseph and Levi are not listed as part of the twelve tribes that make up the army. This is because Jacob adopted Joseph's two sons, Ephraim and Manasseh, essentially giving their father a double portion of the inheritance. The thirteenth tribe of Levi serves as the spiritual officers and guardians of the sanctuary and is not considered a military unit. They are encamped between the twelve tribes and the sanctuary.

Numbers 3 and 4 list those who are to care for the sanctuary and minister within it. God declares the tribe of Levi will take the place and do the work that was formerly done by the firstborn of each family, therefore making it spiritually responsible for the people. The reason for this new arrangement is because they are now an organized nation, and a new structure is needed. This tribe is chosen because they did not participate in the worship of the golden calf.

The three sons of Levi

The three sons of Levi and their descendants have different sanctuary responsibilities. Gershon camps on the west side and cares for its coverings; Kohath camps on the south side and cares for its furniture; and Merari camps on the north side and cares for its frame and structure.

The sons of Aaron are to minister within the sanctuary. They camp at the front of the sanctuary (or on the east side) and their work symbolizes the ministration of the coming Messiah. They must be thirty years of age in order to officiate—just as the future Redeemer will be when He begins His ministry. The ancients believe that a man is not mature until the age of thirty, and public responsibilities of a spiritual nature should not be assumed until that age.

Protection all around

The organization of the tribes of Israel as a military encampment, with the sanctuary in the center, geometrically portrays the whole camp as a military fortress, with the Lord's house/palace at the center. Its form is a perfect square, indicating there is no weak side for attack. The Lord protects them from the inside, and they, in turn, have the responsibility to protect Him from the outside. The fact that He is always in the center of their camp demonstrates that He is the commander-in-chief.

The geometric layout of the sanctuary also depicts, in a literal way, the true meaning of the sanctuary given in Exodus 25:8, "And let them make Me a sanctuary, that I may dwell among them." This indicates that He is the One who redeems them back, after the separation caused by sin. The Lord is the spiritual fortress and strength for His people; He's ever present, and when the camp moves, He remains always with them. It displays God's great love for them, along with His tremendous desire to be the center of their lives. The fact that there are four groups of three tribes surrounding the sanctuary symbolically indicates they have the responsibility to keep the influences of the world from affecting the sanctuary.

On a larger scale, the layout of the whole encampment reflects that the Lord is the heart of the cosmos. The closer the ground is to Him, the holier it is—similar to taking a compass and making smaller and smaller circles around Him.

The smallest circle is the Most Holy Place of the sanctuary. The second largest space is the Holy Place.

The third largest is the court of the sanctuary.

The fourth realm is that of the Levites, who are the ministering priests in the sanctuary.

The fifth realm is that of the descendants of Gershon, Kohath, and Merari, who supply and maintain the sanctuary.

The sixth largest space is occupied by the encampment of the twelve tribes.

And finally, the largest and final concentric circle is occupied by the "mixed multitude," composed mainly of Egyptians who have chosen to join the Hebrews in the exodus.

Through this geometrical layout of the encampment, the Lord is able to teach valuable spiritual lessons to His people in a very literal way. It demonstrates that He is the center of everything, that He is redeeming them back to Himself. He is their military protector from marauding groups while they are in the wilderness, and He is their spiritual leader. Most importantly, it demonstrates in a graphic way that they belong to Him.

CHAPTER SIXTY-SIX

True Justice for the Defenseless

Based on Numbers 5

In Numbers 5:11–31, we find the Lord giving little-known and seemingly strange instructions to Israel on how to deal with the case of a jealous husband who suspects his wife of adultery.

In such situations, the wife has no means of defending herself, because the whole process of judgment is in the hands of men. Since a woman does not have equal status with her husband, she will be judged guilty on the *suspicion* of her husband. The weight of shame, guilt, and trial will rest squarely upon her. However, the Lord elaborates a process that results in true justice for such cases.

The immediate context for the case of the jealous husband is found in the opening verses of the chapter that deal with two cases, one of physical uncleanness and one of an unrepented sin. Both of these will compromise the entire camp if they are not dealt with and put out of the camp until they are resolved. In the same manner, marital infidelity will bring harm into the whole camp. Being unfaithful to one's spouse was classified as being unfaithful to the Lord.

Guilty and not guilty

Two different situations are given. The first is when a wife is unfaithful, but there are no witnesses or evidence of wrongdoing. The other is when a wife has remained faithful, but her husband becomes suspicious and jealous, despite the lack of proof.

In mercy to the woman, the husband is instructed to bring her to the priest with a grain offering that consisted of one-tenth of an ephah of barley meal (approximately two quarts). The offering is called the grain offering of jealousy (literally in Hebrew it is plural, "jealousies") that is stated to be an offering for remembering. This implies that it is to bring sin into remembrance. The plural in Hebrew indicates that if she is guilty, it is an offense against both her husband and the Lord. Also, more than one person is guilty.

Barley meal is a coarse food used only by the poor, and in this case is indicative of the coarseness and grossness of the possible sin. No oil or frankincense is to be added to the offering, since this is a very serious matter and not a festive occasion.

The waters of bitterness

The priest is to bring her before the Lord, indicating she is taken to the sanctuary. He will use holy water that is probably taken from the laver in the courtyard, and add dust that is considered holy because it is from the sanctuary floor, mixing both in an earthen vessel. This is the cheapest of vessels, and again corresponds to the coarseness of the flour and grossness of the sin. The literal Hebrew translation for this mixture is the "waters of bitterness" that bring the curse. The water has a small amount of dust that probably does not give it a bitter flavor. Instead, it is more likely an indication that, for a guilty person, there will be bitter results.

The priest stands the woman before the Lord, uncovers her head as a sign of shame and places the grain offering in her hand. He holds the holy water in his hand, then places her under oath saying that if she is innocent, nothing negative will happen; but if guilty, the Lord will make her a curse among her people and cause her thigh to waste away and her abdomen to swell. The woman says, "Amen, so be it," (Numbers 5:22; the Hebrew literally says, "Amen, Amen"). By saying it twice, she is essentially saying, I am giving a double witness that I understand the issues and am in agreement with them.

The priest writes the curses on a scroll, then washes or scrapes them off into the holy water. The grain offering is then waved before the Lord and taken to the altar, where a portion is burned. Next the priest makes the woman drink the water. She has not only heard the words of the curse, but also in a dramatic sense she is to drink them. By this act, the awful sense of taking the curse into one's body is experienced. Finally, the Lord takes over by producing incontestable visible effects of guiltiness, or no effects at all.

If the woman is found to be guilty of infidelity, the water she drinks will become bitter, meaning she shall suffer the negative effects of the curse. "Her thigh will rot," apparently meaning punishment to her reproductive organs as she becomes "a curse among her people" (verse 27). A guilty woman would have the inability to bear children—a terrible shame to the ancients.

If no curse comes upon the woman, she is considered innocent and free from iniquity. As a result, she will have children and be considered most honorable, in spite of the fact that her husband was jealous of her.

Ultimately, the Lord has brought the trial of this accused woman to His supreme court, and found her pure in accord with the issue dealt with in the early part of the chapter. He has brought real justice to both the guilty and innocent. He has shamed man's injustice in the earthly legal system where a woman would be considered guilty without any tangible proof and be condemned to death—without any chance to defend her innocence.

Here, the Lord has established the principle that one is considered innocent until proven guilty. He has clearly gone against the norms of the day by elevating the status of women and providing true justice.

CHAPTER SIXTY-SEVEN

Jealousy and Judgment

Based on Numbers 12

To prepare Moses to lead the Israelites out of Egypt and through the desert, God leads him into Midian, where he worked as a shepherd for the Midianite priest, named Jethro, and married his daughter Zipporah. God also called his brother Aaron to be the high priest for His people, and his talented sister Miriam, who after crossing the Red Sea, was a prophetic voice leading the song of victory over the Egyptian army (Exodus 15).

Because they help Moses throughout the plagues and the crossing of the Red Sea, and the problems at Sinai, they allow self-exaltation to lead them into thinking they are equal leaders of Israel.

A resentment brews

At this point, Miriam apparently has a resentment against Moses' wife Zipporah. Instead of marrying a Hebrew, he has chosen a woman of another nation. Miriam takes this as offense to her family and national pride and treats her sister-in-law with thinly disguised contempt.

Although ethnically a Midianite, the Bible clearly calls her an Ethiopian. As a descendant of Abraham through Keturah, she is a blood relative to the Hebrews and a worshiper of the true God. However, being an Ethiopian, her skin is apparently darker than the Israelites.

While the Hebrews are camped in the desert, Jethro brings Zipporah and their two sons out to live with him. Observing Moses' heavy workload, Jethro counsels him to choose elders to help judge the matters brought by the people, and his counsel is confirmed when the Lord tells Moses to appoint seventy elders to help judge the people's problems. However, this brews trouble with Miriam and Aaron.

Miriam and Aaron assume (probably correctly) that their brother's wife has spoken to her father about this. Even worse, Moses has left them out by not choosing them as judges—or even consulting them, for that matter!

Outright rebellion

The ringleader seems to be Miriam, since she is listed first, and the Hebrew verb used is both feminine in gender and singular in number. However, Aaron apparently sympathizes, since he is named with her. Their jealousy results in rebellion against God's appointed leader of His people, and they say. "Has the LORD indeed spoken only through Moses? Has He not spoken through us also?" (Numbers 12:2).

Moses apparently does not react to their criticism because Scripture states that he is very humble, more than all men on the earth. He has just gone through a terrible ordeal mentioned in Numbers 11, instigated by the "mixed multitude" consisting primarily of Egyptians who have left Egypt with the Hebrews. They cry for meat, and not just manna. Their insurrection has spread through the whole camp and Moses, in desperation, turns to the Lord and says, "Where am I to get meat to give to all these people?" (Numbers 11:13).

All this is too much for Moses to bear, and he breaks down and begs the Lord, "Please kill me here and now" (verse 15). On top of all this, he faces jealousy and rebellion from his own brother and sister!

Swift judgment

The Lord hears the complaints of Miriam and Aaron and knows that their real issue is in the form of a question, *Why is Moses the Lord's favorite? Are we not as good as he?*

The Lord immediately reacts to defend His faithful servant, and suddenly commands Moses, Aaron, and Miriam to "Come out, you three, to the tabernacle of meeting!" (Numbers 12:4).

Personally descending in a pillar of cloud, the Lord stands in the door of the tabernacle and calls Aaron and Miriam to step forward. Then He says,

> "Hear now My words:
> If there is a prophet among you,
> I, the LORD, make Myself known to him in a vision;
> I speak to him in a dream.
> Not so with My servant Moses;
> He is faithful in all My house.
> I speak with him face to face,
> Even plainly, and not in dark sayings;
> And he sees the form of the LORD.

Why then were you not afraid
To speak against My servant Moses?" (verses 6–12).

As He asks this, the Lord's anger is aroused. He has spoken to them in poetic form, meaning His words have great significance because they are compressed into the fewest words. The effect of biblical poetry is the feeling or experience that one receives from the impact of the words. Imagine the fear that grips their hearts when they hear the Lord's awful question.

The poetry has expressed the sovereignty of the Lord in the way He deals with prophets. Essentially, Miriam and Aaron are common prophets through whom He communicates with in a variety of ways. Moses, on the other hand, is a special prophet because the Lord speaks to him intimately, on a face-to-face basis.

The Lord's anger is aroused against them and He swiftly departs in the cloud as His presence leaves the sanctuary. The disappearance of the pillar of cloud underscores the heat of His wrath! This is perhaps the only place the Bible records the pillar of cloud departing.

Instantly, divine judgment falls on Miriam as she becomes as white as snow, covered with leprosy! For them, leprosy is apparently not Hanson's disease but some form of skin disease that is contagious. Since Miriam becomes leprous and Aaron does not, it must be concluded that Miriam is the main offender.

When Aaron sees her condition, he begs Moses, "Please do not lay this sin on us, in which we have done foolishly and sinned. Please do not let her be as one dead, whose flesh is half consumed when he comes out of his mother's womb!" (verses 11, 12). This is apparently making reference to the appearance of a stillborn child.

Moses prays, asking the Lord to heal her, and the Lord answers, "Let her be shut out of the camp for seven days and then she can again return to the camp" (verse 14). Being leprous, she is unclean and must be quarantined or isolated until the priest declares her cured. During this period, she has plenty of time to think over her sin, since none of the people may go out to see her until she is brought back into the camp.

The irony
Don't miss the irony! Miriam, who criticizes Moses' wife dark skin color, becomes white—*with leprosy!*

Once again, divine judgment and punishment appropriately fit the crime. Criticism against the one whom the Lord has chosen is clearly a serious sin and something we should carefully consider ourselves. However, we must note that in His great love and mercy, God uses leprosy to restore Miriam and Aaron back to Him.

CHAPTER SIXTY-EIGHT

Disbelief, Rebellion, and Judgment

Based on Numbers 13; 14; 16; and Deuteronomy 1

The Hebrews depart Mount Sinai and travel through the wilderness to Kadesh Barnea.

In preparation to enter Canaan, they are in the staging area for an assault. Here, the people propose sending twelve spies, one from each of the twelve tribes, into the land to discover the best routes for a successful assault. When Moses brings this to the Lord, He approves.

Moses instructs the spies to check the land and its fertility, the cities, the people, check for forests, and bring back some of the fruit. In their forty-day trip, they travel to the far north and the far south, as well as to the hill country of central Canaan—a distance of about 250 miles in each direction.

They return with a cluster of grapes carried between two men on a pole, as well as pomegranates and figs. The place where they find the fruit is called the valley of Eshcol, which in Hebrew means "the valley of the cluster." Since they've been in the wilderness for more than a year, the fruit no doubt causes great excitement—thinking they had discovered Eden!

The spies' report

The spies report that the land "flows with milk and honey"(Numbers 13:27), a description from a pastoral stand point, since milk is the product of herds, and honey may be either the honey from bees or the syrup from dates. From an agricultural perspective, it means productivity and abundance.

However, they also report that the people who dwell in the land are strong; the cities are fortified and very large; and "moreover we saw the descendants of Anak there" (verse 28). As the people hear this, their hearts are filled with fear, as they're led to believe that the cities are impregnable, and that the descendants of Anak are giants! The Hebrew word *nephilim* can either be translated as "giants," or the "fallen ones" (such as in Genesis 6:4). Here, clearly, the spies refer to their stature, adding, "we were like grasshoppers in our own sight, and so we were in their sight" (Numbers 13:33).

Caleb counters, "Let us go up at once and take possession, for we are well able to overcome it" (verse 30). But ten of the spies continue their negative report, saying, "We are not able to go up against the people, for they are stronger than we" (verse 31).

All the people weep that night and complain against Moses and Aaron. "If only we had died in the land of Egypt!" they say. "Or if only we had died in this wilderness! Why has the LORD brought us to this land to fall by the sword, that our wives and children should become victims? Would it not be better for us to return to Egypt?" (Numbers 14:2, 3).

Then they say to one another, "Let us select a leader and return to Egypt" (verse 4) and according to Nehemiah 9:17, they actually *did* appoint a leader to lead them back.

Faithful spies

Moses and Aaron fall on their faces before the congregation while Joshua and Caleb tear their clothes in mourning and run through the people, begging them not to rebel against the Lord. They say, "The land we passed through to spy out is an exceedingly good land. If the LORD delights in us, then He will bring us into this land and give it to us, 'a land which flows with milk and honey.' Only do not rebel against the LORD, nor fear the people of the land, for they are our bread; their protection has departed from them, and the LORD is with us. Do not fear them" (verses 7–9). However, the mob picks up stones to kill them!

Suddenly, the glory of the Lord lights up the sanctuary in the midst of the rebellion, and the people are terrified. The Lord says to Moses, "I will strike them with pestilence and disinherit them, and I will make of you a nation greater and mightier than they" (verse 12). However, Moses pleads for his stiff-necked people, arguing that their enemies will say, "The LORD was not able to bring this people to the land which He swore to give them, therefore He killed them in the wilderness" (verse 16). The point is clear, the argument is that the Lord's reputation is at stake!

The Lord accepts Moses' argument, but says, "All these men who have seen My glory and the signs which I did in Egypt and in the wilderness, and have put Me to the test now these ten times, and have not heeded My voice, they certainly shall not see the land of which I swore to their fathers, nor shall any of those who rejected Me see it" (verses 22, 23). Then the Lord instructs Moses to take the people back out into the wilderness.

Punishment and defiance

As punishment for their rebellion, all who are twenty years and older of this first generation out of Egypt will die in the wilderness. Except for Caleb and Joshua, only the younger ones will enter Canaan. The Lord continues, "But as for you, your carcasses shall fall in this wilderness. And your sons shall be shepherds in the wilderness forty years, and bear the brunt of your infidelity, until your carcasses are consumed in the wilderness. According to the number of the days in which you spied out the land, forty days, for each day you shall bear your guilt one year, namely forty years, and you shall know My rejection" (verses 32–34). The number forty has a negative connotation in Scripture, beginning with the Flood and including the length of Jesus' temptation in the wilderness.

A plague breaks out that kills the ten wicked spies and the people mourn deeply. The following day, the people directly disobey God's orders, and decide to enter Canaan, after all. Moses reminds them that the Lord is not with them, and that the ark of the covenant will stay in the camp. These defiant ones go anyway, and die by the sword of the Amalekites and Canaanites.

The Lord has done marvelous things for this generation. He has miraculously brought them out of Egypt with the intent to lead them to the Promised Land, He has miraculously led them through the Red Sea, He has revealed Himself at Mount Sinai, He has established His covenant of grace with them, He has withstood their constant complaints in the desert, led them to the borders of the Promised Land, put up with ten rebellions. In spite of all this they still haven't learned to trust Him. At the moment He is about to fulfill His ancient covenant promise to lead them into Canaan, they rebel against Him and refuse to go in.

There are many lessons in this story, but one is very clear—it is a *terrible* thing to rebel against the Lord, and when we do, our fate will be the same as theirs.

CHAPTER SIXTY-NINE

Swallowed Alive

Based on Numbers 16 and 17

Following the amazing exodus from Egypt and the wondrous revelation of the Lord at Sinai, Moses and Aaron expect the journey to the Promised Land will be quick and easy. Instead, they are constantly plagued by rebellions. They continually have to fall on their faces before the Lord to determine what to do.

Korah is a Levite camped next to the tribe of Reuben on the south side of the sanctuary. Dathan and Abiram are Reubenites who combine with Korah and the 250 leaders of the tribes to organize a jealousy-based revolt against Moses and Aaron.

"You take too much upon yourselves, for all the congregation is holy, every one of them, and the LORD is among them," they say to Moses and Aaron (Numbers 16:3). "Why then do you exalt yourselves above the assembly of the LORD?" (verse 3).

Moses and Aaron are old men at this time, so these younger men are jealous and want to take over their leading positions. Their declaration is that all the people are holy, and therefore qualified to minister as priests within the sanctuary. They believe the ministering priesthood should not just be limited to Aaron, his sons, and his family.

Korah is from the family of Kohath, and being camped alongside the sanctuary, he has the responsibility of maintaining the sanctuary furniture. Aaron is also from the tribe of Levi but is charged, along with his sons, to serve as ministering priests within the sanctuary. Aaron is the high priest and his four sons serve as common priests.

A holy challenge

When Moses hears what Korah is doing, he humbly prostrates himself before the Lord seeking to determine what to do. When he rises, he immediately realizes that neither he nor his brother are under attack—but the Lord, Himself! He firmly addresses Korah, the leader of the group saying, "Tomorrow morning the LORD will show who is His and who is holy, and will cause him to come near to Him. That one whom He chooses He will cause to come near to Him. Do this: Take censers, Korah and all your company; put fire in them and put incense in them before the LORD tomorrow, and it shall be that the man whom the LORD chooses is the holy one" (verses 5–7).

Moses is putting before them a significant challenge by telling them to bring censers, fire, and incense to the sanctuary. They are to do what only the priests do, and the Lord will decide if they are to be priests!

Then Moses adds, "Hear now, you sons of Levi: Is it a small thing to you that the God of Israel has separated you from the congregation of Israel, to bring you near to Himself, to do the work of the tabernacle of the LORD, and to stand before the congregation to serve them; and that He has brought you near to Himself, you and all your brethren, the sons of Levi, with you? And are you seeking the priesthood also? Therefore you and all your company are gathered together against the LORD. And what is Aaron that you complain against him?" (verses 8–11).

Moses essentially says that the Levites have already been appointed to a very sacred office—is that not a very significant honor? Therefore, they are extremely presumptuous in wanting to seek the priesthood too. Aaron did not seek the office, for the Lord appointed him.

Next, Moses calls Dathan and Abiram to the sanctuary courtyard but they answer, "We will not come up!" (verse 12). The Hebrew expression, "to come up" means to appear before a court of law. They are not willing to come before Moses to face charges.

Instead, they verbally attack Moses, saying, "Is it a small thing that you have brought us up out of a land flowing with milk and honey, to kill us in the wilderness, that you should keep acting like a prince over us? Moreover you have not brought us into a land flowing with milk and honey, nor given us inheritance of fields and vineyards. Will you put out the eyes of these men? We will not come up!" (verses 13, 14).

By saying, "We will not come up!" a second time they have given a double testimony that their decision is final and their sin is unpardonable.

The expression to "put out the eyes" is a way of charging Moses with blinding men to his true intentions of bringing them out of the land of milk and honey (Egypt) to kill them in the wilderness.

Moses becomes angry and defends himself, saying to the Lord not to accept their incense offering because he has taken nothing that would enrich himself, not even a donkey.

Again, Moses tells Korah, "Tomorrow, you and all your company be present before the LORD—you and they, as well as Aaron. Let each take his censer and put incense in it, and each of you bring his censer before the LORD, two hundred and fifty censers; both you and Aaron, each with his censer" (verses 16, 17).

They all obey the command and stand at the door of the sanctuary with Moses and Aaron, while Korah gathers the congregation against them at the sanctuary. At that moment, the glory of the Lord appears to all the congregation and He says, "Separate yourselves from among this congregation, that I may consume them in a moment" (verse 21). Then, Moses and Aaron call on the Lord, asking if He will be angry with the whole congregation because of one man's sin?

The Lord informs Moses to tell the congregation, "Get away from the tents of Korah, Dathan, and Abiram" (verse 24). Moses explains what is at stake with these words, "By this you shall know that the LORD has sent me to do all these works, for I have not done them of my own will. If these men die naturally like all men, or if they are visited by the common fate of all men, then the LORD has not sent me. But if the LORD creates a new thing, and the earth opens its mouth and swallows them up with all that belongs to them, and they go down alive into the pit, then you will understand that these men have rejected the LORD" (verses 28–30).

No sooner does Moses finish his words and the ground opens up and swallows Korah, Dathan, and Abiram alive along with their households and goods. The children of Korah apparently did not rebel with their father because they did not die according to Numbers 26:11.

The wages of sin is death, and going alive into the grave is the fulfillment of the prediction of Moses. This clearly establishes him as a true prophet of the Lord.

A fiery end

The glory of the Lord has appeared to all the congregation, now it breaks forth in fire and consumes the 250 men who are offering incense. The Lord often uses fire as judgment to cleanse and purify, and in spite of the fact that all these men have seen the destruction of Korah, Dathan, and Abiram, they did not repent of their rebellion.

Now the Lord tells Aaron's son Eleazar to gather up the bronze censers from the decomposing dead bodies and hammer them into a bronze plate to cover the altar of whole burnt offering. The high priest is not asked to do this because it will make him unclean. Surely Eleazar will have to be purified after his work is done.

The bronze censers are considered holy because they are used with the sanctuary, so they must be preserved. This bronze plate, made from the censers, becomes a memorial that no one that is not a descendant of Aaron should approach the Lord with incense.

A terrible plague

On the next day, the rebellion continues when the congregation accuses Moses and Aaron of killing the Lord's people. They use a strong Hebrew emphatic "you" in their accusation that Moses and Aaron are responsible for their death. Perhaps they believe that Moses and Aaron should have pleaded with the Lord for their forgiveness, rather than letting the Lord bring judgment upon them.

Suddenly, the cloud of the Lord's glory again covers the sanctuary. The Lord then tells Moses to get away from the sanctuary so He might consume the congregation with fire. Immediately Moses and Aaron fall on their faces in intercession before the Lord as a plague from the Lord breaks out among the congregation.

Moses urges Aaron to "take a censer and put fire in it from the altar, put incense on it, and take it quickly to the congregation and make atonement for them; for wrath has gone out from the LORD. The plague has begun" (Numbers 16:46).

Aaron takes a censer with incense and runs into the congregation, making atonement among the dead and the living, stopping the plague. The number that die in the plague are fourteen thousand seven hundred, which is in addition to those who died before. It is interesting to note that the censer—the instrument used in the rebellion—is now used by Aaron in his priestly work of bringing reprieve from the plague.

The dlossoming rod

The issue of the continued rebellion is not totally settled, so the Lord again speaks to Moses saying, "Speak to the children of Israel, and get from them a rod from each father's house, all their leaders according to their fathers' houses—twelve rods. Write each man's name on his rod. And you shall write Aaron's name on the rod of Levi. For there shall be one rod for the head of each father's house. Then you shall place them in the tabernacle of meeting before the Testimony, where I meet with you. And it shall be that the rod of the man whom I choose will blossom; thus I will rid Myself of the complaints of the children of Israel, which they make against you" (verses 2–5).

The twelve rods each bear the name of the staff's owner, representing their tribe.

Aaron's name is inscribed on the staff for the tribe of Levi. Moses takes all of the rods into the sanctuary and lays them before the Lord to see which one He will choose.

The next day, Moses goes into the sanctuary and sees that Aaron's rod has sprouted, put forth buds, blossomed, and produced ripe almonds overnight—a stunning miracle!

Moses then brings the rods out for the people to see, and each takes his own rod. All the people can see that the Lord has chosen only Aaron's rod, and if they rebel against the Lord and Aaron, they will die. Aaron's rod is kept in the sanctuary as a perpetual reminder that the Lord has only chosen him and his descendants to serve as priests.

It takes four divine judgments to vindicate the Lord, and make clear whom He has chosen for the ministering priesthood. First, Korah, Dathan, and Abiram are swallowed up by the earth. Second, 250 princes are burned up from a fire from the Lord. Third, the Lord sends a plague that kills fourteen thousand seven hundred,from the congregation. But none of the Lord's individual judgments seem to make any significant mark on the thinking of the people, since they still believe they are holy enough to serve in the same capacity the future Messiah will serve in. For this reason, the Lord has to have a fourth judgment of the twelve rods, indicating His decision to choose Aaron and his family. The Lord has had to show beyond any doubt that He is the only one to determine who is worthy to minister within His sanctuary.

CHAPTER SEVENTY

A Bronze Snake Lifted Up

Based on Numbers 21

Numbers 21:4–9 tells a short story in six verses that makes little or no sense in our eyes using rational, logical thinking. However, through the eyes of the ancients, it has profound meaning, since they know the stories of their history and understand the deep significance of symbolism.

Here is the story: "Then they journeyed from Mount Hor by the Way of the Red Sea, to go around the land of Edom; and the soul of the people became very discouraged on the way. And the people spoke against God and against Moses: 'Why have you brought us up out of Egypt to die in the wilderness? For there is no food and no water, and our soul loathes this worthless bread.' So the LORD sent fiery serpents among the people, and they bit the people; and many of the people of Israel died.

"Therefore the people came to Moses, and said, 'We have sinned, for we have spoken against the LORD and against you; pray to the LORD that He take away the serpents from us.' So Moses prayed for the people.

"Then the LORD said to Moses, 'Make a fiery serpent, and set it on a pole; and it shall be that everyone who is bitten, when he looks at it, shall live.' So Moses made a bronze serpent, and put it on a pole; and so it was, if a serpent had bitten anyone, when he looked at the bronze serpent, he lived."

Check out the background

In order to better understand the story, some consideration of the contextual background is necessary. After the sanctuary is built and the priesthood is established, Aaron becomes their mediator, instead of Moses. However, now he is dead and they mourn for him. His passing is a blow after all of his years of service for them, and now they are moving on from Mount Hor, where Aaron has been buried.

Next, the king of Arad attacks them and takes prisoners, and the Hebrews turn to the Lord, vowing that if the He will deliver them, they will destroy their enemy's cities. They meet with success, and name the place Hormah, which means "destruction."

Now, Moses kindly asks permission of Edom to march north through their territory, and Edom refuses twice, forcing the people to circumvent the land. First, they head back south in the direction of the Red Sea, then go east when they really want to go north and west. This makes the Hebrews unhappy because they are delayed and getting farther away from the Promised Land. The route they have to take is hot, difficult, and much longer than going through Edom.

Complaining about everything

In anger, they murmur against the Lord and Moses saying, "Why have you brought us up out of Egypt to die in the wilderness? For there is no food and no water, and our soul loathes this worthless bread" (verse 5). They revert to their old story that Egypt was better, including the food, even though they are now getting manna from heaven—which they describe as horrible.

Because of their rebellion, the Lord sends "fiery serpents" among the people that bite them. Their venom causes the flesh to become red with inflammation, resulting in the death of many. The Hebrew word "fiery" comes from the root, "to burn." The ancients, immediately associate this with fire, knowing that the fire is sent to cleanse and purify them.

They've just seen the 250 princes destroyed by fire. They've seen Nadab and Abihu burn up as their own sin offering. They've observed that the whole burnt offering that represents the sinner is completely burned on the altar in the sanctuary courtyard. The sin and guilt offerings are partly burned on that altar, and the remainder is burned outside the camp.

As a result of divine judgment, the people come to Moses saying, "We have sinned, for we have spoken against the LORD and against you; pray to the LORD that He take away the serpents from us" (verse 7). So Moses prays for the people, and the Lord tells him, "Make a fiery serpent, and set it on a pole; and it shall be that everyone who is bitten, when he looks at it, shall live" (verse 8).

The people understand what this means by recalling their own history. In Genesis 3, the serpent is associated with the sin their ancestors committed in the Garden of Eden.

The bronze serpent Moses makes is imagery of the original serpent, and symbolizes sin. But when Moses sets it on a pole, in military terms it becomes an "ensign" or "standard" to rally behind or follow.

The Hebrew word for "pole" literally indicates it is something to look to or be led by. In Genesis 3:15, the first biblical promise of a Messiah occurs with the Seed of Eve. At this point, the Hebrews have been taught the meaning of the sanctuary, offerings, priests, and rituals. They understand that the Messiah will suffer death as the penalty of sin, in place of the sinner.

In sanctuary terms, the Messiah is the great "sin offering" that will bring life and salvation for man. The bronze serpent is a symbol of the Messiah, who is made sin for the people (2 Corinthians 5:21). They must look to Him for healing and life.

This story, which seems so strange for us, is clearly understood by the ancients as they first see that their discouragement and anger against Moses and the Lord brings them justifiable divine judgment for their sin. They also understand that the serpent represents sin, and that the Messiah will take the sin of the world and will become sin, Himself, when He becomes the curse of the covenant and is lifted up on the future cross (Deuteronomy 21:23). By faith, they may look to Him for healing and salvation.

CHAPTER SEVENTY-ONE

An Unexpected Outcome

Based on Numbers 22–24

Israel is camped on the plains of Moab, ready to invade Canaan. Their encampment causes gut-wrenching fear to the Moabites, since the Lord has delivered the Hebrews from Egypt, and has recently given them victory over the powerful kings of the neighboring Amorites.

Pagan king, Balak, goes to the elders of Midian, who are normally his enemies, and says, "Now this company will lick up everything around us, as an ox licks up the grass of the field" (Numbers 22:4). For pastoral people, it is appropriate to compare Israel to an ox, since it is an emphatic symbol of strength that can take over the fragile grasslands of the country.

Bring in the diviner

Balak's solution is to call the internationally famous diviner from Mesopotamia, to curse Israel, so he sends his princes on the four-hundred-mile trip to offer Balaam great rewards for his services. This distance will take about two weeks of travel.

Balak believes that Balaam, through his divination practices of studying animal entrails or observing natural phenomena, can determine the will of the gods and place a curse upon the Israelites. In their thinking, a curse brings the wrath of their god on Israel—based on their belief that the spoken word has great power.

Obviously, Balaam has been a prophet of the Lord, because he tells the princes he cannot "go beyond the word of the LORD my God" (verse 18). However, he's clearly covetous of the gifts, and wants to go with the princes. He asks them to spend the night, but the next morning, tells them that the Lord refuses to let him go; and upon returning to Balak, the princes report, "Balaam refuses to come with us" (verse 14).

Balak is desperate, however, so he sends more princes of higher rank with promises of greater rewards. They tell Balaam, "Thus says Balak the son of Zippor: 'Please let nothing hinder you from coming to me; for I will certainly honor you greatly, and I will do whatever you say to me. Therefore please come, curse this people for me' " (verses 16, 17).

Once again, Balaam insists they stay the night so he can determine what the Lord will tell him. He insists with the Lord that he needs to go, and the Lord accommodates Balaam's rebellious decision, telling him, "If the men come to call you, rise and go with them; but only the word which I speak to you—that you shall do" (verse 20).

The condition on which he is to go is *if they come to him in the morning*. However, they *do not* come and have already started their journey home since they believe Balaam will not receive a different answer than the time before.

In spite of this, Balaam is so eager to go that he saddles his donkey and pursues them with two servants. Although he rides his humble donkey, he is traveling with more than humble motives, because he wants to be greatly enriched by king Balak.

A donkey is normally used for common and humble activities. Later Absalom rides a humble donkey into Jerusalem, trying to present himself as the new king—a common person, attractive to the common people. This actually becomes the Hebrew style of royal entries of kings, as can be seen by the royal entry of Jesus into Jerusalem. This style is in great contrast to the arrogant royal entries of victorious Roman kings and generals, who pompously ride white steeds.

The angel of the Lord

Suddenly, Balaam's donkey turns into a field, because it sees the angel of the Lord with a sword in His hand, blocking the way. The angel blocks the way because Balaam is riding with covetous motives and against the Lord's instructions.

Balaam strikes the donkey, but later, the angel again appears and stands in a narrow path, between two walls. This is vineyard territory, so it is fenced or walled. Frightened by this apparition, the donkey crushes Balaam's foot against the wall in an effort to avoid the angel. Infuriated, Balaam beats the poor animal again.

Finally, the Angel blocks the way completely in a narrow place, and the donkey lays down in terror. In a rage, Balaam beats his donkey mercilessly with his staff, and at this point, the Lord opens the mouth of the beast, and she asks, "What have I done to you, that you have struck me these three times?" (verse 28). By striking the donkey three times, it indicates to the ancients that Balaam has given the ultimate and maximum abuse to his animal.

In sheer surprise, he rages, "Because you have abused me," adding, "I wish there were a sword in my hand, for now I would kill you!" (verse 29).

The donkey answers, "Am I not your donkey on which you have ridden, ever since I became yours, to this day? Was I ever disposed to do this to you?" (verse 30).

Balaam reluctantly answers, "No," and suddenly, the Lord opens his eyes, and he sees the angel standing in the way with a drawn sword.

Stricken with fear, Balaam throws himself down on his face. The Angel asks, "Why have you struck your donkey these three times? Behold, I have come out to stand against you, because your way is perverse before Me. The donkey saw Me and turned aside from Me these three times. If she had not turned aside from Me, surely I would also have killed you by now, and let her live" (verses 32, 33).

Balaam responds, "I have sinned, for I did not know You stood in the way against me. Now therefore, if it displeases You, I will turn back" (verse 34). But the angel responds, "Go with the men, but only the word that I speak to you, that you shall speak" (verse 35).

Curses turned to blessings

When Balaam arrives, Balak meets him in his eagerness up at his northern border and says, "Did I not earnestly send to you, calling for you? Why did you not come to me? Am I not able to honor you?" (verse 37).

Balaam answers, "Look, I have come to you! Now, have I any power at all to say anything? The word that God puts in my mouth, that I must speak" (verse 38).

Balaam goes with Balak to Kirjath Huzoth where preparatory sacrifices of oxen and sheep to appease his god are already being offered, in expectation of the cursing of Israel.

The next day, Balak takes Balaam to one of the high places of Baal worship where he can see the extent of the camp of the Hebrews. Balaam has seven altars built, and he offers a bull and a ram on each, apparently trying to imitate Israel's sacrifices by using the number seven. He tells Balak to stand by the altar to tend it while he goes to a desolate place where he hopes the Lord will communicate with him. He tells the Lord, "I have prepared the seven altars, and I have offered on each altar a bull and a ram" (Numbers 23:4). He hopes the fourteen expensive sacrifices will impress the Lord to communicate with him.

The Lord communicates His message to Balaam in poetic form, indicating that His words are very important. Repeating God's words, Balaam blesses Israel, rather than cursing them! The final words of blessing are:

> "Who can count the dust of Jacob,
> Or number one-fourth of Israel?
> Let me die the death of the righteous,
> And let my end be like his!" (verse 10).

Then Balak says to Balaam, "What have you done to me? I took you to curse my enemies, and look, you have blessed them bountifully!" (verse 11).

Balaam answers, "Must I not take heed to speak what the LORD has put in my mouth?" (verse 12).

Then Balak says, "Please come with me to another place from which you may see them; you shall see only the outer part of them, and shall not see them all; curse them for me from there" (verse 13).

He takes Balaam to the top of Mount Pisgah, where just a portion of the camp is visible. Maybe smaller numbers might aid in the cursing. But seven more altars and fourteen sacrifices later, Balaam blesses them again and further emphasizes Israel's unique relationship with God. He closes with these words of their strength:

> "Look, a people rises like a lioness,
> And lifts itself up like a lion;
> It shall not lie down until it devours the prey,
> And drinks the blood of the slain" (verse 24).

Balak, in frustration, finally says, "Neither curse them at all, nor bless them at all!" (verse 25).

Balaam answers, "Did I not tell you, saying, 'All that the LORD speaks, that I must do'?" (verse 26).

Then Balak thinks of moving the third time and says, "Please come, I will take you to another place; perhaps it will please God that you may curse them for me from there" (verse 27).

Balaam is taken to the top of Mount Peor, another place of Baal worship. Again, fourteen sacrifices are offered, amounting to a total of forty-two expensive animals; but Balaam cannot help himself and blesses Israel, prophesying about the coming Deliverer and Israel's future dominion.

"His king shall be higher than Agag,
And his kingdom shall be exalted.

"God brings him out of Egypt;
He has strength like a wild ox;
He shall consume the nations, his enemies;
He shall break their bones
And pierce them with his arrows" (Numbers 24:7, 8).

Balak is beyond furious, and striking his hands together, says, "I called you to curse my enemies, and look, you have bountifully blessed them these three times!" (verse 10). The three times indicate that Balaam has effectively completed his blessing. As a result, Balak orders Balaam to go home, apparently without pay!

Balaam responds, "I am going home, but before leaving I will advise your people what Israel will do to your people in the latter days when the Lord destroys Moab and its neighbors" (author's translation). Then he prophesies of the coming Messiah:

"I see Him, but not now;
I behold Him, but not near;
A Star shall come out of Jacob;
A Scepter shall rise out of Israel,
And batter the brow of Moab,
And destroy all the sons of tumult" (verse 17).

Balaam leaves and goes home after being able to only bless Israel as the Lord said. He is frustrated because his covetous desires of riches have not been satisfied.

To comprehend much of the significance of this whole story, we westerners need to see and hear it through the eyes and ears of the ancients, who see much symbolism in this story because it is linked with previous stories. To start with, they will see a linkage with the story of Moses, Aaron, and Pharaoh when the gospel is presented to him by the Lord's revelation of Himself though the plagues. Pharaoh sees that the Lord is the true God because He has power over his gods by making them impotent.

The experience of Balak with Balaam parallels this with the God of the Hebrews being revealed through the words of blessing of Balaam and the impotence of Baal to cause cursing.

The ancients will see a parallel between Mount Sinai and the mountain or mountains of Moab, where the message of the Lord is being proclaimed. At Sinai Moses is the divine agent, revealing much of the Lord's covenant, while Balaam is the Lord's mouthpiece, revealing the words of the Lord to Balak.

The Sinai covenant has both blessings and curses—Balaam gives three blessings, but when told to go home without pay, he pronounces curses.

Last, but not least, the blessings Balaam pronounces on Israel echo much of what has been stated to Israel's forefathers in the covenant promises—ending with the magnificent promise of the coming Messiah!

CHAPTER SEVENTY-TWO

Balaam's "Success"

Based on Numbers 25 and 31

Israel is camped on the plains of Moab, across the Jordan from Jericho at Shittim, which literally means "acacia trees." This is the staging area for the conquest of Canaan.

The time marks the end of the forty years of Israel's wilderness wanderings, and at issue is their tenth and final rebellion. All the previous rebellions in Numbers have involved murmurings against the Lord, Moses, and Aaron. The Israelites have repeatedly provoked the Lord by complaining about food, water, and by refusing to believe the Lord would lead them into Canaan. However, in Numbers 25, their rebellion is unique, because it involves the worship of a pagan deity—echoing the worship of the golden calf.

In Numbers 31, the Bible indicates that the rebellion's instigator is Balaam, whom king Balak of Moab hired to curse Israel. After failing to curse them three times—and blessing them, instead—he returns home, but is still conniving to get his hands on Balak's riches. Now, he returns to Moab with a new plan, and he must be pretty sure of himself, to take three trips totaling twelve hundred miles for his scheme! His idea is to use the women of Moab to lure the Israelites into immorality and then invite them to participate in a Moabite Baal festival.

Participating in the festival will give the Israelites the opportunity to eat meat as a welcome change from the everyday manna. However, participation in a festival to a foreign god is a definite breach of the divine covenant. Their actions will definitely forfeit their divine blessing and prepare them for the divine judgment of death.

Harlotry

Our story begins unfolding with the people committing harlotry with the Moabite women. In the ancient, Near Eastern context, references to sexual imagery, as this story describes, link this immorality with pagan religious rites of prostitution. Normally the Hebrew verb for committing harlotry is applied to women, but here it is applied to men.

Next, the Moabite women invite the Israelite men to their pagan sacrifices. They participate by eating the sacrificial meal and even bow down to worship Baal, proclaiming that they are now followers! Baal is known as the god of rain and fertility.

Finally, the Lord's grace is completely spent, and He tells Moses to have the judges of Israel execute the leaders who fall under their jurisdiction that have participated in the worship. Their position among the people and their indulgence in the feast make them primarily responsible. After they are killed, they are hung "out in the sun" (Numbers 25:4) at the tabernacle before the Lord as a deterrent—so the fierce anger of the Lord (literally, the "reddening of His nose") may be turned away from the rest of them.

Meanwhile, a plague has broken out among the congregation that kills thousands throughout the camp.

Arrogance

As an act of highest arrogance, Zimri, a notable prince of the tribe of Simeon strides into the camp with Cozbi, the daughter of Zur, one of the five Midianite kings. It needs to be recalled that the Midianites combined with the Moabites in trying to get Balaam to curse Israel.

Zimri parades Cozbi around in deep disrespect before Moses, the faithful members of the congregation who are weeping at the door of the sanctuary, and as an arrogant affront to the Lord.

Suddenly, Aaron's grandson, Phinehas, takes a javelin, pursues Zimri into his tent, and with great physical force impales them both in one stroke.

This act stops a plague sent by the Lord that by now has killed twenty-four thousand. The number of casualties indicates the seriousness of the sin, because it far exceeds any numbers of those who have perished from divine retribution during their wilderness journey.

Israel's final rebellion completes the death of the old generation that refuses to enter Canaan at the time of the twelve spies. It is the final object lesson for the new generation of those who were twenty or younger when their parents refused to enter the Promised Land. They are to avoid a mixed religion that combines the worship of the Lord with that of a pagan god.

Then the Lord speaks these words to Moses, saying, "Phinehas the son of Eleazar, the son of Aaron the priest, has turned back My wrath from the children of Israel, because he was zealous with My zeal among them, so that I did not consume the children of Israel in My zeal. Therefore say, 'Behold, I give to him My covenant of peace; and it shall be to him and his descendants after him a covenant of an everlasting priesthood, because he was zealous for his God, and made atonement for the children of Israel' " (verses 11–13). When He gives him a covenant of peace, it undoubtedly includes protection for him from "blood vengeance" of the relatives of Zimri. It also involves confirming Phinehas and his descendants as the ministering priests for succeeding generations.

Through the killing of Zimri and Cozbi, Phinehas makes an atonement that saves the rest of the congregation, similar to what Aaron did with the censer and incense when he stopped the plague that killed fourteen thousand in Numbers 16:46–50.

Zimri's name means "My Remembrance" in praise to God, however, after this incident, his name sadly takes on a very negative connotation.

Cozbi's name, after the incident, means "My Lie" or "Deception." Although she comes from a noble family, she has been memorialized as a seductress for religious immorality—a prototype of Jezebel.

A command to attack

After the incident with Zimri and Cozbi, the Lord speaks to Moses, saying, "Harass the Midianites, and attack them" (verse 17), in divine judgment for tempting the Hebrews to sin.

The Lord informs Moses that this is the last war he will be involved in before he dies.

In Numbers 31 organization takes place to execute the Lord's command. Moses has the people recruit one thousand men from each tribe to form an army to attack the Midianites.

Then, he sends these twelve thousand to war with Phinehas, the priest. He takes with him the undefined holy articles and the signal trumpets made of metal—separate from the shofar, which is made from a ram's horn. They kill all the males of military age, take captive the women, and bring back all the spoil of war.

Final defeat

Balaam thinks that the great success of his plot to curse Israel through heathen women and the worship of Baal will bring him high rewards. However, his great "success" only brings him final defeat as he is killed with the Midianite men.

As can be seen by this story, the Hebrews can only be defeated when they depart from the Lord. They continually receive blessings as long as they remain loyal to the Lord, but receive covenant curses when they depart from Him. Sadly, for the older generation that came out of Egypt, this covenant curse is final for them.

Balaam is a prophet of the Lord to bless Israel as long as he seeks the Lord for his message, but when he proposes the plot to entice the Hebrews in sin, the words spoken are his own and the end result for him is death. Ironically, the curse that he had put on Balak and his people also becomes his.

CHAPTER SEVENTY-THREE

A Type of Christ

Based on Numbers 20 and Deuteronomy 1–34

Israel is now camped east of the Jordan River during their fortieth year of wandering, awaiting the Lord's orders to cross into the Promised Land.

Moses, still brokenhearted, knows he cannot lead the people into him into Canaan because of his sin at Kadesh.

Let's look back at that story. During the forty-year wilderness journey, the Hebrews camped at Kadesh, and had no water, and they contend with Moses, saying, "Why have you brought up the assembly of the LORD into this wilderness, that we and our animals should die here? And why have you made us come up out of Egypt, to bring us to this evil place?" (Numbers 20:4, 5).

Moses and Aaron fall on their faces before the Lord, who tells Moses, "Take the rod; you and your brother Aaron gather the congregation together. Speak to the rock before their eyes, and it will yield its water; thus you shall bring water for them out of the rock, and give drink to the congregation and their animals" (verse 8).

Previously, when the Hebrews lacked water at Rephidim, the Lord instructs Moses to *strike* the rock. However, here He instructs him to only *speak* to the rock. This is to teach the people that there is no power in the rod but only in what the Lord has spoken.

A serious mistake

Moses assembles the people before the rock and says to them, "Hear now, you rebels! Must we bring water for you out of this rock?" (verse 10). He is clearly very angry with them and reacts by stating that *he and Aaron* must bring water out of the rock, and as he speaks, he emphatically strikes it twice.

Moses' sin is in not having faith in the Lord or believing that He will perform the miracle, and the Lord immediately informs him that his sin will preclude him from leading the people into the Promised Land.

Later, in Deuteronomy 3, Moses says that despite his pleadings, the Lord said, "Enough of that! Speak no more to Me of this matter. Go up to the top of Pisgah, and lift your eyes toward the west, the north, the south, and the east; behold it with your eyes, for you shall not cross over this Jordan" (verses 26, 27).

By not allowing Moses to enter the Promised Land, He portrays His true justice by not allowing even his faithful servant to escape the penalties of sin.

A grand farewell

Before Moses dies, he gives a grand farewell to the second generation of Hebrews that came out of Egypt, who are now on the verge of entering the Promised Land. This farewell, recorded in the whole book of Deuteronomy, is a restatement of the divine covenant given at Sinai to the first generation that came out of Egypt, but continually rebelled.

The word Deuteronomy means "Second Law," because Moses is restating the divine law or covenant. It follows the basic elements of ancient covenants, beginning with a prologue, identifying who is giving the covenant. First, it refers to Moses, who is speaking, and secondly, to the Lord, who originally gave the covenant.

The next covenant element is the historical prologue that gives the history of the relationship between both Moses, the Lord, and the people. The history that is mentioned is from the time they leave Mount Sinai all the way to the eastern border of Canaan. It includes the people's refusal to enter Canaan and the Lord' s victories over their enemies.

The next covenant element is the stipulations, elaborating the covenant expectations of the Lord in light of what He has done for them during the historical prologue, and what He has given them at Sinai. This includes the Ten Commandments, the seventy statutes, and miscellaneous laws to govern their lives.

The Stipulations are followed by the blessings and curses. The blessings show what the Lord will do for them if they remain faithful to Him and His covenant. They will be prosperous and considered the head and not the tail on earth. Secondly the curses demonstrate His grace and mercy to try to bring them back to Him if they become unfaithful and do not keep the terms of the covenant. The final curse is exile in a foreign country and slavery.

Since the covenant is a legal document there are public witnesses—and two of them are needed to guarantee the covenant is genuine. In this case, they are cosmic witnesses, since they are *heaven* and *earth*.

The final element is a provision for public reading. The covenant is to be reread at the end of every seventh year to the whole congregation during the Feast of Tabernacles. The idea for the periodic reading stems from the fact that people have short memories, and many details will be forgotten. In addition, many of the younger generation have only heard bits and pieces of the covenant from their parents or others.

Moses finishes his repetition of the covenant with a final appeal to choose life over death, and blessing over cursing, so all the covenant promises given to Abraham, Isaac, and Jacob will be theirs.

After repeating the whole covenant, Moses orders that it be stored in the Most Holy Place with the ark. Then Moses composes a long song in poetry that the congregation is to learn. Since most of them cannot read, a song in poetic form is the means to remember something very important. Its purpose is to remind them of their covenant relationship with the Lord. It tells of what the Lord has done for them and that in the future they will apostatize. However, it ends with the beautiful and gracious words, "He will provide atonement for His land and His people" (Deuteronomy 32:43).

A new leader

The final chapters of Deuteronomy record the transfer of leadership to Joshua. Moses, Joshua, and Eleazar, the high priest, go before the people, as Moses appoints Joshua as the new leader. Moses charges him to be strong and of good courage, because the Lord will go with him.

Before he dies, Moses blesses the tribes of Israel in geographic order, corresponding to their territories. (Simeon is omitted because it will be absorbed into Judah.) Then he climbs Mount Nebo—the highest peak in the Pisgah mountain chain, where the Lord gives him a panoramic view of Canaan, along with the promise that it will all be given to his descendants. It appears that Canaan is the new Eden and the new sanctuary, if one goes back to Genesis 2 and observes that the boundaries of Eden are described by the four named rivers that mark off its boundaries. These appear to correspond to the land of Canaan that is given to Abraham in the covenant promises. Imagery of the original Eden is also the prototype of the new Eden, and the new sanctuary of the earth made new of Revelation 21 and 22.

Moses dies alone and the Lord Himself buries him in a secret place in the valley of Moab, near his people. He dies at 120 years of age and his life is divided into three parts of forty years each. To the ancients, the three-part total has great significance because it shows that his life ends with completeness, a finished work, and great leadership. Jude 9 says that Moses is resurrected by Michael, and later appears on the mountain of Jesus' transfiguration.

A type of Christ

Moses' death ends an era of rebellions. The older generation, Miriam and Aaron, and Moses—who struck the rock—have all passed away. His life bears many similarities to that of the Messiah—with the exception of his recorded sin, which stands in sharp contrast to Christ's exemplary life of obedience.

He, like Christ; is born poor; taken to Egypt; and becomes the greatest prophet, lawgiver, teacher, and leader of his people. He casts himself with his sinful people by asking the Lord to blot his name out of the book which He has written. He dies alone because of sin but is resurrected into glory, and lives through eternity.

The book of Matthew portrays Christ as the antitype of Moses. He's called from Egypt, goes up a mountain to give the law (the covenant, including the blessings), gives five discourses that correspond to the five books of Moses, casts His lot with sinful humanity, dies alone for His people's sins separated from His father, is resurrected, and will live throughout eternity.

Epilogue

As I reflected on my experience of writing *Through the Eyes of the Ancients: The Books of Moses,* it soon became obvious that I needed to alter my thinking. Much of what I had previously been doing to understand the Pentateuch (the books of Moses) and its context was either incorrect or inadequate. I was reading much of my own thinking, context, and many of my concerns into the text.

Here is a list of some of the things I needed to either learn or greatly improve upon to understand the message more fully and improve my methodology of study:

1. I've learned that the Bible is a big story

I realize that many times I've read the Bible to establish correct doctrine by using the "proof text" method of study. However, I now realize that this methodology distorts Scripture and does not permit us to either correctly understand the context, or its message as the original audience understood it. It finally dawned on me that the Bible was primarily *written as a story,* and the central message is revealed little by little. That was the way the ancients learned and remembered things. They effectively learned things through stories and retained them by retelling the stories. That is why the gospel writers wrote portraits of Jesus in story form, and Jesus taught the people in parables.

2. I've realized that typology is really important

I was surprised that the use of typology was far more extensive than I ever realized. In simple terms, typology means that *anything that is similar to something else is likened to it.* Stories are linked with previous stories; similar people are linked together; numbers and even colors are linked, as well. The governing principle is, "like is like." This ties the big story together, showing that all parts of the story are parts of the whole, and each contributes something to the complete story.

3. Symbolism is more important than I thought

I soon perceived that the *use of symbolism* was far more significant and important than I ever dreamed. A few examples of the numerous symbols are: light, darkness, the two trees in the midst of Eden, numbers (2, 3, 4, 6, 7, 10, 12, and often multiples), sanctuary, Sabbath, serpent, lion, man, calf, eagle, circumcision, birthright blessing, Passover, whole burnt offering, sin offering, Day of Atonement, high priest, and Sinai. Each symbol adds many facets of meaning, enriching the overall story. Most symbols are used repeatedly, thereby connecting different aspects of the big story.

4. I've been inserting my own background

I read my language, culture, and way of thinking into the message of Scripture. However, since the language of the Pentateuch is Hebrew, I needed to learn how the language functioned in describing things. *Hebrew is a verbal language*, where all parts of speech are derived from a verbal root. This makes it an action language, where normally, the action of the verb is written first, and the subject is considered secondary and placed after the verb. This affects how people and things are viewed. God and people are known by their actions, not by what they were. We describe people or things by their attributes or characteristics, while the Hebrew language describes them by what they do. This is why we are *judged by works*, even though *we are saved by faith and grace*. The verbal emphasis provides a clear revelation of what God and sinful man really do.

5. I need to use all my senses

I needed to learn that the ancients acquired all their *knowledge by experience* in using their five senses of sight, hearing, touch, taste, and smell. Much of my knowledge comes from rational thought that did not begin until much later, in the time of the Greeks. This makes their knowledge much more trustworthy than mine.

6. I need to set aside my Greek thinking

Because of my training in logical reasoning, based on Greek philosophical categories, I view ideas and experiences in a much different light then they did. When I think of God's law, I think in terms of moral law, ceremonial law, criminal law, ethical law, and so on. They did not atomize

God's law into many different kinds. God's law was God's law—all of it! They viewed everything by using *all knowledge as a whole*. Today, we tend to specialize in some branch of knowledge and exclude other branches when thinking about what we are focusing on.

7. It's easy to forget the context

I was imposing much of my own context and thinking on Scripture. When I read the first chapter of Genesis, I immediately thought of it in terms of the doctrine of Creation, or began to impose science on it by thinking in terms of creationism versus evolution.

The real context of Genesis takes into account who wrote the message, to whom was it written, why was it written, and what message were the people supposed to receive. *Their context* indicates that God provided a self-revelation to the Hebrews by showing He is a God of love, in the way He created them, provided for their needs, and created a lovely home for them.

8. Genealogy is not boring

I had to learn that *genealogy is significant* and not boring. I needed to learn that when Adam was personally created by God, that he became God's son, and was created in His image and likeness. God ordered the genealogy to continue when He told Adam and Eve to be fruitful, multiply, and fill the earth. He had Moses tell Pharaoh, "Israel is My son, My firstborn" (Exodus 4:22). While several who are not *chronologically* the firstborn are *classified* as firstborn and given the birthright blessing, it appears that only those of the *spiritual lineage* receive the distinction of "son" or "firstborn." Israel, as a nation, is the Lord's, so they can be called His son and firstborn.

When Cain killed Abel, God said, "The voice of your brother's blood cries out to Me from the ground" (Genesis 4:10). In Hebrew, the word for blood is plural, giving the connotation that the killing of Abel cut off all the future offspring of his brother. In the same manner, the tree of life in Hebrew is the tree of lives, indicating that whoever eats of it will continue living through the successive generations of his offspring.

After Abel is killed, Adam had a son in his own likeness and image who he named Seth, as a replacement for Abel. When Seth is born, he is said to be in Adam's own likeness and image, the same terminology used when God created Adam. From the time of Cain and Seth onward, two genealogical lines are listed, the ones faithful to the Lord are the sons of God, while the wicked line is known as the offspring of men. All of this shows the great importance of son, firstborn, fathers, generations, and genealogies.

9. We degenerate quickly

I learned how *quickly and drastically man's nature degenerated morally* when sin entered the world. Based on the context that the Pentateuch is written in—the verbal language of Hebrew—it follows that the nature of sinful man is revealed by his actions. Immediately after sinning, Adam blames Eve for giving him the fruit, then blames God for giving her to him. Eve blames the serpent for deceiving her. Cain kills his brother because Abel's sacrifice is accepted, while his is not. Lamech is a bigamist with two wives and becomes violent, killing a young man that wounded him. Sin spread so quickly that the whole earth became corrupt and filled with intolerable violence, forcing God to destroy it with the Flood. After the Flood, men tried to be independent of God by building the tower of Babel. War between groups of people became commonplace. Idol worship, brought on by the worship of other gods, became prevalent and was accompanied by immoral rituals.

Sin affected the whole plan of governance for the earth. However, sin went far beyond just morally affecting mankind. When Adam and Eve violated the relational integrity of love between one another and their God, they began a whole new governing principle that changed their system of rulership under the Lord. The earth now was under the rulership of a foreign lord, named Satan. He became the unseen spiritual force that changed the thoughts, impulses, and deeds of man. He set forth new principles of governance that were in his image—governance by selfishness and force. Adam and Eve attempted self-exaltation before God by eating of the fruit of the tree of knowledge of good and evil. Men began to subordinate women to the point that much of the time, the name of their spouse was not even given in Scripture. After the Flood, men especially sought strength and force, giving rise to Nimrod, the mighty hunter, from whom emerged the first empire. Monarchy became the normal governing system of fallen humanity.

Slaves became the permanent property of owners. Israel became enslaved in the Egyptian empire that was ruled by a Pharaoh who considered himself to be a human god.

10. God reveals himself slowly

I learned that *God's message of restoring sinful man to the image and likeness of Himself is revealed in the Pentateuch—little by little.* This indicates that too big a dose of even the wonderful message of salvation is too much for sinful man to absorb and put into practice all at once. God did not ask Abraham to sacrifice his son when He first called him but only when his faith had considerable time to mature.

By reading the whole Pentateuch, it became clear that God's principle message begins with the creation of a son with free will in the perfect Garden of Eden. Adam's relationship with God was intimate and designed to be permanent and everlasting. Their relationship was based on the foundation of love. Humans were created under God and given dominion over the earth. The significance of this arrangement lies in God's governing principle of love, because true love is other-centeredness, so that neither entity tries to rule over the other. Other-centered love provides complete freedom with no domination by anyone.

With the sin of Adam and Eve, the story makes a tragic shift that imposes an interruption of God's original plan. This interruption is caused by Satan (represented by the serpent) who deceives humanity into believing a misrepresentation of God. This interruption nearly effaces the image of God from the original son of God, making Adam unable to transmit God's likeness and image to his succeeding offspring. Restoration of man to the likeness and image of God will have to happen within the human situation, with a new Adam who will become the new head of the human race.

The rest of the story found in the Pentateuch provides, little by little, the details of what God will do to restore mankind. The first glimpse of this comes in Genesis 3:15, where a Redeemer will emerge among Eve's offspring to ultimately vanquish Satan and his offspring. No further details are furnished until covenant promises are made to Abram, when he is promised numerous offspring that will be a blessing to the earth and land, later revealed as Canaan. These three promises are repeated to Abram, furnishing more detail. This covenant is ratified between him and the Lord, guaranteeing that God will fulfill His promises. The Lord's covenant promises are restated by God when Abram is ninety-nine years old; this time adding that he will have a son, in spite of his old age. The Lord also tells him that he will be a father of many nations, and that his name will be changed from Abram, "exalted father," to Abraham, "father of many." God also makes the covenant more prominent with the addition of circumcision.

Abraham was one hundred years old when Isaac was born, and when he grew into a young man, the Lord told Abraham to go to the land of Moriah and offer his son on a mountain there. Solomon built the temple at Jerusalem on Mount Moriah, so it is clear that Abraham was sent to what is later called Jerusalem to offer his son in sacrifice. When the knife was lifted to slay him, the angel of the Lord called to Abraham not to slay his son. Suddenly, Abraham saw a ram caught in a thicket, and he sacrificed the animal. The Lord here has added the details that the sacrifice was to be at Jerusalem, and the sacrifice is to be provided by the Lord, symbolized by the ram.

The Lord's covenant promises are repeated to Isaac and Jacob, who will have twelve sons that will eventually be called Israel. Jacob's son Joseph is sold as a slave to Egypt, and saves the whole nation, and his relatives, from starvation. This makes him a type of Christ. After Jacob died, Joseph's brothers are afraid that Joseph will repay them for the evil they had done to him in his youth. But instead, Joseph assures them that he has forgiven them and would provide for their needs—just as the future Messiah will do for mankind by restoring them back to God.

Then Moses is born, another type of the Messiah, like Joseph. Further details of what the Messiah will do are given through Moses' leadership. He is used by the Lord to liberate His people from bondage and lead them to Sinai, where the promises of the divine covenant are repeated in full detail.

The type of covenant that the ancients make, and is used in the divine covenant, is very different from human covenants, today. The covenant parties are not equal, because the superior party elaborates all the covenant conditions, and the inferior party only has the choice to either accept or reject them. In the Pentateuch, the covenant is often called the divine law, a term easily misunderstood in our society, where anything dealing with the law generally has a punishment factor if the law is broken. However, for the Hebrews, the law is *relational*. It was termed "Torah" in Hebrew, and stems from the verbal root "to teach." The covenant type in the Lord's covenant, as well as those made by kings who had vassals ruling under them, was one of grace. Man has rebelled against the Lord and deserves to die, but through repentance and grace, the Lord will restore him to be His son, again. He will also be restored to his rulership position under the Lord, and all rulership will be once more based on love and other-centeredness.

The Lord has clearly revealed Himself to both the Hebrews and the Egyptians that He is the only true God. He leads His people to Sinai, where He established His covenant, giving far greater detail than He's ever been given before. The principles of His government are revealed, showing they are based on love.

The restoration of sinful man back to the Lord is revealed with the building and functioning of the sanctuary as well. Through its offerings and services and the priesthood, the Lord symbolically reveals the plan of salvation. Through a literal sanctuary, He demonstrates how He will deal with sin, save mankind, and restore humans back to Himself. The result of the Lord's actions will be that men and women will, once again, be in God's likeness and image as His sons and daughters.

After the Exodus from Egypt, the Lord leads them by the pillar of cloud that provides the people comfort, and a visible sign of the Lord's constant presence is with them. He furnishes them with food, water, and protection. He reveals His patience and long-suffering as they constantly complain and rebel. At the end of his life, Moses gives a great farewell discourse, where he repeats the history of how the Lord has led them. He finishes by once more repeating the covenant.

The Hebrews finally came to the border of the Promised Land, but the adults who came out of Egypt have completely rebelled and rejected the Lord. So He reveals that He is a just God by not allowing them to enter Canaan because of their multiple rebellions. They die in the wilderness, instead. The Lord's justice is even further evident when Moses in not allowed to enter Canaan, either, because of his sin in striking the rock in anger and frustration. However, God's faithful servant is still allowed to view the Promised Land from afar.

The Lord has clearly revealed Himself through the long story of the Pentateuch. It has been done gradually, but He has plainly shown how He deals with sin and sinful man. He has demonstrated how He will ultimately redeem them from sin and restore them back into an intimate relationship as His sons and daughters. They will once again be restored to the exalted position of rulership of the earth, under the Lord.

The story of the Pentateuch ends with a challenge to the children of the parents that the Lord brought out of Egypt. Will they serve the Lord and cross over the Jordan River to the Promised Land, or will they rebel, like their parents did after they heard the report of the spies, and refuse to go into the Promised Land?

We have looked through the long story of the Lord and His people through the writings of Moses as revealed in five books, 187 chapters, and 5,853 verses. We have seen how the Lord historically reveals Himself from the beginning of Creation to the borders of the Promised Land. We have observed how the Lord creates humans in His image and likeness with the responsibility to govern and care for the earth. But the humans sin, and much of their image and likeness as offspring of the Lord is lost. However, the Lord, through incredible love and unending patience, has gradually revealed how He is restoring us to the relationship and position we had before sin. All of this I have attempted to describe through the eyes of the ancients who first received the message.

Today, as the secondary audience, we are confronted with the very same story. What will our reaction be to this message? We are on the borders of the Promised Land as well. Will we respond to the Lord's loving message and join Him in the long-promised Land?